FLOURISH
A Field Guide *for* Spiritual Growth

Flourish: A Field Guide for Spiritual Growth
Identify the who, what, where, when, and why of your God story

Copyright © 2025 Mary Alice Hall

All rights reserved. No part of this publication may be reproduced in a retrieval system, or transmitted in any form or by any means—electronic, mechanical, photocopying, recording, or otherwise—without the prior written permission of the publisher.

Scripture quotations marked (NLT) are taken from the Holy Bible, New Living Translation, copyright ©1996, 2004, 2015 by Tyndale House Foundation. Used by permission of Tyndale House Publishers, Carol Stream, Illinois 60188. All rights reserved. | Scriptures taken from the Holy Bible, New International Version®, NIV®. Copyright © 1973, 1978, 1984, 2011 by Biblica, Inc.™ Used by permission of Zondervan. All rights reserved worldwide. www.zondervan.com The "NIV" and "New International Version" are trademarks registered in the United States Patent and Trademark Office by Biblica, Inc.™ | Scripture taken from the New King James Version®. Copyright © 1982 by Thomas Nelson. Used by permission. All rights reserved. | Scripture quotations marked TPT are from The Passion Translation®. Copyright © 2017, 2018 by Passion & Fire Ministries, Inc. Used by permission. All rights reserved. ThePassionTranslation.com. | The Holy Bible, English Standard Version® (ESV®) Copyright © 2001 by Crossway, a publishing ministry of Good News Publishers. All rights reserved. ESV Text Edition: 2016. | Scripture quotations taken from the Amplified® Bible (AMP), Copyright © 2015 by The Lockman Foundation. Used by permission. www.lockman.org. | Scripture quotations taken from the American Standard Version of the Bible (ASV), public domain January 1, 1957.

While precaution has been taken in the preparation of this book, the publisher and author assume no responsibility for errors or omissions, or for damages resulting from the use of the information contained herein.

Illustrations provided by Uliana Tsaprilova.

This book is set in the typeface Minion Pro designed by Robert Slimbach in 1990 for Adobe Systems.

ISBN: 978-1-955546-89-8

A Publication of *Tall Pine Books*
PO Box 42 Warsaw | Indiana 46581
www.tallpinebooks.com

| 1 25 25 20 16 02 |

Published in the United States of America

Identify the *who, what, where, when* and *why* of your God story

FLOURISH

A Field Guide *for* Spiritual Growth

Foreword by JENNY DONNELLY
MARY ALICE HALL

ENDORSEMENTS

"In *Flourish*, Mary Alice Hall will captivate you with powerful and practical principles of spiritual growth. She will take you on a journey that mirrors the stages of natural growth, from seed to blossom, all while uncovering spiritual truths that are transformative to your life. Her approach is deeply rooted in the Word and offers not just a theoretical guide, but practical tools to apply to everyday life."

—Anastasia & Vik Fomenko

Speakers and Pastors of *Kingdom Movement,* author of *No Longer Afraid*

"If you're desiring to discover who God made you to be and what His unique calling is for your life, then this book will walk you through that process step-by-step and so much more. You will be equipped to flourish in your spiritual growth, gaining vision and understanding for your life. Mary emphatically lives what she teaches. This book is not just a wealth of teaching and insight; it's an impartation from the overflow of her life. You will be richly blessed as you read these pages."

—Stefanie Overstreet

Speaker and Founder of the *PEACE Method Program for postpartum support*

"Mary is a master at bringing life to her family, friends and community. Let this book bring life to you while invigorating your faith and cultivating your identity through the simple illustration of a tree. Get to the root of spiritual formation and Flourish!"

—Shawna Danberg

Pastor and Speaker, author of *Go There Mama Bear*

"As I read *Flourish,* I simultaneously felt challenged in my view of God and awakened to my righteousness in Him. Mary writes with such clarity and realness that you will be drawn into intimacy with the Father and be provoked to grow and FLOURISH!"

—Ben Rose

Pastor of *The Collective Church,* Speaker and Founder of *Cross the Island*

For all of my children — the ones who stay and the ones who come and go. You are my most precious gifts and most worthy investments. I pray that you will freely receive the love of Jesus and freely give His love away all the days of your lives. I love you to the heavens and back again.

CONTENTS

Foreword
By Jenny Donnelly xi

Introduction
How do you get the most out of this journey?
Identifying your Guide 1

1. **Seed**
   How do you hear God's voice?
   Identifying your intrinsic value and inheritance 7

2. **Plant**
   How do you experience true life?
   Identifying God's nature and your need for surrender 33

3. **Cultivate**
   How do you receive nourishment for transformation?
   Identifying your thoughts and beliefs. 55

4. **Root**
   Who has God created you to be?
   Identifying your true identity. 79

5. **Grow**
   How do you remain connected with your true source of growth?
   Identifying God's presence 107

6. **Pollinate**
   How were we created to flourish in community?
   Identifying your kingdom family and legacy 131

7. **Branch**
   Where are you called to serve?
   Identifying your burden and reach 157

8. **Weed**
   How does the enemy entangle you?
   Identifying hindrances to your freedom 179

9. **Sprout**
   When is God asking you to act?
   Identifying your unchanging purpose and seasonal assignments ... 205

10. **Blossom**
    What gifts has God given you to blossom?
    Identifying your unique giftings 231

11. **Prune**
    How do you develop and multiply?
    Identifying your purpose in testing 253

12. **Flourish**
    Why were you created?
    Identifying your mission and the motivation of your eternal destiny 275

    Appendix
    Answering FAQs with the Holy Spirit and Scripture 301

    Acknowledgements 311
    Meet the Author 315
    References 317

FOREWORD
by Jenny Donnelly

W E HAVE ALL SEEN a child's fast food meal paired with a small toy or a cheap coloring book. But there is only one place I know that includes an item that is completely unexpected. Burgerville, an iconic Northwest fast food restaurant, gifts a packet of seeds with every kid's meal.

I have to give them credit for being unique, but I have yet to hear one of my kids shout with excitement as they pull out a pack of onion seeds with their fries. I wonder how many people go home and plant them? With the hopeful idea that someday I will become a green thumb, I toss them into the kitchen drawer.

As I collected a few packets over time, I began to think about the power of seeds and how similar they are to you and me. Seeds left in a packet have no real purpose. They only hold the *potential* to become more than they are at the present moment.

Like seeds, each person holds great *potential,* a God-given destiny code embedded in us in our mother's womb. But also like a seed, we do not just automatically blossom into our full God-purpose without an intentional process that must take place! The seed must come out of its packet and be buried in the ground, in soft nutrient-rich soil. It also must be watered so that it can break open. And of course, the sun rays must interact with the seed, causing it to grow according to the DNA instruction that is written inside the seed.

In this incredible book, you will find that you too must go through a similar process of being thrown out of your place of familiarity (out of your packet), planted in a spot where you are now in over your head (buried in the dirt), placed in a soft and nutrient-rich environment (a community or organization), stretched outside of your own self-imposed limitations (break out of your shell), and interact with the Son (Jesus Christ) so that he can cause the destiny code on the inside to begin to burst forth out of you.

And the analogy just keeps going! You end up multiplying and blossoming into someone who is impacting the world with great value... only to soon wonder why the pruning shears are clipping you down to a state of humble dependency on God all over again.

I will never open the junk drawer in my kitchen to a surprise bushel of onions! No, the packet of seeds will remain in a state of potential until the process I have described is activated. You, my friend, are not meant to sit passively in your life, striving for safety and predictability. It has been said that ninety-eight out of every one hundred people are "drifters." Meaning, they just flow with the current of life and never activate the potential that lies within them. They strive for comfort and smallness, fearing life outside the packet, outside the drawer.

My friend Mary has not just written a guide for you to live out the destiny code that God has placed inside of you, but she has lived it. She was willing to place her life in the conditions that require great surrender, faith, and sometimes pain. But her life has now blossomed into a great harvest where children are able to have a mother and a family they otherwise would not have.

Pray this prayer if you want to become all that God has destined for you:

Father God, I thank you for placing destiny inside of me as I was in my mother's womb. I ask you to help me see myself the way you see me and to empower me to live out my destiny to the fullest! Help me to completely depend on you and trust you. Walk with me daily as I breathe in your love, your presence, your forgiveness, your peace and your joy. When I see the impossible tasks in front of me and I am overcome with doubt or fear, I ask that you blow fresh faith through me and remind me that it is not by my own power or might that I will be able to accomplish what you've asked, but by your Spirit! I pray these things in the precious name of Jesus Christ.

So he answered and said to me:
"This is the word of the Lord to Zerubbabel:
'Not by might nor by power, but by My Spirit,'
Says the Lord of hosts.
(Zechariah 4:6)

—Jenny Donnelly
Author of *Still: Seven Ways to Find Calm in the Chaos,*
Wake Up Dead: Dying to Self to Experience New Life,
The One Degree: Small Adjustments in Leadership that Reap Big Rewards.
Founder, *Her Voice Movement* | www.hervoicemvmt.com
Founder, *Her Voice Action* | www.hervoiceaction.com

INTRODUCTION

How do you get the most out of this journey?
Identifying your Guide

"But they delight in the law of the LORD,
meditating on it day and night.
They are like trees planted along the riverbank,
bearing fruit each season.
Their leaves never wither,
and they prosper in all they do."
(Psalm 1:2-3 NLT)

WHAT WE BELIEVE DETERMINES our spiritual growth. The psalmist declares that when we meditate and delight in the Word of God, we become like flourishing trees.

The Christian life is full of opportunities to grow into the mature, fruitful believer illustrated in Psalm One. This is one of those opportunities and I believe you are not reading this book by accident. You are holding an invitation for spiritual growth designed to function like a microscope that, with the illumination of the Holy Spirit, can help you investigate your unique destiny seed. Understanding the divine design of our spiritual DNA changes our thoughts which are the seeds of belief. Beliefs are not just what we know to be true intellectually, but also what we know to be true experientially. All transformation starts with the identification of our thoughts and beliefs.

Though I have experienced the fruit of this transformation in my own life, I have no seminary degree or persuasive theological rhetoric to offer you. Jesus tells us that the *Spirit of Truth* will guide us into all truth (John 16:13). My job is simply to determine, like Paul, to "know nothing… except Jesus Christ and Him crucified," and say, "follow my example, as I follow the example of Christ" (1 Corinthians 2:2, 11:1 NIV).

I have only one answer that I will point back to again and again and again. His name is Jesus. Ultimately, I have nothing to give you except Him. The good news is we need nothing but Him, because he is everything. I can only guide you on the path of spiritual growth the Holy Spirit is guiding me on. All growth, direction and transformation come from you connecting to God Himself. No one can do that for you.

With that said, I cannot encourage you enough to test everything I say against the inspired Word of God. If something I have written challenges your theology or interpretation of Scripture, I simply ask that you do not immediately disregard it. Ask the Holy Spirit to be your teacher. The Bible was written to an Eastern audience in a cultural context that is foreign to most of us. We read the Bible wearing a Western lens clarified by commentaries from Western theologians. Sometimes we see askew.

Thankfully, the Author himself is available to us to help us interpret what he wrote when we invite His presence into our time of reading and study. We need the revelation of the Holy Spirit to supernaturally bridge the divide of every cultural and contextual gap. In over thirty years of being a Christian, I have built up a lot of theology based upon human understanding, not truth. Are you willing to humbly examine the areas that perhaps you have, too?

While it is important to deconstruct wrong beliefs, it is equally important to not deconstruct to the point of unbelief. Deconstruction is defined by Merriam Webster as, "the analytic examination of something (such as a theory) often in order to reveal its inadequacy." "Deconstruction" is a current trend that has tragically led many to disconnect from Jesus, the Church, and their purpose. Deconstruction of non-biblical beliefs does the opposite: it leads to closer connection to Jesus, the Church, and our purpose. We only want to deconstruct what is bringing disconnection in our lives.

Your degree of connection to Jesus and others is the primary determinant of impact on this journey. Adventures are always more fun and successful with companions! I encourage you to invite a few friends to go through this book together. God created us to flourish in community.

This book is designed as a field guide for discipleship both for the one being discipled as well as the one discipling. Using the illustration of a tree, we will identify essential components of spiritual growth. Every chapter includes teaching keys and testimonies. At the end of each chapter are Field Notes that will invite you into a conversation, activation, and encounter with Jesus. Personal reflection and observation are vital for true transformation, so it is my prayer that you will give yourself plenty of time for this. It is not what I have written, but what the Holy Spirit speaks to you through it that will yield good fruit in your life.

I pray this book is full of revelation that we *grow into* on our spiritual journey rather than mere understanding that doesn't take root in our hearts and produce change within us. It's just as essential for the person who has been a Christian for fifty years to ask self-examining questions as it is for the person who is newly born again. Paul instructs us to take every thought captive (2 Corinthians 10:5) and be transformed by the renewing of our minds (Romans 12:2). This field guide will walk you through both as we examine our beliefs under a metaphoric microscope, starting with what we believe about our own intrinsic value.

"There are far, far better things ahead than any we leave behind."
- C.S. Lewis

SEED I

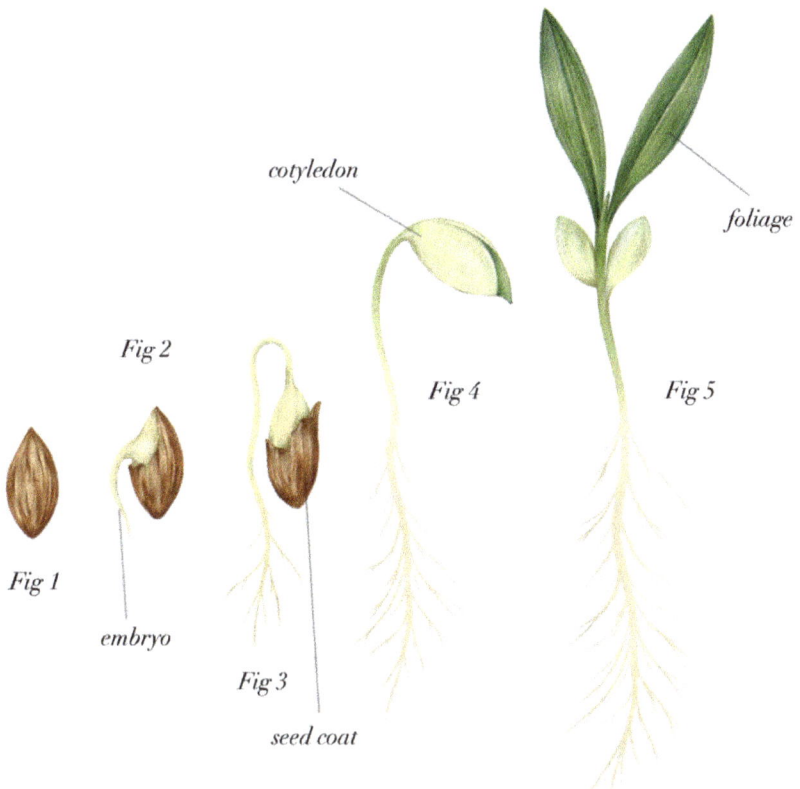

Figure 1: Seed Figure 2: Embryo
Figure 3: Seed Coat Figure 4: Cotyledon Figure 5: Foliage

SEED
Chapter One

*How do you hear God's voice?
Identifying your intrinsic value and inheritance*

"I AM THE ANSWER TO every question." Jesus spoke these words to me and, like a seed, they implanted in my heart. Every bit of spiritual growth in my life is connected to this conviction that Jesus is my answer. And He is yours, too.

For as long as I can remember I have loved Jesus, but truthfully, Jesus has not always been my *only* answer. At the youngest possible age I received the gift of salvation, but it remained wrapped up in the gift box of religion that it had been presented to me in. As I grew up, I grew more conflicted by the gift box. Deep in my spirit, I knew that this glorious gift was not meant to be kept in a man-made box. After all, what gift is? I was convinced there had to be more to the Christian life than what I had yet experienced, but I settled for letting the Holy Spirit out just enough to get a glimpse of Him, and then back into the box He went.

Despite my longing for more, I eventually learned to accept compartmentalized Christianity as a way of life. I would jump into my God box for morning devotions and jump right back out for the rest of my day. I would jump into my God box for church and then jump out as soon as I heard, "Amen" at the end of the closing prayer. I would jump into my God box to pray when I needed something from God, but rarely stayed long enough to connect to God and hear His voice. Everything was right and wrong. Open and shut. On and off. In and out.

The more I added to my to-do list of spiritual disciplines, the more I realized something was not adding up. I, for sure, was not adding up. Jesus plus my best efforts should be the solution for any problem, right? Yet somehow all my striving for spiritual growth was never enough.

"What am I missing?!" I practically yelled at the Lord in frustration one day. In response to my desperate question, the Holy Spirit began to dismantle the gift box of religion to reveal the fullness of the gospel and the transforming power I had unknowingly been carrying all along. Once the box that kept God bound by my own understanding, reasoning and fear had been removed, I was left with the gift of salvation in the form of a seed.

Without any mention of what I *should* do to nurture this seed, the Master Gardener came and began to tend to the soil of my soul by telling me *who I am*. In the place of *doing*, God asked me to focus on *believing*, assuring me that what I believe I will become. He began revealing to me how He created my destiny seed purposefully with unique spiritual DNA. Through gentle care and the utmost intentionality, the Holy Spirit watered roots of love while simultaneously uprooting weeds that were thriving on lies rooted in fear.

After twenty-five years of being a Christian, I could see the full gospel for the first time. Scales of religion fell off of my eyes as I realized the problem was not that I was *missing* anything. The problem was that I was trying to *add* to the perfect and complete finished work of the cross. The answer is not Jesus PLUS me; it is Jesus IN me. Jesus replaces me. Jesus alone is the answer. Salvation is not a ticket to Heaven; it is the empowerment to live a transformed life that brings Heaven to Earth. When we receive the seed of salvation we are both transplanted into Heaven for eternity and planted presently on earth to see His kingdom come here and now. *Sozo*, the original Greek word for salvation, does not just mean saved; it also means healed, delivered, and made whole![1]

Wholeness comes with the revelation that Jesus is the whole equation. He is the beginning, and He is the end. I am not enough, but He is! Without Jesus I can never measure up, but I am no longer without Jesus.

---

1. Strong's Greek: 4982. Σώζω (Sózó) -- to Save.

My question changed from, *"What should I do?"* to, *"Who is Christ in me?"*

I embarked on a journey of asking questions and expecting, in faith, that Jesus would not just answer me, but *be* my answer. The Holy Spirit began inviting me to encounter Him in the most ordinary moments. At the simple mention of His name, His glory met me there.

I was delighted to discover that whenever I look for God within, I find Him. This happens most frequently at the kitchen sink or in the midst of piles of dirty laundry or crying babies refusing to be comforted. Seeking and finding has become a divine way of life for me that transforms the mundane into the sacred.

As God's children, it is truly incredible that He does not tire of our questions. My own children often have more questions than I have answers for. One day in particular, I loaded the kids into their carseats in pursuit of some quiet time to pray. I had been answering my toddler's questions for ten straight minutes when I heard myself say, "Finn, you need to ask God your questions. I'm going to talk to him, too."

Finn did not miss a beat. "God, why does mama have to stop at stop signs? …. Mama! God says they keep us safe!" His questions and answers continued for some time. I couldn't believe this simple strategy worked. I forgot the questions I was attempting to ask the Lord moments before. The sound of my four year old, with child-like faith, having an effortless conversation with the Creator of the world made me tear up. The tangible presence of the Lord filled my car, and everything I had felt needed to be sorted out fifteen minutes earlier escaped my mind. He *was* the answer.

My son has not stopped asking questions, so I get to practice welcoming them like my Heavenly Father welcomes mine. On another drive Finn asked, "Do trees grow until they reach Heaven?" "Yes, Finn," I responded. "Trees can grow until they die. And like trees, you and I are meant to grow spiritually until we reach Heaven."

As I answered my son's question, the Holy Spirit illuminated truth to my heart. The moment before, I had been beating myself up for what I had measured as slow spiritual progress in one area of my life. When we allow the Holy Spirit to be our guide, we cannot run ahead of him (as I am often tempted to) or lag behind him. We are meant to step in time with him, stride by stride.

The Created Seed

We all begin as a seed, one conceived in the very image of God. How incredible is that?! In our Heavenly Father's likeness, in the purest love, He created you and me! Our very substance was formed by the spoken word of God like a seed implanted into the fabric of our being.

At this point of conception, before any growth or development, our seed had intrinsic value. Our worth was established from the beginning in who we are and who we were created by, not in what we do.

Chances are, if you are a Christian, you do not disagree with me. This truth, after all, is woven throughout scripture. But I have to ask, do you really believe it?

For most of my life, I did not. This misalignment with what I thought I believed and what I spent the majority of time rehearsing in my mind kept me from experiencing real transformation. I would take one step forward and then one step back, unable to progress on the path God had planned for me.

All of us live with some degree of disconnect between what we profess to be true and what our lives demonstrate that we actually believe. For twenty-five years of being a Christian, if you told me, "You are loved by God." or "You are intrinsically valuable!" my response would have been, "Yes, I know." On this journey we are going to cover a lot of topics that might seem basic to you. If your response to the Word of God is an unenthusiastic, possibly offended, "Yes, I know," you have likely been taught the truth but have not yet encountered Truth. Truth has a name. Jesus is Truth personified.

Truth is not meant to be theorized. It is meant to be realized. If a loving father hugs His child and says, "I love you!" the child would not shrug it off and say, "I know" (unless, perhaps, they are a teenager). A connected child would hug their dad back and say, "I love you, too!" And so it is with us. As we receive the love of our Father, our love for Him grows. Truth experienced through relationship is not stagnant. It is always growing.

The blocks we have in our reception of the love of God reveal themselves in our struggles to love the people around us. When we know how to live in the love of God, we do not have to muster up love for others; we overflow with the love we have already received.

"We love because he first loved us." (1 John 4:19 ESV)

God loves you.

Does that make you uncomfortable? I can hear some of you saying, "Yeah… but," or "Sure, sure," eager to move on to more important things. But there is nothing more important.

God is divinely in love with you.

This truth should cause us to run into the arms of Love. It makes me want to drop everything to just be with Him because I do not just know about His love; I experience it. My heart longs to spend the rest of eternity in the presence of this divine, undeserved love.

There is nothing more important than our response to the love of God. The primary purpose for which we were created was to experience and mirror this divine love to the world. In scripture, God intentionally establishes *who we are* — children made in the image of a loving father — *before* He states what we are made to *do*.

> **"God created man in his own image**, *in the image of God he created them; male and female he created them. And God blessed them. And God said to them,* **"Be fruitful and multiply** *and fill the earth and subdue it, and have dominion over the fish of the sea and over the birds of the heavens and over every living thing that moves on the earth." (Genesis 1:27-28 ESV, bold text mine)*

Did you catch the purpose of each seed stated here? From the very beginning, God declares that the mission of each seed is to be fruitful and multiply. When we are growing in the love of God, we respond by taking dominion, confidently occupying the spaces God created us to fill. Taking dominion is not a suggestion; it's a command. Even more importantly, it is God's first command of man. I believe the problems we see in the world today are a direct result of us as the children of God abdicating our roles instead of fulfilling our God-given assignments.

On our journey together, we will grow into the *who, what, where, when* and *why* of our God story. To begin we will focus on how we step into our God story. But before we can do that, we have to establish the who that is God, and the who that is you. There is no way to reach our destiny without connection to God. He is True North. Until we see ourselves the way He sees us, our impact will be limited. Anyone who, deep down, believes themselves to be worthless will not contribute much lasting worth to the world.

If we are not fully convinced of our inherent value and God's love for us personally, we will be powerless to fulfill our purpose. We cannot give away that which we have not fully accepted first for ourselves. Living the *who, what, where, when,* and *why* of our destiny story starts with us journeying back to our origin story.

As a natural achiever, the truth that my value is based upon who I am and not what I produce is hard for me to accept. I still catch myself in performance mode, attaching my self-worth to what I accomplish. In these moments, I like to recite Psalm 139 out loud to renew my mind.

I feel a warning is needed before I share this Scripture for those who have been Christians for some time. We must be careful that we do not allow the Word of God to become common to us. When the Bible becomes familiar to our natural minds, but not alive in our hearts, it can lose its potency and power.

The beliefs of the psalmist become a love letter to God. Likewise, the way we see ourselves can become an act of worship to our Creator. Take a moment to read this Scripture out loud to God as if you were reading it for the first time:

> *"For you created my inmost being; you knit me together in my mother's womb. I praise you because I am fearfully and wonderfully made; your works are wonderful, I know that full well. My frame was not hidden from you when I was made in the secret place, when I was woven together in the depths of the earth. Your eyes saw my unformed body; all the days ordained for me were written in your book before one of them came to be. How precious to me are your thoughts, God! How vast is the sum of them! Were I to count them, they would outnumber the grains of sand— when I awake, I am still with you." (Psalm 139: 13-18 NIV)*

We were created as a tiny seed in our mother's womb, handcrafted by our Creator, fully known and loved before we even came to be! The intrinsic value of life is displayed in the joyful mother who just found out she is pregnant and already feels immeasurable love for her tiny baby.

It is displayed in the mother who had an early miscarriage but still experiences devastating grief. Many women share stories of finding out about their pregnancy during a miscarriage yet, despite not having previous knowledge of the baby, feeling unexplainable pain at the loss of life.

It is displayed in the testimony of friends who carried the suppressed trauma of abortion in their bodies for years until they faced the reality that they chose an act that killed an immeasurably valuable life. Tragically, the babies are not the only victims of abortion. I personally know many women who testify of a part of themselves dying on the table during their abortion procedure as the trauma caused them to disassociate. In the termination of life, they were left with deep shame and unworthiness. For men and women who have been deceived into believing abortion was their only option, healing is unlocked when the truth of that child's inherent worth is confessed and real repentance is released.

There is a war raging against intrinsic value. One-fourth of our generations are missing because of abortion and with it, invaluable destinies that can never be fulfilled.[2]

The enemy has been attempting to devalue human life since the very beginning. He knows that if we, the children of God, know who we are, we will be unstoppable. The fact that the most heated political debate of our day revolves around the value of life shows us the reality of the spiritual war that we are in.

Every seed is created with divine skill and vision. Like an olive seed that carries the DNA code of an olive tree before it is planted and can begin to grow, you are created not only with unique DNA but with a unique destiny code. Each image bearer reflects a facet of God both in the natural and the spiritual realm. Just as we grow physically by our genetic code, as we grow spiritually our destiny is unlocked.

> *"For we are his workmanship, created in Christ Jesus for good works, which God prepared beforehand that we should walk in them."* (Ephesians 2:10 ESV)

Good works, like blueprints of Heaven, are embedded inside us. And yet, God does not value us based upon the potential of our destiny but simply by our *being*. The word for "workmanship" in the Greek is *poiēma*

---

2. Number of Abortions in US & Worldwide - Number of Abortions Since 1973.

which is where we get our word poetry.[3] We are His divine poetry! We are a beautiful expression of the Divine Artist who created us.

Unlike an olive seed whose value is only in its potential for growth and production, God's love for us is not measured by what we produce. Olive trees were created by God but not in God's image. As a child of God, His lavished, undeserved love is our inheritance. It is a gift that we could never earn.

> Good works, like blueprints of Heaven, are embedded inside us. And yet, God does not value us based upon the potential of our destiny but simply by our being.

I will never forget the moment I held my children for the first time. Immediately, unexplainable love rushed over me like a flood. Before my children could do a single thing, I loved them unconditionally. And scripture says my love is evil compared to the love of God (Matthew 7:11)! How much more does He love us, His sons and daughters, regardless of what we do?!

The Polluted Seed

We cannot hide from the fact that we were born into a fallen world polluted by sin. Genesis 4:7 says, "...sin is crouching at the door. Its desire is contrary to you, but you must rule over it" (ESV). This verse shows us that sin is an exterior pressure coming against us, not our truest nature dwelling within us. The definition of contrary is "opposite in nature." Sinfulness is inherent to our fallen nature, but it is opposite to our new, redeemed nature!

The sin that entered the world through Adam and Eve corrupted our seed. "All have sinned and fall short of the glory of God" (Romans 3:23 NIV). The DNA of Heaven inside of each of us has been polluted by the toxic sin of the world. Sin's pollution causes a smog of deception that hides our true nature.

The Bible describes sin like a sickness. Just as sickness does not determine a person's value, sin does not determine our value. But the disease of sin requires a cure or it will destroy us. Sin leads to death (James 1:15). So Jesus took our sin by dying for us. He rose again and is now the cure for sin and death.

Before sin entered our story, God had a rescue plan in motion. He

---

3. Strong's Greek: 4161. Ποίημα (Poiéma) -- a Work.

sent His son Jesus to replace our corrupted seed with an incorruptible one! He redeems our pollution and restores us to purity.

Romans 8:19 says, "For the earnest expectation of the creation eagerly waits for the revealing of the sons of God." The word "revealing" can also be translated, "uncovering." There are many Christians who have received salvation from their sins but have not uncovered their true identity as children of God. The understanding of our sinfulness without the revelation of our sonship leaves us powerless to reflect the image of our Father.

Ephesians 1:5 says that even before we chose God, He chose us! He predestined us for adoption so that we could become children of God. Knowing that sin would separate humanity from His love, God put the destiny code for redemption inside of us. Jesus' blood unlocks the code. It cleanses us from our sin, giving us a brand new nature as sons and daughters of God!

The Implanted Seed

Did you know there is a parable where Jesus tells His disciples that if they do not understand it, they will not be able to understand *any* of His parables? It is "The Parable of the Sower" found in Mark 4. Hopefully I've provoked your curiosity enough to ask, "What is the key to unlocking all of Jesus' teachings?" The key to understanding the kingdom of God is the revelation that the Word of God is like a seed intended to be implanted deep into our hearts. Luke 17:21 reiterates this truth by declaring "For indeed, the kingdom of God is within you!"

One of my favorite quotes is from the book *Experiencing the Depths of Jesus Christ* by Madame Jeane Guyon. She says, "The Lord is found only within your spirit, in the recesses of your being, in the Holy of Holies; this is where he dwells. The Lord once promised to come and make His home within you (John 14:23). He promised to there meet those who worship Him and who do His will. The Lord will meet you in your spirit. It was St. Augustine who once said that he had lost much time in the beginning of his Christian experience by trying to find the Lord outwardly rather than turning inwardly."

> *Sinfulness is inherent to our fallen nature, but it is opposite to our new, redeemed nature!*

As the sons and daughters of God, it is our birthright to hear the voice of our Father. James 1:18 says God's word is implanted in us like a seed because, "He chose to give us birth through the word of truth, that we might be a kind of firstfruits of all he created," or as other translations say, "his prized possession," and "the favorite ones out of all his creation" (NIV, NLT, TPT).

God spoke, and with His word we were created. Without the voice of God, we would not exist. If receiving the spoken word of God was essential for our creation, why would it not also be essential to sustain true life?

In John 1:14 Jesus is described as the Word made flesh. This means the seed of Father God inside of Jesus was in full form. This seed grows bigger and bigger inside of us the more we hear and believe God's word.

When we allow God's word to be implanted deep within us, we are transformed. As we allow information to transfer from our minds to our hearts, it becomes revelation that changes us. Revelation grows in us through spiritual formations like hearing and reading the Word of God.

Maybe when you hear or read the word "word" you think of the written Word of God, the Holy Scriptures. The Bible has sixty-six books with forty different authors. There are approximately twenty-five hundred prophecies in scripture, two thousand of which have already been fulfilled without a single error. The odds of this happening is less than one in 10^{2000}.[4] The Bible is without doubt the inspired Word of God!

Two Greek words for "word" in scripture are *logos* and *rhema*. *Logos* is "divine utterance" or the spoken word of God.[5] The Bible is God's *logos*, transcribed through the written words (Greek, *graphe*) of men. In John 1:14, Jesus is called the *logos* made flesh. The person and life of Jesus is God's message to the world. *Rhema* is the word God is continually speaking.[6] In Matthew 4:4, Jesus says, "It is written, 'Man shall not live on bread alone, but on every word that proceeds out of the mouth of God'" (NASB). *Rhema* is also the word used in Romans 10:17, "Faith comes from hearing, and hearing through the word of Christ" (ESV). God is speaking *rhema* to us that once we receive, gives birth to belief.

---

4. Reasons to Believe, "Fulfilled Prophecy: Evidence for the Reliability of the Bible - Reasons to Believe."
5. Strong's Greek: 3056. Λόγος (Logos) -- a Word (as Embodying an Idea), a Statement, a Speech.
6. Strong's Greek: 4487. Ῥῆμα (Rhéma) -- a Word, by Impl. A Matter.

As we open His *logos* Word, the Holy Spirit highlights the *rhema* words we need.

If you have accepted Jesus as your Savior, you have personally heard God speak. It is impossible to be saved without the presence of the Holy Spirit making Jesus real to us. At the moment of salvation we are given a brand new seed (Matthew 13:23)! As we receive, believe and respond to God's word, our tiny seed grows into a flourishing tree.

A Christian who does not daily hear the voice of God is living like an orphan instead of the son or daughter that they are. Just like God provided manna in the wilderness for the Israelites, He provides fresh bread from Heaven for His children today. God sets a glorious table for us in His Word and through His words to us throughout the day. It is our choice if we will come and feast, taking our honored seat with Jesus at the right hand of the Father or live off scraps like orphans.

Hearing God's voice is something we must get better and better at if we wish to grow and mature in our relationship with Jesus. In Deuteronomy 6:7, God instructs the Israelites to tell their children truth continually: "...when you sit in your house, and when you walk by the way, and when you lie down, and when you rise" (ESV). This is the way God teaches us, His children. Our Father desires to journey and talk with us throughout our day. The question is: Do we hear Him?

Jesus says in John 10:27: "My sheep hear my voice, and I *know* them, and they follow me" (ESV, italics mine). According to John, in order to know God personally we must listen to His voice.

The Greek word for "know" used in this Scripture is *ginosko*.[7] It does not mean intellectual knowing but rather being known or becoming known in a relationship. It is used as an idiom in Jewish culture to describe intercourse between a husband and wife.[8]

All spiritual growth is relational. Our purpose is *to be known by* and *to know* Jesus, the Family of God, and the people he calls us to serve. True discipleship can only happen in the context of relationship.

In scripture we are instructed to ask for, "a spirit of wisdom and revelation" (Eph. 1:17 ESV) and to, "lean not on your own understanding" (Prov. 3:5 ESV). It's crucial that we catch the difference between revela-

---

7. G1097 - Ginōskō - Strong's Greek Lexicon (Kjv).
8. Ginosko Meaning - Greek Lexicon | New Testament (KJV).

tion truth and intellectual knowledge built on our own understanding. 1 Corinthians 8:1 explains that there is a type of knowledge (Greek, *gnósis* meaning doctrine) that puffs up our pride, but love (experientially knowing the One who calls Himself Love) builds us and others up.[9]

I grew up in a church that taught through the entire Bible, chapter by chapter, verse by verse. While I am very grateful for the love of the Word and biblical foundation established in me at a young age, there was a downside to this style of intellectual teaching. The truth is, I often left Wednesday night Bible study more prideful than when I arrived. Sometimes this pride would manifest as judgment of others who didn't have the same interpretation of scripture that I had been taught. Most frequently, pride would manifest in the form of false humility.

I would say things like, "I'm *just* a sinner saved by grace" believing that focusing on my sinfulness made me humble. In twenty-five plus years of Bible study, I do not remember one time that I asked Jesus for a Spirit of wisdom and revelation to teach me the Word of God. I read the Bible daily on my own, but I relied on my own thoughts and the instruction of my pastor to interpret scripture.

Have you ever learned something that you forgot in less than twenty-four hours? This happens because we quickly grow out of intellectual knowledge once we attain it. In contrast, we *grow into* revelation knowledge because it is based on a relationship that is not stagnant.

Modifying our behavior based on information that requires only independent application does not produce true transformation. Revelation is transformational because of the work of the Spirit on our behalf, not because of our own effort and striving. It is a supernatural gift that produces the fruit of the Spirit in our lives when we surrender to it. I pray that, like Paul, you will encounter a spirit of wisdom and revelation as you read this book.

Since knowing and hearing come from following, let's focus on some keys to practically follow the voice of our Shepherd.

We gain confidence in following God's voice by testing what we hear and assessing it against the nature of God and the entire counsel of the Word. The enemy's voice sounds like accusation, discouragement, con-

---

9. Strong's Greek: 1108. Γνῶσις (Gnósis) -- a Knowing, Knowledge.

demnation, and hopelessness. Our own voices are often full of doubt. God's voice is the voice of love and truth.

Ask these questions: Does it line up with scripture? Does it bring glory to God? Does it lead to freedom? Does it produce the fruits of the Spirit? Does it edify, encourage and build up?

1. Attention

To follow someone requires our attention and a turning from other distractions. Love is expressed first through our attention. Attention requires intentionality to turn away from lesser things. Attention is like currency and we "pay" attention to what we value.

When God is wanting to speak, there is always an invitation for our spirit to come to attention. Often the Lord gently nudges me and says, "Pay attention" before He speaks to me in any number of ways.

God speaks in a still, small voice. In 1 Kings 19, Elijah, a prophet of God, is waiting to hear God speak to him. God instructs him to stand on a mountain in the presence of the Lord. He looked for God to speak through a mighty windstorm, then an earthquake, then fire, but God was not there. One translation says God was found in a gentle whisper (1 Kings 19:12 NIV).

Elijah the prophet had experienced many wild encounters with God and heard the audible voice of the Lord countless times, so it is interesting that God chose to speak to him in a still, small voice. I believe this encounter was a prophetic picture of how God planned to continually speak to us under the new covenant after the outpouring of the Holy Spirit.

God still encounters people in dramatic ways involving fire, wind and even earthquakes. There are many people alive today who have heard the audible voice of the Lord, but also many, including myself, who have not. While God does still speak audibly, most of the time He speaks by simply whispering to our hearts. He does this so we have to lean into Him and pay close attention to hear Him.

To follow something we have to focus on it. Colossians 1:15 says "Christ is the visible image of the invisible God" (NLT). God speaks through our free flow of thoughts when we fix our eyes on Jesus. We are living in a period of history where continual distraction and disconnection has become normal. It is said that the average attention span of an adult is now less than a goldfish. There is an all out war for our attention.

1 John 4:8 says: "God is love," so His voice is the voice of love. What is the voice of love speaking to you right now?

I do not believe God ever grows tired of our questions, but not all of our questions are good for us. Anxiety is often attached to questions that are based on a need to figure things out rather than to trust God to lead us one step at a time. One of the ways God speaks to me is through books I read to my children and the shows they watch. I remember one Friday family movie night in particular. We had all eagerly climbed on to the couch with popcorn to watch the new Mary Poppins. I was distracted with a text message when the Holy Spirit got my attention with the line, "When you are on the edge of an adventure, don't spoil it with too many questions!"

When my head is swirling in problem-solving mode rather than resting on the Lord, I will simply fix my eyes on Jesus and His eyes like fire will burn away my unnecessary questions. It is in these moments that I am realigned and find once again, Jesus is the answer to every question.

"I will instruct you and teach you in the way you should go; I will guide you with My eye." (Psalm 32:8)

2. Surrender

Following requires allowing someone else to lead. We must deny our flesh and be impulsed by the Spirit to follow Jesus. The Holy Spirit is the seed growing inside us. We surrender to the Holy Spirit by turning inwardly to the indwelling Christ in us.

When we talk about the biblical concept of following Jesus we have to get the idea out of our head that life is somehow like social media. We cannot follow multiple people at the same time, all going in different directions. To follow we have to surrender to the leading of the Holy Spirit and give Jesus supremacy in our hearts. He is the Way; there is no other way. He is the Truth; there is no relative truth. He is the Life; there is no heavenly, eternal life apart from union with Him.

In 1 Corinthians 3:4-6, Paul addresses a trap the people of Corinth fell into that we often fall into today: "When one of you says, 'I am a follower of Paul,' and another says, 'I follow Apollos,' aren't you acting just like people of the world? After all, who is Apollos? Who is Paul? We are only God's servants through whom you believed the Good News. Each of us did the work the Lord gave us. I planted the seed in your hearts, and Apollos watered it, but it was God who made it grow" (NLT).

Doesn't this sound familiar? "I follow Bill Johnson; I'm a Pentacostal" or "I follow John Piper; I'm a Baptist." We are not called to be followers of churches, denominations, pastors or evangelists. We are followers of Jesus! Being a Pentacostal, Baptist, or any other denomination association is not our identity. We absolutely need to be led by leaders in the Church, but ultimately it must be Jesus whom we are following.

> *It is in these moments that I am realigned and find once again, Jesus is the answer to every question.*

Paul said, "Follow my example, as I follow the example of Christ" (1 Corinthians 11:1 NIV). When we allow someone else to guide us we must be sure that it's the Holy Spirit guiding them and not their own opinions, human understanding, or their flesh. When we remain connected to the Holy Spirit we will be able to discern when we are not being led by truth.

3. Faith

In order to follow someone, we must have faith in them. Remember Romans 10:17, "So then faith comes by hearing and hearing by the word of God." To hear the voice of our Shepherd, we have to suspend all thoughts of doubt and expect God is going to speak.

God often answers my questions with scripture. One day, in prayer I asked, "God how can I expand my receptors to hear you more?" He answered with Acts 2:17. "In the last days, God says, I will pour out my Spirit on all people. Your sons and daughters will prophesy, your young men will see visions, your old men will dream dreams."

Because I was not used to God speaking to me through dreams and visions, I had to trust the Holy Spirit to sanctify my imagination. The Lord created our imaginations to encounter Him. Our imagination is part of our soul. In the soulish realm there is a continual battle between good and evil. Scripture is clear that not all of our imaginations are from

God. 2 Corinthians 10:5 instructs us to cast down all imaginations and anything that exalts itself against the knowledge of Christ. When we take our thoughts captive out of obedience to Jesus, as the verse goes on to instruct, it frees our imagination from the lies of the enemy. Jesus is Truth, therefore He cannot manifest in a lie. When we confess the lies and capture our thoughts, our imagination becomes a place of sanctification and encounter.

My first step of faith was to write down my dreams and pray for an interpretation. When I did so I was shocked by the level of revelation God would give me. Surprisingly, it is often the abstract or seemingly insignificant dreams that God speaks the most significant revelation to me through. Hearing God in the night hours opened up new depths in my relationship with Him.

When we worship, when we read the Word, and when we pray we have to engage our imagination. Our God is alive! It is by faith that we engage with Him.

The first vision I ever had was of a simple olive branch. I asked God for revelation on the olive branch and here I am years later, writing an entire book based on an illustration not just of a branch, but of a whole tree. The Lord always responds to our hunger and faith.

4. Pursuit

In order to follow, we must take action steps in the footsteps of another. Matthew 7:7 says, "Ask and it will be given to you; seek and you will find; knock and the door will be opened to you." There is always pursuit involved in hearing God's voice. We are called to follow Jesus one step at a time. And so it is also with hearing His voice.

Psalm 119:105 gives us a word picture for this idea. The psalmist writes, "Your word is a lamp to my feet and a light to my path." A lamp at our feet, one foot step at a time, eventually leads to an illuminated path. If we do not step out in faith we will never be able to see the full destiny God has written for us.

God intentionally hides truth so we will discover it by pursuing a personal relationship with Him. This means we can chase the words he is speaking to us like a holy scavenger hunt. While western culture teaches through direct information and evidence, eastern culture (in which Jesus grew up) teaches that truth cannot be learned without it being uncovered in a process of personal discovery.[10]

The best example of this is how Jesus spoke in parables. Doing so meant only those truly hungry for the message of God received understanding. The Lord leaves us breadcrumbs that, when picked up in faith, lead to a whole loaf. The Father leads us into revelation when we are mature enough to receive it.

Hebrew scholars wrote commentaries on scripture that were compiled and called the Midrash. This rabbinic literature does not just state revelation that scholars discovered in the text like our western commentaries do. Instead, they wrote parables and allegories to help guide their readers on a process of discovery. This is how Jesus, a Jewish rabbi, taught His disciples.[11]

God is always beckoning us to find Him and can be found in the beauty all around us. Proverbs 25:2 says, "*It is* the glory of God to conceal a matter, but the glory of kings *is* to search out a matter."

Sometimes God speaks to me by dropping one word in my spirit. Often He will have me look up the definition of the word or show me an image in my mind and, as I follow the Holy Spirit, I am able to piece together what He wants me to know.

Often, when God prompts me to share encouragement with someone, He will only give me one word. When I open my mouth and speak it out in faith, more clarity comes. An example of this that always makes me chuckle is the time God told me to tell a stranger just one strange word: "cabbage." Does it get any more random than that?

I will give you a little background. For our ten year anniversary, my husband and I went to a spa in a beautiful mountain town. This was the first child-free trip we had taken since the birth of our kids four years prior. With this rare break from the constant noise of expressive toddlers, I was eagerly anticipating uninterrupted time with my husband and the Lord.

I asked God to speak to me as I laid down on a massage table about to enjoy a time of relaxation. As soon as the massage therapist put her hands on my back I heard God say one word: "cabbage." I immediate-

---

10. Discipleship, "The BEMA Podcast."
11. Discipleship, "The BEMA Podcast," n.d.

ly knew in my spirit that God wanted me to say this word to the massage therapist. For the next forty-five minutes I wrestled with the Lord. I asked for more insight. I tried to make sense of the word with my natural reasoning and I couldn't. I tried to talk myself into just blurting it out, but then I'd talk myself out of it. What could God possibly be saying to this woman through the word cabbage? Surely, I'd made it up. God did not really say that, right?

The massage ended and the massage therapist walked me to the front desk. I knew I would regret not responding to the voice of the Lord, so with a surge of courage I said, "This is going to sound crazy, but does the word cabbage mean anything to you?" Her eyes filled up with tears and she asked, "How do you know that?" I told her that I believed God wanted to speak to her but He only shared that one word with me. She went on to explain that she and her son affectionately call each other cabbage because they both have round faces and it's the only common physical trait they share. She said she had been worrying about her son and their relationship. From there, God began to give me words of prophetic encouragement to minister hope to a hurting mom.

It would have been so easy to give into doubt and disregard the word I heard God speak instead of responding with obedience. Sadly, there have been plenty of times when I have done just that and chosen not to step out in faith. There is certainly an abundance of mercy for these times, but I believe God trusts us with more of His heart when we listen with a willingness to obey.

If we are having a hard time hearing God speak, it could be that we are listening with no intention of responding. When God calls Samuel's name in the night in 1 Samuel 3:10, the priest Eli instructs him to respond: "Speak, your servant is listening" (NLT). In the original language this Scripture was written in, this is essentially saying, "Yes, to whatever you are about to say."

In Hebrew the word for "hear" is *akouó* and it also means to listen to comprehend and to respond.[12] In Matthew 13:13, Jesus speaks of some that listen to His teaching and says, "though hearing, they do not hear or understand." There is actually no Hebrew word that means to "obey"

---

12. Strong's Greek: 191. Ἀκούω (Akouó) -- to Hear, Listen.

as we would translate it in English. God is not looking for our reluctant compliance; He is after our hearts. To hear is to listen and follow.

Have you ever noticed that the disciples were not afraid to ask Jesus direct questions? In Matthew 13 the disciples ask Jesus why He spoke in parables. Let's read Jesus' reply:

> *"He answered and said to them, "Because it has been given to you to know the mysteries of the kingdom of heaven, but to them it has not been given." (Matthew 13:10)*

Wow! Jesus clearly makes a distinction between the disciples who were able to know the mysteries of the kingdom because of their relationship with Jesus. He goes on to describe the spiritual blindness and deafness of those who did not have intimacy with Him.

> *"For whoever has, to him more will be given, and he will have abundance; but whoever does not have, even what he has will be taken away from him. Therefore I speak to them in parables, because seeing they do not see, and hearing they do not hear, nor do they understand. And in them the prophecy of Isaiah is fulfilled, which says:*
>
> *'Hearing you will hear and shall not understand, And seeing you will see and not perceive; For the hearts of this people have grown dull. Their ears are hard of hearing, And their eyes they have closed, Lest they should see with their eyes and hear with their ears, Lest they should understand with their hearts and turn, So that I should heal them.'*
>
> *But blessed are your eyes for they see, and your ears for they hear; for assuredly, I say to you that many prophets and righteous men desired to see what you see, and did not see it, and to hear what you hear, and did not hear it." (Matthew 13:11-17)*

We want to be those who do not just hear God's voice, but also understand and heed it. When we say to children, "Why aren't you listening?" what we are really asking is, "Why aren't you responding?" Revelation of something without a willingness to obey gives the enemy an open door for condemnation. This further blocks us from hearing God speak. When we ask the Lord a question and are determined to obey whatever He speaks, He trusts us with more.

I challenge you to give your full attention to the following Field Notes. Ask God these questions in faith with a willingness to respond when He speaks. Let Him take you back to your origin story. Allow His words to water the seed of destiny growing inside you.

SEED FIELD NOTES

Identify how you hear God's voice

Find a quiet place and start by breathing in God's love for four seconds. Hold that breath for four seconds imagining His presence filling you up like a balloon. Now, for four seconds breathe out whatever negative emotion is weighing you down. Repeat this exercise until you feel settled and present. Ask the Holy Spirit the following questions. Then journal the free flow of thoughts that comes to your mind as you fix your eyes on Jesus.

Questions:

Holy Spirit, how do you feel about me? What lies have I believed about your thoughts towards me?

_____
_____
_____

How have I been blocked from receiving your love?

_____
_____
_____

How do you like to speak to me personally?

_____

_____

_____

How do you want me to open up to hearing you more?

_____

_____

_____

How can I limit the distractions keeping me from living connected to your voice?

_____

_____

_____

Activation:

In the next twenty-four hours, listen for God to speak in a way you haven't been open to hearing Him before. Journal about those experiences.

_____

_____

_____

_____

_____

Encounter:

Pick one verse from Psalm 139:1-18. Find a moment to sit in total stillness before the Lord focusing solely on that verse. Imagine yourself tasting the word of God, then carefully chewing it, then slowly swallowing it. Continue to digest this one Scripture all week while the seed of revelation takes root inside of you.

Recommended Resources:

Bible Hub is an excellent, free tool that allows you to examine the original language through the Strong's Concordance and access Bible commentaries that can provide important historic context; access it at Biblehub.com.

The YouVersion Bible App is another great resource for comparing different translations; access it at Bible.com

PLANT II

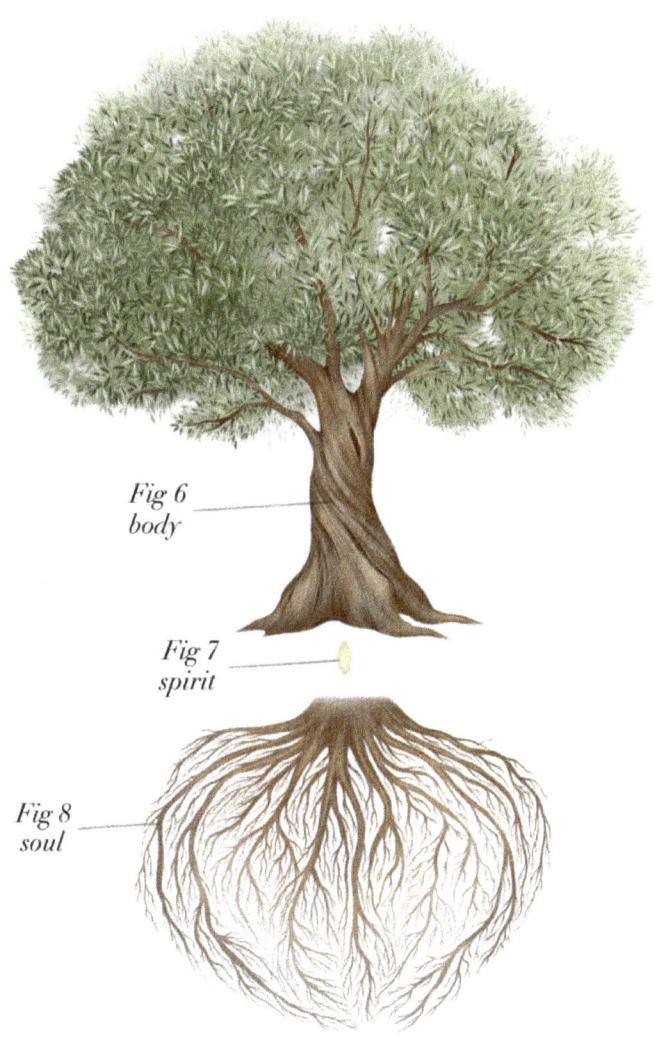

Figure 6: Body – The Seen   Figure 7: Spirit – The Eternal
Figure 8: Soul – The Unseen

PLANT
Chapter Two

How do you experience true life?
Identifying God's nature and your need for surrender

The Planted Seed

INSIDE EACH OF OUR destiny seeds is a beautiful and unique part of the kingdom of God that we were created to bring to the earth. This is wonderful and exciting! But there is a catch.

Jesus says in John 12:24 that unless a seed goes into the ground and dies it will never reap a harvest. When a seed is planted the shell has to be crushed so it can crack open, allowing the roots to emerge. We cannot experience true life without death to self, and we will not submit to the dying process with a wrong view of God's nature.

Remember, the seed implanted in us at our first birth has been corrupted with sin's decay. The penalty for our sin is eternal death. God is a just judge and justice demands a price be paid for our transgressions. Each of us deserves the death penalty.

Imagine an olive seed being burned in a fire. No amount of effort or good works could restore that seed to its original intent and function. The damage has been done and the seed is dead. Because the seed has been corrupted, it can never grow into an olive tree that produces good fruit.

The good news is that Jesus died so we can experience a new birth!

He paid the price for our sins on the cross and pleaded guilty so we could be pardoned. He took the punishment for our sins so we could be cleansed and justified before God, just as if we had never sinned.

He doesn't improve our corrupted seed; He replaces it completely with a brand new seed!

> "Therefore, if anyone is in Christ, he is a new creation. The old has passed away; behold, the new has come." (2 Corinthians 5:17 ESV)

Many of us were taught that receiving salvation is as simple as confessing our sinfulness and declaring that we believe Jesus is Lord. And it is that simple, but it's not that easy. Jesus tells His disciples to count the cost. The requirement is that we lay down our lives to follow Jesus. We were bought with a price, and our life is no longer our own. If we actually believe that Jesus is Lord, we have to allow Him to be Lord of every area of our life. The evidence that we have established true Lordship is our willingness to surrender control. Simple? Yes. Easy? Certainly not.

One of the main areas of my life I have battled with allowing God to be Lord is my marriage. My lack of surrender looked different in various seasons. Sadly, for the first eight years of my marriage I found myself repeatedly trading one version of control for another.

My husband and I met in Drawing 101 at Olivet Nazarene University. For our first assignment, our professor led us out to the Quad to sketch trees with charcoal. Feeling the pressure to do well on the first day of my college career, I gripped the charcoal tightly, attempting to control my strokes. The tighter I gripped, the worse the drawing got. This turned out to be a prophetic picture of the next several years of my life with the man I was about to meet.

I was so tense that I hardly noticed the student sitting next to me attempting to make a joke. Seeing my distress, he offered to help me. I was convinced he was an upper class art major and his advice was genuinely helpful. I found out later that he was a biochemistry major who had never taken a drawing class in his life. Because he simply did not take himself too seriously, he excelled in the class.

Michael really got my attention a week later after I was quarantined for the swine flu. He delivered a care package to my door and randomly wrote my life verse on the card to encourage me. Since I do not believe in random coincidences, it softened my heart and I took it as a sign that I should get to know him. During my week-long quarantine, we messaged back and forth and Michael promised to make me dinner and take me to Chicago once I was better. He kept his promise, with a cinnamon chicken dinner that was surprisingly good and the first of many day trips to Chicago's Chinatown for authentic chinese food – the way to my heart. We fell in love and got married two years later on a hot summer day in Southern Oregon. Unfortunately, my desire for control stayed with me, and I quickly discovered that Michael was not as easy going in other areas of his life as he was in Drawing 101.

For the first couple years of our marriage, I was determined to stand up for my rights and needs. I genuinely believed that I was responsible for my happiness, and I was willing to fight for it. I made myself judge and jury. As a result, I was destroying my husband, our marriage and myself.

One day, as an act of great mercy, the Lord convicted me of my selfishness. He told me that I was not my husband's Holy Spirit. He reminded me that He alone is responsible for the conviction and correction of my husband. I saw how my way was not working, and I genuinely repented. I wanted to experience transformation, but I believed that it was my job to right my wrongs. In so doing, I denied the very power that could actually transform me. Instead, I became determined to *try harder* and *do better* to be a godly wife.

> He doesn't improve our corrupted seed; He replaces it completely with a brand new seed!

I completely overcorrected. I got a hold of a book that misused scripture and convinced me I was created to please my husband. By agreeing with this lie, I traded one version of bondage - selfishness, for another - false responsibility. Believing I was responsible for Michael's happiness became a crushing weight that I was never meant to carry. Somewhere along the way I lost my voice completely.

When I did not see transformation in my husband, I believed it was because I was not behaving good enough or praying hard enough. The occasional times I felt I did well, I would end up feeling prideful about my effort. The majority of the time I did not measure up to the impossible standard I set for myself. This left me tormented by guilt, shame and even hopelessness. These cycles always ended with me promising myself I would try harder and do better.

How did I get here? One of the primary tactics of the enemy in this season of my life was to twist scripture like 1 Peter 3:1: "Likewise, wives, be subject to your own husbands, so that even if some do not obey the word, they may be won without a word by the conduct of their wives" (ESV). This is a powerful verse when understood in proper context. Unfortunately, the enemy deceived me into thinking that my husband's behavior, either good or bad, was a reflection of my own behavior. I believed the lie that his behavior was my responsibility.

Change in any relationship absolutely can come from one person being willing to be the change. The heart cry, "Lord start in me!" is one of the most powerful prayers we can pray. The problem in my case was a lack of surrender. I was no longer operating like my husband's Holy Spirit, but now I was operating like my own Holy Spirit. Instead of surrendering to Jesus, the only one responsible for true transformation, I relied on my own religious striving and behavior modification for the next several years.

By relying on myself, I was not allowing God to be the Lord over my marriage. One day, after another cycle ended in guilt and shame, I finally reached a point of full surrender. When I got to the end of myself, the Father was waiting to rescue me. God promised me that He was going to restore my marriage and make us ministers of reconciliation for other families. He told me I was spiritually blind and that He was about to open my eyes.

The truth is, I did not know who I was for the first eight years of my marriage. I was blind to my identity and my kingdom authority. True self-denial requires self-agency.

"To die to self we have to have a sense of self. Jesus had a self." The Lord spoke this revelation to my friend Lynelle Garrison after she discovered that her husband was not the honorable man everyone thought him to be and her happy marriage of thirty years was a mirage. When she shared her testimony at our Tuesday night Bible study, her words hit me like a ton of bricks. They sum up the main problem with my first eight years of marriage: I was trying to die to a self I did not know or value.

Self-hate has no place in self denial. Jesus says love your neighbor as you *love yourself* (Matthew 22:39). Self-love does not have to lead to selfishness, self-obsession, and self-promotion like the world models. Biblical self-love leads to self-denial. I do not know that it is even accurate to label it "self-love" because for the love of self to be pure it has to first funnel through the love of God. Remember, we only love because He first loved us.

Danny Silk teaches that powerful people say, "You matter and so do I," while passive people say "You matter and I don't," and aggressive people say, "I matter and you don't." Do you think Jesus ever questioned if He mattered as much as other people? Think about the power and authority He carried as He stepped into a room. Jesus, the ultimate model for self-denial, had a self. Until I understood my identity and inheritance as a child of God, I did not have the power to authentically give of myself to my husband or to anyone for that matter.

I had to learn that I could surrender control without abdicating my role.[13] Once I completely surrendered my marriage and the other areas of my life that I was trying to hold onto the reins, it was like I was born again, again! After twenty-five years of being a Christian, my spirit was awakened and my spiritual eyes were opened. It felt like I could see in color for the first time. Life became vibrant.

> "Therefore it says, "Awake, O sleeper, and arise from the dead, and Christ will shine on you." (Ephesians 5:14 ESV)

After this spiritual awakening, God began to teach me about my true identity starting with the truth that we are three part beings: body, soul and spirit. When we receive salvation, our spirit is now one with the Spirit of God. This truth became the catalyst for all my spiritual transformation.

The Implanted Spirit

> "Having been born again, not of corruptible seed but incorruptible, through the word of God which lives and abides forever;" (1 Peter 1:23)

When we are planted in the Lord and receive salvation, our seed is replaced with an incorruptible seed! The very spirit of God is implanted in us.

---

13. Concept articulated by Heather Rose, co-pastor of The Collective Church.

"But he who is joined to the Lord becomes one spirit with him." (1 Corinthians 6:17 ESV)

We are not given a new seed that we can quickly corrupt again with our sin. We are given God's seed: Jesus to live in us.

"I have been crucified with Christ. It is no longer I who live, but Christ who lives in me." (Galatians 2:20 ESV)

This is the greatest exchange of all time. God takes our dead spirit and replaces it with the Holy Spirit. Jesus told His disciples that it would be better if He left them because He was going to send the Holy Spirit as a helper to infill them (John 16:7).

The disciples surely had a hard time imagining what could be better than Jesus with them in the flesh. They had no idea the radical power they were about to experience on the day of Pentecost. One seed now eternally multiplied in everyone who chooses to receive new life. This is the wonder-working resurrection power of Christ!

"The Spirit of God, who raised Jesus from the dead, lives in you. And just as God raised Christ Jesus from the dead, he will give life to your mortal bodies by this same Spirit living within you." (Romans 8:11)

If Jesus is Lord of your life, the same Spirit that raised Jesus from the dead lives inside of you. As He is, so are you in the world!

"Love has been perfected among us in this: that we may have boldness in the day of judgment; because as He is, so are we in this world." (1 John 4:17)

Does your life look like the life of Jesus? In more than two decades of being a Jesus-loving Christian, my life certainly did not. Up to this point I had never seen the sick healed, demons cast out and the gospel preached with a demonstration of power. Then I read John 14:12 for what felt like the first time.

"Most assuredly, I say to you, he who believes in Me, the works that I do he will do also; and greater works than these he will do, because I go to My Father."

How is it possible for us to do greater works than Jesus? This was a mystery to me. However, just because our natural mind may not fully understand a scripture, does not mean we can disregard it. The entire narrative of scripture is consistent with the truth that no one will ever be greater than Jesus. I believe Jesus is referring to the work that comes after His ministry on the earth, after His death, resurrection, and ascension. Jesus' A.D. ministry in union with us is greater than His ministry while He walked the earth. Why? Because He conquered death and sent the Holy Spirit to live inside each of us! Now, through individual partnership with each believer, we get to be a part of the greatest work on the Earth. The absolute honor and responsibility that comes with this truth is sobering.

So what is the disconnect from the Spirit alive inside of us and the tangible power of the Spirit displayed in our lives? Jesus addresses this also in the gospel of John.

> *"Jesus said to her, "I am the resurrection and the life. Whoever believes in me, though he die, yet shall he live, and everyone who lives and believes in me shall never die. Do you believe this?" (John 11:25 ESV)*

Do you believe this? Four words that should cut to the core of our being. *Do you believe?* Do you actually believe you are a new creation? Do you believe the same power that raised Jesus from the dead lives in you? Right now Jesus is asking you the same question He asked His disciples over 2,000 years ago, "Do you believe this?"

The gap that lies between what we live and what scripture says is with what we actually believe. This disconnect is like having unlimited funds, but only accessing a few pennies a day. We withdraw in faith what has already been deposited into our account. We only have access to what we believe we have.

We have been given the Spirit of the living God, but our soul and body are still in a process of renewal. The more we believe in the work God has done on our behalf, the more our souls and our bodies reflect our already transformed spirit.

Does scripture teach that our body, soul and spirit are all essential components of our sanctification? In 1 Thessalonians 5:23 Paul blesses the Church of Thessalonica by saying, "Now may the God of peace himself **sanctify you completely**, and may **your whole spirit and soul and body** be kept blameless at the coming of our Lord Jesus Christ" (ESV, bold text mine).

Imagine your spirit as a seed that has been planted in good soil. The underground root system that grows from this seed is your new identity. What sprouts up from the seed of truth becomes a reflection of Jesus to the world. This is your destiny, the true life you were created for.

The battle for our spirit has been won and Christ has been victorious! Thank you, Jesus! But as long as we are on this side of eternity, the war over our soul and body continues. This is the war against our flesh:

> *"For those who live according to the flesh set their minds on the things of the flesh, but those who live according to the Spirit, the things of the Spirit. For to be carnally minded is death, but to be spiritually minded is life and peace. Because the carnal mind is enmity against God; for it is not subject to the law of God, nor indeed can be. So then, those who are in the flesh cannot please God. But you are not in the flesh but in the Spirit, if indeed the Spirit of God dwells in you." (Romans 8:6-9)*

The flesh is at war with the spirit. The only way we can grow in victory is by daily dying to the desires of our flesh and yielding ourselves completely to the impulses of the Spirit.

> *"But I say, walk by the Spirit, and you will not gratify the desires of the flesh. For the desires of the flesh are against the Spirit, and the desires of the Spirit are against the flesh, for these are opposed to each other, to keep you from doing the things you want to do. But if you are led by the Spirit, you are not under the law. (Galatians 5:16-18 ESV)*

Imagine thousands of weeds planted next to the seed of the spirit. Each of these weeds has their own roots that entangle the roots of the spirit. This is a picture of your soul and actually resembles the neural pathways of the human brain. The weeds are your sin, flesh, demonic oppression, fear and trauma.

The sanctification of the soul happens through the watering of the seed of the spirit *(refer to figure 7)* and the uprooting of the weeds of the flesh.

The tree that is visible above ground represents the body *(refer to figure 6)*, or what is seen. The roots reflect what is unseen, growing in our soul *(refer to figure 8)*. This is an overview of the illustration that we will unpack in more depth in future chapters.

The Implanted Nature

In order for our new spirit to be reflected in our soul and body, we need to have a true understanding of the nature of the God we are reflecting. We become what we behold. Like little children, we mirror the expression and nature of our Father when we experience His delight for us.

Dr. Edward Tronic conducted a revolutionary study in child development called the Still Face Experiment.[14] This experiment showed that babies have the ability to regulate their emotions and understand their world right from the start. They need to know the answer to three questions: Do I belong here? Am I loved? Can we build a world together?

It is natural for us to be expressive with our face and body language as we engage with babies. We smile, mimic the noises they make and engage them through our expressions of delight. During the Still Face Experiment parents were instructed to start off by actively engaging with their babies in this way. Then, after a minute of unrestricted attention and loving expressions, they were instructed to make their facial expressions go completely still.

When this happens, the babies immediately begin to experience unrest. They went from smiling and laughing to fussing in a matter of seconds. They tried to engage their parents in the way that they had previously. When the parents did not respond, they began to cry out for the expressions they needed to feel safe and loved. As time goes on you watch trauma begin to set in. At this point the experiment is concluded and parents return to their normal interaction and loving engagement with their babies.

We may outgrow our need to interact with our parents in this way, but eye contact with those we love remains a core need for adults. This is

---

14. Lisitsa, "The Research: The Still Face Experiment."

where the invention of the cell phone has created a war on connection. Our souls desperately need eye contact with people around us, but there is a magnetic, addictive pull to look at our devices instead.

If eye contact with people is a core need of humans, how much greater is the need for face to face time with our Creator? The reality is, we never outgrow our need to look to the face of our Heavenly Father and experience His love for us. It is here that we receive the love and security we need and are able to address the same questions we subconsciously asked our parents as infants. "Do I belong here? Am I loved? Can we build a world together?"

> We can only know ourselves by knowing God.

Devastatingly, the majority of people will not look to the face of their Creator and to His Word daily to have these subconscious questions answered. Instead, they will give their gaze to social media, the news, work, YouTube, and TV, forgetting God and in turn, forgetting their true selves.

What happens when we have an entire population looking to the world to answer these three core questions: "Do I belong here? Am I loved? Can we build a world together?" A massive global identity crisis. Now, one in four high school students in the U.S. identify as LGBTQ, deceived into thinking that God made a mistake when he created them.[15] Suicide rates have increased 36% since the same time period smart phones became available.[16] There has been a 13% increase in mental health disorders in the last ten years,[17] and 90% of Americans believe we are in a mental health crisis.[18] Also rising at an alarming rate, the number of Americans who profess to have no religion has risen 266% since 1991.[19] A culture who mostly forgets God and mostly thinks of self will lose their true selves completely.

We can only know ourselves by knowing God. "What comes into our minds when we think about God is the most important thing about us,"

---

15. Cochran, "1 in 4 High School Students Identifies as LGBTQ."
16. USAFacts, "US Suicide Rate Trends and States With the Highest Suicide Rates."
17. Oxford Academic. "Mental Health," n.d.
18. Insel, "America's Mental Health Crisis."
19. Bauman, "Is America Becoming Godless? The Number of People Who Have No Religion Rose 266% in Three Decades."

A.W. Tozer writes and continues his thoughts on this concept in his book *The Knowledge of the Holy*:

"The history of mankind will probably show that no people has ever risen above its religion, and man's spiritual history will positively demonstrate that no religion has ever been greater than its idea of God. Worship is pure or base as the worshiper entertains high or low thoughts of God. For this reason the gravest question before the Church is always God Himself, and the most portentous fact about any man is not what he at a given time may say or do, but what he in his deep heart conceives God to be like. We tend by a secret law of the soul to move toward our mental image of God. This is true not only of the individual Christian, but of the company of Christians that composes the Church. Always, the most revealing thing about the Church is her idea of God."[20]

This concept of a secret law of the soul that moves toward our mental image of God is profound. It is also concerning as many believe God is mad at them and desires to punish them. Others believe God to be disappointed in them. Then there are those who have confronted the wrong belief that God is angry with them, but they still believe God to be indifferent towards them or still faced. This thought can be just as detrimental as believing God feels anger and desires vengeance when He thinks of us.

If we have a still faced God in our mind, we will always perform for acceptance when acceptance is not something that can be earned. Acceptance is our birthright as the beloved sons and daughters of God. Ephesians 1:6 says, "to the praise of the glory of His grace, by which He made us accepted in the Beloved." This scripture does not say He *is making* us accepted because He already has. We tend to confuse sanctification and acceptance. Sanctification is the growth process we are in that requires our participation, but acceptance is something we have already obtained from our Heavenly Father.

Whether we realize it or not, our life experiences play a part in creating our theology, either accurately or devastatingly inaccurately. Intellectually believing God to be good and experientially living in the goodness of God are two different things. Our first beliefs about our Heavenly Father come from our relationship with our earthly father. When these emotions are suppressed, they become a subconscious force that keeps

---

20. Tozer, *The Knowledge of the Holy*.

us separated from the freedom and joy of the Lord.

WM. Paul Young, author of *The Shack,* says, "It took me fifty years to wipe the face of my father off the face of God."

What happens when the face of our imperfect fathers has taken the place of our perfect God? Our vision is blurred. In our blindness, we cannot see God rightly and therefore we do not see ourselves rightly as children created in the image of God.

Before God challenged my view of His nature, I believed all the right things about God. I knew He was good. I knew He was faithful. I knew He was steadfast. I knew He was different from my earthly father because He is perfect. I had even experienced His goodness, faithfulness and steadfastness in my life. The misalignment was with how these truths related *to me.* Even though, deep down I believed God was good, the belief that *I* was not good enough kept me from freely receiving the goodness of God. The truth is, we *are* undeserving, but that is only half of the gospel. The other half is that grace gives us everything we do not deserve! The more we learn to receive the underserved goodness of God, the more good we become. Not from trying harder to be "good Christians" but from challenging our wrong beliefs about God and about ourselves.

Under the New Covenant, God never turns His back on us. We get to live in the delight of God from now until eternity! Understanding Jesus' sacrifice forever unlocks the pleasure of God towards us like Heaven on Earth. Now everything we do is reflecting from His gaze, not striving for love, but abiding in the love that He freely, lavishly gives.

It is God's kindness that leads to repentance (Romans 2:4). When we sin, we turn our back on God. Experiencing His loving-kindness makes us feel safe to turn back to Him, time and time again. Repentance simply means to change our mind and change direction. True repentance always involves us changing our mind about God or ourselves. As a result of this mind change, we change directions and move towards God.

Worship is the gift God gave us to turn our hearts back to Him so He can embrace us with open arms. We do not worship God to remind Him who He is. We worship God so we can be reminded of who He is and open our hearts to receive from Him. As we remember the nature of our Father, we naturally rest securely in His arms. Worship is not about us; it's about God. By remembering God, we are transformed.

When we have wrong thoughts, singing songs of deliverance and declaring the truth out loud are two of the most effective weapons of warfare that we have. Try counting down from one hundred in your mind. Are you counting? Now, keep counting and speak out loud your name and address. Did you lose count? Of course you did. Because the words we speak are always more powerful than our thoughts.[21]

Since we are made in the image of God, we cannot know who we are until we know God. Everything bad we believe about ourselves we believe at some level about God.

Say these out loud to God as a declarative act of worship. If your heart is not agreeing with any of these characteristics of God, say them anyway. Then look up the Scripture references and let the Holy Spirit illuminate truth to you.

God, you are Creator – *Elohim*. (Genesis 1:1, Revelations 4:11)

God, you are All Sufficient – *El Shaddai* (Genesis 17:1-2)

God, you are God Who Sees Me – *El Roi* (Genesis 16:14-15)

God, you are Everlasting – *El Olam* (Genesis 21:32-33)

God, you are Provider – *Yahweh - Yireh* (Genesis 22:14, Philippians 4:19)

God, you are Master – *Adonai* (Psalm 16:2)

God, you are Healer – *Yahweh Rapha* (Exodus 15:26, Psalm 103:1-3)

God you are Prince of Peace – *Yahweh Shalom* (Judges 6:22-24, Isaiah 9:6)

God, you are Holy – *Qedosh Yisrael* (Isaiah 6:3, Exodus 15:11, Leviticus 19:1-3)

God, you are My Shepherd – *Yahweh Roi* (Psalm 23:1)

God, you are Present – *Yahweh Shammah* (Ezekial 48:35)

God, you are a Consuming Fire – *El Kanna* (Exodus 34:14)

God, you are My Rock – *Yahweh Tsuri* (Psalm 18:2)

God, you are Strength – *El Sali* (Psalm 18:1)

God, you are My Father – *Abba, Pater* (2 Corinthians 6:18)

God, you are Mercy – *Yahweh Hesed* (Nehemiah 9:17)

God, you are My Righteousness – *Yahweh Tsidqenu* (Jeremiah 23:6, 2

---

21. Fomenko, "Destroy Fear, Panic and Anxiety with Debra Arnott."

Timothy 4:8)

God, you are With Us – *Emmanuel* (Matthew 1:22-23)

God, you are The Beginning And The Ending – *Alpha kai Omega* (Revelation 22:13)

God, you are Potter (Isaiah 64:8)

God, you are My Hope (Psalm 71:5)

God, you are Protector (Psalm 3:3)

God, you are My Strong Tower (Psalm 18:10)

God, you are My Great Physician (Matthew 11:5)

God, you are Faithful (1 Corinthians 1:9)

God, you are Love (1 John 4:7-8)

God, you are Kind (Ephesians 2:7)

God, you are Just (Deuteronomy 32:4, Psalm 89:14)

God, you are Steadfast (Psalm 33:5)

God, you are Forgiving (Ephesians 4:32)

God, you are Gracious (Isaiah 30:18)

God, you are Trustworthy (Psalm 20:7, Proverbs 3:5-6)

God, you are all Powerful (Psalm 147:5, Jeremiah 32:17, Luke 1:37)

God, you are Humble (Philipians 2:8)

God, you are Patient (2 Peter 3:9)

God, you are Wise (Proverbs 3:19, Job 12:13, Isaiah 55:9)

God, you are Perfect (2 Samuel 22:31)

God, you are Joyful (Nehemiah 8:10)

God, you are Beautiful (Psalm 27:4)

God, you are Victorious (Deuteronomy 20:4)

God, you are Compassionate (Psalm 116:5)

God, you are Worthy (Revelations 4:11)

God, you are Light (1 John 1:5)

God, you are Working (Romans 8:28)

God, you are Generous (James 1:17)

God, you are Stable (Isaiah 33:5-6)

God, you are Great (Psalm 145:1)

God, you are Glorious (Hebrews 1:3, Revelation 5:13)[22]

If you are not yet convinced that God is not mad at you or indifferent towards you, the majority of the time this comes from unhealed places in our heart towards our fathers and/or misunderstandings about the old and new covenant. Stay sensitive to the guidance of the Holy Spirit as we journey on and boldly confront these things.

---

22. "O.T. Names of God - Study Resources," Blue Letter Bible, n.d.

PLANT FIELD NOTES

Identify how you misunderstand God's nature and how to give Him Lordship over your life

Find a quiet place and start by breathing in God's love for four seconds. Hold that breath for four seconds, imagining His presence filling you up like a balloon. Now, for four seconds breathe out whatever negative emotion is weighing you down. Repeat this exercise until you feel settled and present. Ask the Holy Spirit the following questions. Then journal the free flow of thoughts that come to your mind as you fix your eyes on Jesus.

Questions:

Holy Spirit, how have I misunderstood your nature? Who do you say that you are?

_____
_____
_____

How am I resisting your sovereign authority in my life?

_____
_____
_____

How can I surrender completely to you? Are there any areas of my life that I have not yet made you Lord over?

_____

_____

_____

Activation:

Go back through the list on pages 45-47 and circle three to five characteristics of God that the Holy Spirit highlights to you. Look up the scripture references and ask God for further revelation on each particular part of His nature. Add as many characteristics as you would like to the list. God, you are_____ . Say these statements out loud to your Heavenly Father. Make these declarations of God's nature a part of your daily routine.

Encounter:

Kristi McLelland notes, "We live in such a way that we stare at our lives and glance at God" It should not be this way! Let's take a minute and intentionally stare at God."

It should not be this way! Let's take a minute and intentionally stare at God.

Find a quiet moment, close your eyes and listen to the song Show Me Your Face by Steffany Gretzinger, available on all streaming platforms. Afterwards, read the following slowly using your sanctified imagination.

Imagine yourself stepping through the veil of separation.

All your filthy garments are taken off. You are robed in His righteousness.

The Accuser is silenced. Jesus takes the enemy's words, like darts out of your back, and throws them into the depths of the sea.

There is nothing shameful or faulty about you anymore.

You now can come boldly before the throne of grace with confidence.

Look at your Father's face. Remember, Jesus is the image of the invisible God.

Take all record of your sin and shame and hand it to the Father.

Can you see His delight?

Bask in the warmth of His smile.

Lock into His love.

Sense His passion.

His desire is for you.

Engage with His gaze.

Settle into the pleasure He has for you, His beloved child.

You are brand new, a reflection of Jesus.

Rest in love's embrace.

Abide in this place of acceptance.

Remain in the pleasure of your Father.

Recommended Resource:

The Still Face Experiment. Gottman.com/blog/research-still-face-experiment.

CULTIVATE III

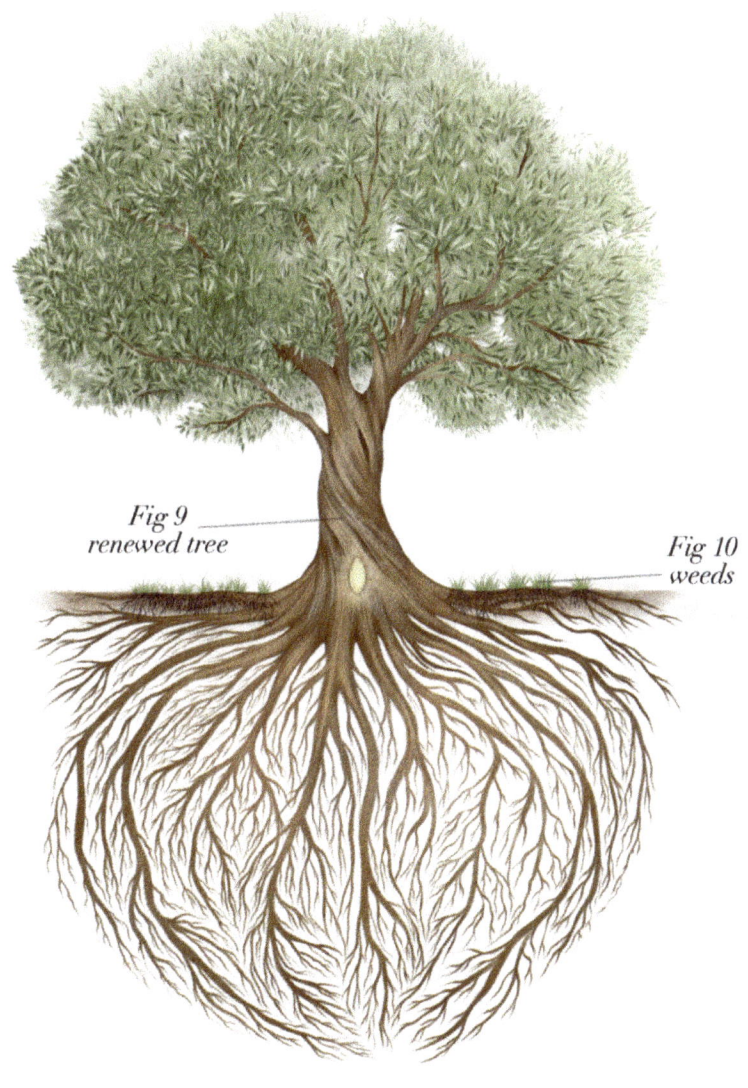

Figure 9: Renewed Tree   Figure 10: Weeds Invading Soil

CULTIVATE

Chapter Three

How do you receive nourishment for transformation?
Identifying your thoughts and beliefs

"I AM JUST NOT A patient person." This is a toxic thought that I have had most of my life. I remember the last day I fully agreed with this thought. It was an ordinarily stressful day with my two little kids only a year apart. Children are excellent magnifiers of the unhealed places of our hearts. In this instance, I was unwilling to confront the frustration I had just expressed to my children so I consoled myself with the all too familiar thought, "I'm just not a naturally patient person."

My immediate agreement with this thought was an excuse to remain the same. Accepting my weakness in this way felt like humility, but in that moment the Holy Spirit spoke a word of correction to me that I will never forget. He said, "If you keep believing you lack patience you will always be impatient. The fruit of my Spirit is patience and I live inside of you. What you believe you will become."

This is a foundational truth that has changed my life. What we believe we will become.

I chose to repent by changing my mind at that moment. I walked out my repentance by renewing my mind daily with the truth that I *am* patient because I am a new creation in Christ. By doing this I have grown tremendously in the area of patience.

Sadly, there are still times when my flesh takes over and I express impatience, but my reaction towards this expression of my old nature is different now. When we express characteristics of our old nature, like impatience, we do not need to beat ourselves up and agree with the enemy's lies that say impatience is a part of who we are. Repentance is not saying "I'm sorry." Repentance is choosing to change. The way we choose to change is by cultivating our thoughts which create our actions.

Now, anytime we are convicted of impatience, we can take the opportunity to thank God that our old nature is dead and Christ's perfect patience is alive in us! In the same way, we can turn from any and all expressions of our old, dead nature. We crucify our flesh by surrendering to the power of the Holy Spirit. The same power that raised Jesus from the dead lives in us. We do not just need this power to heal the sick, cast out demons and share the gospel. The primary function of the Holy Spirit's power is to *change us* by revealing Jesus to us. We need supernatural power to be patient and loving towards the cashier at Target, the old lady in traffic, and certainly our own family.

For most of my life, I tried my hardest to be patient. It did not matter how hard I tried, impatience still oozed out of me every uncomfortable chance it got. And it was not just impatience, other characteristics of my flesh showed up in all the places I wanted to hide them the most. This religious striving is exhausting and ineffective. It is an absolute miracle that because of the power of the Spirit and a renewed mind, the fruit of patience is evident in my life.

Scripture says everything we need for godliness is already planted within us. We access this abundant supply through partnership with God's divine nature. This is an incredible truth, but it can only produce fruit in our lives if we believe it. The truth in the Word of God has the power to change us far more than any self-help book or even commentaries on Scripture can. I challenge you to take a minute to read the following passage with focused faith.

"By his divine power, God has given us everything we need for living a godly life. We have received all of this by coming to know him, the one who called us to himself by means of his marvelous glory and excellence. And because of his glory and excellence, he has given us great and precious promises. These are the promises that enable you to share his divine nature and escape the world's corruption caused by human desires.

In view of all this, make every effort to respond to God's promises.

Supplement your faith with a generous provision of moral excellence, and moral excellence with knowledge, and knowledge with self-control, and self-control with patient endurance, and patient endurance with godliness, and godliness with brotherly affection, and brotherly affection with love for everyone.

The more you grow like this, the more productive and useful you will be in your knowledge of our Lord Jesus Christ. But those who fail to develop in this way are shortsighted or blind, forgetting that they have been cleansed from their old sins.

> "So, dear brothers and sisters, work hard to prove that you really are among those God has called and chosen. Do these things, and you will never fall away. Then God will give you a grand entrance into the eternal Kingdom of our Lord and Savior Jesus Christ." (2 Peter 1: 1-11 NLT)

If we already possess everything we need then why do we sometimes lack characteristics of Christ? Peter tells us it is our own blindness and forgetfulness. When Christians do not exhibit the fruit of the Spirit and the power of God, it's not because something is missing. Rather, that fruit has not been fully realized on the inside of us. To grow the fruit of the Spirit, we must cultivate the soil of our hearts by saturating our thinking, believing and being with truth.

Cultivated Soil

> "Sow with a view to righteousness [that righteousness, like seed, may germinate]; Reap in accordance with mercy and lovingkindness. Break up your uncultivated ground, For it is time to seek and search diligently for the Lord." (Hosea 10:12 AMP)

We all have some measure of uncultivated ground in our heart that is in need of plowing by the Spirit. Hosea teaches us that for the righteous seed to germinate in us we have to sow (to think, to choose, to live) with a view of righteousness. To become righteous we have to view ourselves as righteous, the same way God sees us because of the blood of Jesus.

How do we see ourselves as righteous? By seeking and searching diligently for the Lord like the prophet Hosea concludes in Hosea 10:12. It is only when we behold God, the only one truly righteous, that we become like Him.

In scripture, the heart is a reference to our soul, our minds, will, and emotions. Breakthrough in our lives comes when we intentionally partner with Jesus, the plowman, to break up the stony places of our hearts. Jesus uses the metaphor of soil to describe various heart conditions in the Parable of the Sower.

> *"Therefore hear the parable of the sower: When anyone hears the word of the kingdom, and does not understand it, then the wicked one comes and snatches away what was sown in his heart. This is he who received seed by the wayside. But he who received the seed on stony places, this is he who hears the word and immediately receives it with joy; yet he has no root in himself, but endures only for a while. For when tribulation or persecution arises because of the word, immediately he stumbles. Now he who received seed among the thorns is he who hears the word, and the cares of this world and the deceitfulness of riches choke the word, and he becomes unfruitful. But he who received seed on the good ground is he who hears the word and understands it, who indeed bears fruit and produces: some a hundredfold, some sixty, some thirty." (Matthew 13:18-23)*

Whether or not the seed implanted in us at salvation sprouts and bears good fruit depends on the condition of the soil we are planted in and the nourishment we receive. Jesus did everything for us to obtain salvation, but we have a part to play to remain planted, rooted and growing in truth. The conditions of our growth environment matters for the ultimate success or failure of our development.

The purpose of soil preparation is to break up compacted soil and replenish vital nutrients. Newly germinated seeds have an especially hard time sprouting through soil that has not been cultivated. Good ground is created when we understand, believe and receive truth. We cultivate good soil by cultivating our thoughts. It is the Word of Truth that bears fruit and produces it effortlessly in our life when we agree with it.

The word cultivate means: to loosen or break up the soil; to foster the growth of; to improve by labor, care, or study.[23] When I think of the word

---

23. "Cultivate," in *Merriam-Webster Dictionary*.

cultivate, what comes to mind is intentionality, diligence and supernatural empowerment. These are important biblical concepts necessary for our growth and development.

Others hear the word cultivate and their thoughts turn towards striving, stress and duty. One response provokes yieldedness to the Holy Spirit, while the other creates a self-dependency that hinders the work of the Spirit. We must be able to recognize the difference between striving out of religious duty and cultivating as we abide with Christ.

Good soil has to be continually renewed and restored through a process of cultivation. Our souls are the same. Remember, our spirits have been replaced at salvation, but our souls and body are still in a process of renewal. The seed of salvation has already been sown, but whether or not it springs up to reveal the new life in us depends on the cultivation of our thoughts.

King David models speaking to his soul to change his reaction to his circumstances throughout the Psalms. The writer of Lamentations does the same in Lamentations 3:20-23.

> *"My soul is downcast within me. Yet this I call to mind and therefore I have hope: Because of the Lord's great love we are not consumed, for his compassions never fail. They are new every morning; great is your faithfulness." (NIV)*

If we understood the power we wield when we call to mind the truth about God, we would not ever think about anything else. Our emotions, our thoughts, and our choices will not always reflect what is true. We cannot control our circumstances, but we must cultivate our reactions to our circumstances by calling to mind what is true and worthy of praise. God's mercies are new every morning, because He knows we desperately need to receive them fresh, every day. When our souls are downcast, we call to mind the compassion, faithfulness and mercies of the Lord so renewal can take place within us.

Scripture clearly teaches that all true transformation comes when we change our minds.

> *"Do not conform to the pattern of this world, but be transformed by the renewing of your mind. Then you will be able to test and approve what God's will is—his good, pleasing and perfect will." (Romans 12:2 NIV)*

The word renewing in the Greek is "anakainósis." According to Strong's Concordance it represents a positive change, a process of renewing, and change affected by the Holy Spirit.[24] The concept is a change of heart which leads to a change of life.

Romans 12:2 implies an active participation in this renewal process. In Titus 3:5 the same word is used. "But when the kindness and love of God our Savior appeared, he saved us, not because of righteous things we had done, but because of his mercy. He saved us through the washing of rebirth and renewal by the Holy Spirit" (NIV).

Titus 3:5 clearly states that renewal happens by the power of the Holy Spirit. Only God can change hearts. Apart from the power of the Holy Spirit there is no real transformation. So what active part do we play in the renewal process?

I believe the answer is found in 2 Timothy 1:7. Timothy says, "For God has not given us a spirit of fear, but of power and of love and of a sound mind."

God freely gives us power, love, and a sound mind. The enemy continually offers us fear, rendering us powerless. We choose which we will accept. The role of the recipient is to reject or to receive.

Right this moment God is declaring to us, "I have set before you life and death, blessings and curses. Now choose life, so that you and your children may live" (Deuteronomy 30:19 NIV).

Life or death. Blessings or curses. Love or fear. Whatever we choose to think about becomes a tangible reality in our life. The fruit we see, good or bad, is created first by our thoughts.

Fertilizer of Faith

Faith is like fertilizer that has to be applied to the soil of our hearts for us to grow. Without fertilizer the nutrients in the soil cannot replenish. When soil is not replenished it becomes sterile and unfit for cultivation. Likewise, we cannot grow and produce good fruit without the renewal of our minds through an intentional application of faith.

We have all been given a measure of faith (Romans 12:3), and all we need is faith the size of the tiniest seed to be able to move mountains (Matthew 17:20). If this is true, why do we feel we need to muster up

---

24. Strong's Greek: 342. Ἀνακαίνωσις (Anakainósis) -- Renewal.

more faith? When we lack faith it is not because we do not possess it, but rather because we are not choosing to apply it. If you have ever taken the time to apply fertilizer to anything, you know you are not going to put in the effort if you do not believe in its benefits. In the same way, doubt and unbelief hinder us to the degree that they stop us from applying the fertilizer of faith. Hebrews 11:6 says that without faith it is impossible to please God, because we have to believe in order to choose God and His ways.

All spiritual warfare is a battle for what we believe. Paul repeatedly addresses the war of the mind throughout his epistles. Every piece of the armor of God in Ephesians 6:11 is a metaphor for the protection of our minds, our thinking and our choosing.

Most Christians have been taught that we need to take our thoughts captive, but few know the context of this Scripture and understand why this concept is so vitally important. Without this understanding, capturing our thoughts is just a nice idea, not an everyday discipline.

Let's examine 2 Corinthians 10:3-5 carefully for the why behind the command to take our thoughts captive.

> *"For though we live in the world, we do not wage war as the world does. The weapons we fight with are not the weapons of the world. On the contrary, they have divine power to demolish strongholds. We demolish arguments and every pretension that sets itself up against the knowledge of God, and we take captive every thought to make it obedient to Christ." (NIV)*

Did you spot the why? There is an all out war for our minds. We wrestle not against flesh and blood, but principalities and powers (Ephesians 6:12). Whether or not we know it, we are in a spiritual war right now. There are no bystanders in this war. There are those who choose to enlist in the fight of faith and those who are casualties. This is why taking every thought captive is not a nice suggestion; it is a life-saving command. When we understand that we are in a real war, putting on the armor of God is not optional; it is mandatory.

We looked at Romans 8:6-9 in the last chapter where Paul says the mind of the flesh is at war with the mind of the spirit. Thoughts rooted in deception must be taken as a prisoner of war and made to bow before our Commander, King Jesus.

Every negative thought we have is a direct assault against truth. It is often said that our lives move in the direction of our most dominant thought. Our thoughts are never neutral. They are either fighting for us or working against us. If God did not say it, we cannot agree with it. We can no longer remain passive towards our thought life!

How we perceive something is how we receive from it. Our thoughts determine our attitudes, which determine our beliefs, which determine our actions, which determine our life. The enemy is waging physiological and spiritual warfare, and he does not fight fair.

Our brains are wired for love, not negativity. When we are negative it causes neurochemical chaos within the cells and structure of our brains. The brilliant Creator of our minds tells us how we are to think. Our brains function properly when we meditate on thoughts that are true, noble, just, pure, lovely, good and praise worthy just as God instructs us to do in His word.

> *"Finally, brethren, whatever things are true, whatever things are noble, whatever things are just, whatever things are pure, whatever things are lovely, whatever things are of good report, if there is any virtue and if there is anything praiseworthy—meditate on these things." (Philippians 4:8 NIV)*

Meditation on what is good is the intended function of our brains. This is a biblical truth that is fully backed by neuroscience. Dr. Caroline Leaf, a communication pathologist and neuroscientist specializing in cognitive and metacognitive neuropsychology, teaches extensively on how God created us to be able to rewire our minds. She was one of the first in her field to study how the brain can change (neuroplasticity) with directed mind input. Dr. Leaf says it takes three cycles of 21 days minimum to change a thought pattern. In this war on our minds we must be constantly taking captive toxic thoughts and replacing them with truth.

Dr. Caroline Leaf says, "Our mind is designed to control the body, of which the brain is a part, not the other way around. Matter does not control us; we control matter through our thinking and choosing. We cannot control the events and circumstances of life but we can control our reactions. In fact, we can control our reactions to anything, and in doing so, we change our brains. It's not easy; it is hard work, but it can be done through our thoughts and choices."

"What you are thinking every moment of every day becomes a physical reality in your brain and body, which affects your optimal mental and physical health. These thoughts collectively form your attitude, which is your state of mind, and it's your attitude and not your DNA that determines much of the quality of your life. Research shows that 75 to 98 percent of mental, physical, and behavioral illness comes from one's thought life."[25]

This statistic proves the reality of the spiritual war we face and the weapons God gave us so we would not be victims of the enemy's schemes. Through the intentional application of faith we can go on the offense against the kingdom of darkness as agents of light.

Water of the Word

In order for the fertilizer of faith to absorb into the soil of our hearts we have to be watered by the Word of God. The condition of the soil that our seed either thrives or dies in is created by the nourishment we receive. Throughout scripture water is used as a metaphor for the Word. Isaiah 55:10 -11 says, "As the rain and the snow come down from heaven, and do not return to it without watering the earth and making it bud and flourish, so that it yields seed for the sower and bread for the eater, so is my word that goes out from my mouth: It will not return to me empty, but will accomplish what I desire and achieve the purpose for which I sent it" (NIV).

God sends His word to accomplish His desired purpose on the earth. Each of us has a unique purpose that we cannot achieve without receiving God's living word.

Have you ever been really thirsty and drank soda instead of water? When we do this our stomachs fill with liquid but our bodies do not receive the hydration they need. Our thirst is temporarily quenched, but the proper nourishment our bodies need is not received.

This same principle applies with what we feed our souls. The world offers us many drinks, but only one drink truly quenches the thirst of our soul. In John 14 Jesus says this directly to the woman at the well.

> *"Jesus replied, 'Anyone who drinks this water will soon become thirsty again. But those who drink the water I give will never be*

---

25. Leaf, *Switch On Your Brain: The Key to Peak Happiness, Thinking and Health.*

thirsty again. It becomes a fresh, bubbling spring within them, giving them eternal life.'" (John 14:3-4 NLT)

When we drink from this well, a spring is created within us. We never thirst again not because one drink is enough, but because one true drink produces a fountain within us that can endlessly satisfy every thirst we have for all eternity. However, the choice to drink from this living spring is one we must make daily.

Our problem is that we are far too easily satisfied with lesser things.[26] We have become addicted to additives that have numbed our craving for pure water. I personally have been known to leave my house with no less than three different beverages in my hand. Convenience stores offer hundreds of beverages to choose from other than water. Likewise, each day we are offered drinks for our soul in many forms. Our deepest thirst is for pure connection with God.

Social media, phone calls with friends, tv shows, movies, books, comfort food —can all be forms of counterfeit connection. They are not bad things unless they are replacing our consumption of living water. When we fill up on these forms of connection first, we lose our thirst for the Word of God.

God sent us the Holy Spirit so that there would be no more disconnection between us and the Father. This is the truest longing of our soul. When we cultivate our connection to God's voice first, then we can do the other things that we enjoy in connection with God, rather than using them as a counterfeit connection that cannot satisfy us. If we find our souls are no longer thirsty for God, we must assess what counterfeit spring we are drinking from that is robbing us from experiencing living water.

> *"O God, you are my God; earnestly I seek you; my soul thirsts for you; my flesh faints for you, as in a dry and weary land where there is no water. So I have looked upon you in the sanctuary, beholding your power and glory. Because your steadfast love is better than life, my lips will praise you. So I will bless you as long as I live; in your name I will lift up my hands. My soul will be satisfied as with fat and rich food, and my mouth will praise you with joyful*

---

26. Concept from C.S. Lewis, *The Weight of Glory*.

lips, when I remember you upon my bed, and meditate on you in the watches of the night; for you have been my help, and in the shadow of your wings I will sing for joy. My soul clings to you; your right hand upholds me." (Psalm 63:1-8 ESV)

Is your soul parched? Come to the living water. Are you dissatisfied with the shallow pleasures this world offers? Come to the living water. Are you lacking energy and joy? Come to the living water. There is a fountain of abundant life inside you. The Spirit is beckoning you to come to the living water. "Everyone who thirsts, Come to the waters!" (Isaiah 55:1).

> It does not matter how much scripture we know; what matters is how much scripture we live.

Not receiving enough water can be a major hindrance to our spiritual growth, but it's not the only hindrance. Over watering and receiving contaminated water are dangers we have to be aware of as well. When a tree is overwatered, new growth withers before it's fully grown. Leaves can be fragile and break easily.

Overwatering happens when we focus on the quantity of scripture we are taking in rather than how deeply the word is soaking into our souls. It does not matter how much scripture we know; what matters is how much scripture we *live*. We do not want to move on from a passage of scripture until we sense the heart of God. One word that penetrates to our roots and the core of our being is much better than entire chapters shallowly consumed.

Our leaves will wither quickly when we search the Word for information rather than revelation. Revelation truth is revealed through *relationship* with the Holy Spirit. The Bible is the only book that requires the author to be present while it is read.

Since the Information Age, we have an unprecedented volume of information available to us. "The average global consumer spends eighty-two hours per week consuming information. Assuming an average of seven hours of sleep per night, this means that 69% of our waking hours are engaged in consuming information. We consume almost ninety times more information in terms of bits today than we did in 1940 and four times more than we did less than twenty years ago."[27]

This constant consumption of information has become like a firehose, and most of the water misses its target. We are continuously drowning in information.

The temptation to consume other forms of information instead of the inspired Word of God has never been greater. Also, there is a dangerous temptation to consume scripture the same way we do other information by prioritizing quantity over quality. Even secular researchers conclude that there is a need for greater contemplation and, as a natural result, greater meaning derived from the information we receive.[27]

Just because we read the Word, does not mean that we automatically receive the nourishment we need from it. In her book, *Experiencing the Depths of Jesus Christ*, Madame Guyon writes, "If you read quickly it will benefit you little. You will be like a bee that merely skims the surface of a flower. Instead, in this new way of reading with prayer, you must become the bee who penetrates into the depths of the flower. You plunge deeply within to remove its deepest nectar."

She continues, "To receive any deep, inward profit from Scripture, you must read as I have described. Plunge into the very depths of the words you read until revelation, like a sweet aroma, breaks out upon you. I am quite sure that if you follow this course, little by little you will come to experience a very rich prayer that flows from your inward being."[28]

For us to be trees with leaves that do not wither, we must open the Word with a desire to commune with God, not to consume knowledge. As we pray through the scriptures and meditate on truth, the water of the Word absorbs deep into the soil of our souls.

Newborn Christians have a pea-sized appetite that grows and matures through consistent nourishment. As we regularly learn to consume the Word of God, our appetite grows. If we do not, it shrinks. When our cravings begin to change from carnal to spiritual, we will see our desire to consume media and entertainment decrease, and our desire for spiritual food will increase.

> *Jesus says, "Blessed are those who hunger and thirst for righteousness, for they will be filled." (Matthew 5:6 NIV)*

---

27. Deepwater Asset Management, "Defining the Future of Human Information Consumption | Deepwater."
28. Guyon, *Experiencing the Depths of Jesus Christ*, 8.

Reading the Word without the presence of God is simply a religious duty that will not bear good fruit. Psalm 1 says that we are blessed when we delight in the Word of God and meditate on it, while remaining aware of the presence of God continually.[29]

Regarding the one who does this, the psalmist promises:

"He shall be like a tree
Planted by the rivers of water,
That brings forth its fruit in its season,
Whose leaf also shall not wither;
And whatever he does shall prosper." (Psalm 1:2-3)

Contaminated Water

The water we receive must be filtered through the spirit of wisdom and revelation. When we filter the Word through our own understanding or the interpretation of other teachers, and not the inspiration of the Holy Spirit, we end up with contaminated water.

In order to trust in God we cannot lean on our own understanding (Proverbs 3:5). God's thoughts are not our thoughts and His ways are higher than our ways (Isaiah 55:8).

How do we make sure we are not interpreting scripture in our own understanding or the way that seems right to us? Or perhaps we are interpreting scripture in the way that seems right to the pastors and theologians we respect? Scripture clearly states, "There is a way *that seems* right to a man, but its end *is* the way of death" (Proverbs 14:12, italics mine).

In Ephesians 1, Paul gives us the prayer filter by which we can purify water for our souls. He models praying for the spirit of wisdom and revelation "in the knowledge of Him," in other words, through *personally knowing* Jesus. He continues to pray for the church at Ephesus that the eyes of understanding be opened so they will know their calling, their spiritual inheritance, and the power that lives in them. This is one of my favorite passages of scripture. I challenge you to ask the Holy Spirit to illuminate the following verses to you as you read them aware of the presence of God.

---

29. Derived from the idea that Jesus is Truth so when we meditate on truth we should simultaneously be more aware of his presence.

> *"Making mention of you in my prayers: That the God of our Lord Jesus Christ, the Father of glory, may give to you the spirit of wisdom and revelation in the knowledge of Him, the eyes of your understanding being enlightened; that you may know what is the hope of His calling, what are the riches of the glory of His inheritance in the saints, and what is the exceeding greatness of His power toward us who believe, according to the working of His mighty power which He worked in Christ when He raised Him from the dead and seated Him at His right hand in the heavenly places, far above all principality and power and might and dominion, and every name that is named, not only in this age but also in that which is to come." (Ephesians 1:16-21)*

When we do not understand the Word of God, the enemy can lie to us and contaminate the water that we receive. One thing that the health community unanimously agrees on (while disagreeing on many other things), is the necessity for quality water consumption.

One of the primary ways that the enemy muddies the water of the Word is by covenant mixture. In the old covenant, under the law of Moses, people had to work to earn forgiveness. The law revealed how man's best efforts always fall short of God's standards. The law demonstrates our need for a Savior. Jesus fulfilled all of the requirements of the law for us and sent His Spirit to work through us.

When we mix the old covenant built on the law and the new covenant built on grace alone, we end up with contaminated water. The old and new covenant were never meant to be mixed together.

The law was given as an if/then covenant. God repeatedly says, "If my people... then I will..." (2 Chronicles 7:14). The new covenant is not conditional! Religion can be defined as man's attempt to get to God. Essentially, this is what Jews under the law had to do. When God sent His son to die for us, He tore the veil of separation so we could come boldly before His throne of grace. Religion deceives us into thinking we have to do X, Y and Z to get to God when God already moved Heaven and Earth to get to us!

Scripture says our best deeds are like filthy rags (Isaiah 64:6). Any time we put ourselves into the equation, we create religious contamination. Mixture is thinking Jesus plus us equals change, Jesus plus our best efforts, Jesus plus our best behavior, or Jesus plus our striving. But the gospel is not a formula; it is a completed work. It is the entire equation! Jesus' last word on the cross was *tetelestai* which means, "It is finished." The gospel is so complete that anything we try to add to it is actually a subtraction from it.

It is not 50/50 nor is it Jesus does His part and we do ours. The gospel of grace is Jesus replaces us. Now when God looks at us He sees Jesus. Our spiritual debt has been paid for all of our past, present and future sins. Jesus does everything for us, and we simply surrender and receive like little children. Our job as believers is to *believe*. That's it. That's the too-good-to-be-true good news. The gospel is better than we can imagine.

The New Covenant is unconditional, but we choose whether or not to accept it. Romans 10:19 says, "If you confess with your mouth the Lord Jesus and believe in your heart that God has raised Him from the dead, you will be saved." Remember, the Greek word *sozo* means, saved, healed, delivered and made whole. Our process of sanctification happens the same way we receive salvation, simply through our belief.

When we fail to filter the Word of God through the entire storyline of scripture, we misapply scripture and muddy the waters with our own religious striving.

Many Christians fall into condemnation and judgment when they read verses like 2 Chronicles 7:14 that says, "...if My people who are called by My name will humble themselves, and pray and seek My face, and turn from their wicked ways, then I will hear from Heaven, and will forgive their sin and heal their land." The enemy tells us that God is not healing our land because we are not praying hard enough. This is an example of contaminated water that is killing the Body of Christ! The enemy knows that if he can use scripture to heap condemnation on us that we will lose our appetite for God's Word. Satan used scripture to accuse Jesus, and he does the same with us.

God already heard from Heaven. God already forgave our sins and cast them as far as the east is to the west (Psalm 103:12). This one might surprise you, but God has already healed our land because He exists outside of time. The covenant God established with us after Jesus' death, resurrection and ascension is an *already-but-not-yet* covenant. Do we have a part to play in all of this? Absolutely! But God is not transactional. His hands are not tied because the saints are not praying enough. God created us for divine partnership and our prayers do move Heaven. Instead of begging God to do something He already did, our job is to agree in prayer with His perfect plan of redemption. We spread the Kingdom of God, like fertilized seed, everytime we apply our faith to God's will for the earth.

The world is in its own process of renewal to reflect the salvation and glory of the Lord, just like we are personally. The revealing and sanctification of the sons and daughters of God will be reflected in the sanctification of our land (Romans 8:20-21). When we read 2 Chronicles 7:14 with a proper understanding of the new covenant, we thank God for what He has already done and agree with Him in prayer that the whole earth will soon reflect His healing power.

> *Instead of begging God to do something He already did, our job is to agree in prayer with His perfect plan of redemption.*

A muddied filter reads passages like Psalm 51 where David cries, "God take not your spirit from me," and fears that God will withdraw from us if we are not good enough. A pure filter processes this scripture with the understanding that on the day of Pentecost, God sent His Spirit as a gift to us (Acts 10:45)! We are now the temple of the Holy Spirit (1 Corinthians 6:19) and God does not take back the gifts He gives His children (Romans 11:29).

There are four unconditional covenants in scripture and one conditional covenant. The unconditional covenants are established with God saying, "I will give." These covenants are the Abrahamic (Genesis 17:7), Palestinian (Genesis 13:15; 15:18), Davidic (2 Samuel 7:16) and New (Jeremiah 31:36). The New Covenant replaces the Mosaic Covenant which was a conditional covenant that brought the law.[30]

Religion mixes the old and new covenant and brings confusion and condemnation on the children of God. It is a toxin that contaminates God's word to render it ineffective and even harmful.

> *"Jesus stood and cried out, saying, "If anyone thirsts, let him come to Me and drink. He who believes in Me, as the Scripture has said, out of his heart will flow rivers of living water." But this He spoke*

---

30. Joe Griffin Media Ministries, "The Church of the Living God."

concerning the Spirit, whom those believing in Him would receive."
(John 7:37-39 ESV)

The good news is that Jesus sent His Spirit to wash us from all our religious striving and give us new life. He says those who believe in Him will receive! All we have to do to be nourished by pure living water is believe and receive.

Another example of muddied understanding is around the judgment and wrath of people. We misunderstand the nature of God when we read Old Testament scriptures today and fear that God is doing the same thing now. God poured out all judgment on Jesus! God's righteous wrath and need for justice has been satisfied. Instead of justice, we were granted mercy!

God is not currently judging those who have been redeemed by the blood of Jesus. Yes, we all will stand before the Lord on judgment day, but for those of us who have accepted Jesus as our Savior, God looks at us and only sees the perfection of Jesus. When we read scriptures involving the wrath of God, our hearts should immediately thank the Father for sending Jesus to plead guilty so we could go free.

A final example of muddied water is when we mix faith with doubt and unbelief. James says the person who doubts is unstable in all of their ways. This is the opposite of the deeply rooted tree from Psalm 1 that we all want to grow into!

> *"If any of you lacks wisdom, you should ask God, who gives generously to all without finding fault, and it will be given to you. But when you ask, you must believe and not doubt, because the one who doubts is like a wave of the sea, blown and tossed by the wind. That person should not expect to receive anything from the Lord. Such a person is double-minded and unstable in all they do.*
> *(James 1:5-8 NIV)*

Remember, our problem is not with how much faith we possess. Our problem is what we are tempted to add to our faith in the form of doubt and unbelief. When we believe one moment and doubt the next, our double-mindedness will lead to instability. By taking care with the story we tell ourselves, we can remain congruent with truth.

Thoughts of doubt and unbelief will come, but we choose what thoughts we agree with. What we agree with, we will have to pay for. When I catch myself coming into agreement with thoughts of doubt, the instability usually shows up first in my emotional responses. There are so many subtle ways this can happen on a regular basis.

I may wake up with a thought full of faith, "Thank you God that this is the day you have made!" But that thought quickly switches to, "Here we go again, it's going to be a long day" with the first tantrum of the morning. Sadly, one challenging circumstance is sometimes all it takes to forfeit my faith in God's good plans and partner with double-mindedness. You better believe my reaction to my toddler's attitude will not be full of grace and peace if the enemy has gotten me to agree with the negative storyline of my day.

"I love this man! God has blessed our marriage and it keeps getting better and better," I may think to myself, full of faith after a kiss and a prayer on my husband's way out the door for work. Only to turn around and see that he forgot to take the trash out that he promised to do last night. The enemy serves me this narrative, "You can't ever trust him to do what he says he's going to do. He hasn't changed and he's never going to. He expects you to do everything!" The feelings of emotional instability are already strong, tempting me to agree with the enemy's narrative. But God always gives us a way of escape when we are tempted (1 Corinthians 10:13). No matter what my feelings are telling me, I have the power to choose what narrative to believe. The root of frustration is powerlessness. We get our power back when we choose to cultivate thoughts of faith.

When God speaks to us, faith is activated in us. The enemy will always try to counteract that activation with doubt and unbelief because he knows that if we simply believe God's Word we have everything we need to defeat the devil and live in total victory. He will whisper, "Did God really say?" "You probably made that up" or "That's too good to be true, dream on." When we hold onto the Word of God despite this testing, our faith is strengthened. One of our mantras at my home church, The Collective, is "faith expressed is grace released."

When the Master Gardener sows seeds of fertilizer onto our soil we want to be those with cultivated ground prepared to receive in faith, letting the truth take deep root within us.

CULTIVATE FIELD NOTES
Identify how you think and what you believe

Find a quiet place and start by breathing in God's love for four seconds. Hold that breath for four seconds, imagining His presence filling you up like a balloon. Now, for four seconds breathe out whatever negative emotion is weighing you down. Repeat this exercise until you feel settled and present. Ask the Holy Spirit the following questions. Then journal the free flow of thoughts that come to your mind as you fix your eyes on Jesus.

Questions:

Holy Spirit, how have I agreed with doubt and unbelief?

_____
_____
_____

How am I double-minded? What areas of my life are emotionally unstable as a result of this double mindedness?

_____
_____
_____

How have toxic thoughts poisoned me? What toxic thoughts do you want to address first?

_____
_____

How can I trade these toxic thoughts for true, powerful statements?

_____
_____

How do I prioritize daily receiving the water of the Word?

_____
_____

How have I viewed the Word through a muddied filter?

_____
_____

How are you leading me to exercise and apply faith?

_____
_____

Activation:

Ask the Holy Spirit for three scriptures you can use as a weapon in this season of your life. Pick an area God is asking you to apply your faith and google "scripture on ____" (ex: provision, marriage, trust, redemption, relationships). Read through the list until one lights up in your spirit. Repeat this process until you have three scriptures declarations. Begin reading these scriptures out loud daily.

Encounter:

Prepare communion elements and find a quiet place to be alone with the Lord. Take the cracker or piece of bread and break it in our hands. In your own words thank Jesus for being broken so you can experience wholeness in your mind and body. When you are ready, eat the body, not as a mere symbol, but believing in faith that Jesus is coming in and filling you fresh. Imagine Him invading every part of your mind and giving you the mind of Christ. Now take the juice and in your own words plead the blood of Jesus over your mind and body. Ask Him to cleanse every toxic thought you have. Thank Him for blotting out every sin in your past, present and future. Repent for the agreement you have made with lies that have kept you in bondage. When you are ready, drink the blood staying aware of the high price paid for your freedom and healing. Ask the Lord to keep you in this place of continual communion as you go throughout your day.

Repeat as often as you can, ideally daily.

Recommended Resource:

Neurocycle App - This is an excellent tool that will guide you through three cycles of twenty-one day detoxes scientifically proven to reduce stress, anxiety, depression, and toxic thinking. The program focuses on finding the root of the toxic thought and habit, reconceptualizing the root and rebuilding a healthy new thought pattern and habit. You can access most of the program for free or choose to pay for the full access version at Neurocycle.app.

ROOT IV

Figure 11: Good Fruit   Figure 12: Rotten Fruit
Figure 13: Fear Roots - False Identities   Figure 14: Love Roots - True Identity

ROOT
Chapter Four

Who has God created you to be?
Identifying your true identity

Two Root Systems

THE ROOTS OF OUR tree are our identity which comes from what we believe about God and ourselves. Everything grows from one of two root systems: fear or love. Our fear roots grow when we believe the enemy's lies. Our love roots grow when we believe the truth that God speaks. What's rooted in love is our true identity. What's rooted in fear is our false identity.

In our false identity we self protect, self promote, separate and isolate. We disconnect from God, from community and from our purpose. In our false identity, it is extremely hard to hear God because the lies of the enemy are so loud.

The root system of fear produces rotten fruit like complaining, judgment, worrying, gossip, hatred, pride, anxiety, perversion, depression, division and envy. The root system of love produces the fruit of the Spirit: love, joy, peace, patience, kindness, goodness and self control.

> *"Now the works of the flesh are evident: sexual immorality, impurity, sensuality, idolatry, sorcery, enmity, strife, jealousy, fits of anger, rivalries, dissensions, divisions, envy, drunkenness, orgies, and*

things like these. I warn you, as I warned you before, that those who do such things will not inherit the kingdom of God. But the fruit of the Spirit is love, joy, peace, patience, kindness, goodness, faithfulness, gentleness, self-control; against such things there is no law. And those who belong to Christ Jesus have crucified the flesh with its passions and desires." (Galataians 5:19-24 ESV)

In the last chapter, we identified some of our recurring negative thoughts. Toxic thoughts are judgments of ourselves, others, or circumstances. Do you know it is not our job to measure good and bad? It was the tree of the knowledge of good and evil that got Adam and Eve thrown out of the Garden of Eden. Let's think about that. Adam and Eve's desire to measure good and bad is what separated them from God and their purpose.

Eden means delight. Thanksgiving and praise are the gate to God's presence (Psalm 100:4) and delight is the pathway. Now because of Jesus' death and resurrection, we have access again to the Garden of Eden. We were created to walk with God continually, praising Him and feasting on His goodness. Enjoying God and having an eternal dialog with Him is the primary way that we rewire our brains. God created us for this purpose! The problem is that we are obsessed with assessing things in our life and measuring them based on our man-made metrics. As my pastor Jenny Donnelly says, "God didn't create us to measure anything other than His goodness." When we constantly judge ourselves, others and our circumstances, we throw ourselves out of the garden of delight into the toil of duty, behavior modification and striving.

All throughout scripture we are told not to judge. There is, however, one verse that says we are not to judge based on appearances but we are to judge righteously. This shows us that there are different kinds of judgment. One type fuels our false identity, and the other keeps us rooted in our true identity.

1. Unrighteous judgments are based on our own assessments, measurements, comparison, fear, guilt, shame, and trauma.
2. Righteous judgments are based on the separation of truth from lies and the discernment of spiritual forces.

"Stop judging by mere appearances, but instead judge correctly." (John 7:24 NIV)

Rooted In Lies

In our false identity, we naturally villainize and victimize ourselves and others. This victim mentality deflects blame and refuses to take personal responsibility. The victim spirit is powerless and is perpetuated by pity. Pity is a counterfeit of compassion. Pity prevents us from being encouraging, edifying and faith-filled. Pity blocks prophecy.

When the enemy is not making us feel like a victim, he will deceive us into believing we are a villain. When we are caught in a villainized identity, we will believe lies about ourselves. Common lies are, "I'm a failure; I am evil; I am not good enough; I don't measure up."

When we feel we do not measure up, it's because our measuring stick is from the enemy. The truth is, we can never measure up. We all fall short of the glory of God (Romans 3:23). But, because of Jesus, we have been given a completely new metric. Jesus is our new standard! We are worthy because He is worthy, and He made us worthy. We are only enough because He made us enough. We measure up because God does not measure our sins, instead He measures the perfect sacrifice of Jesus.

> We cannot live a transformed life with an unrenewed mind.

No longer do we measure our worthiness by our attitudes, behavior and actions. When we do, we are measuring our old nature, not our new redeemed nature. This is a trap of the enemy that keeps Christians from living a transformed life, dead to the old nature and alive in Christ.

Most of my life I believed, like many Christians do, that I was not worthy, was not enough and was "just a sinner saved by grace." The problem with this paradigm is that it completely denies the power of the resurrection. If we believe that we are made into a new creation in Christ, then believing ourselves to still be unworthy is void of truth and faith.

It breaks my heart to see countless Christians settle with false humility like a ragged security blanket. We know Jesus died to save us for all eternity, yet we are often fooled into believing that He is somehow powerless to transform our lives presently. We cannot live a transformed life with an unrenewed mind. Scripture is clear that in the last days there will be people who settle with their sinful nature, slanderous, selfish, and lacking self-control. 2 Timothy 3:5 says these people have a form of godliness but deny its power. If we want to reflect Christ as Christians (the word means little Christ), we cannot settle on a powerless narrative about ourselves and others.

> *"But mark this: There will be terrible times in the last days. People will be lovers of themselves, lovers of money, boastful, proud, abusive, disobedient to their parents, ungrateful, unholy, without love, unforgiving, slanderous, without self-control, brutal, not lovers of the good, treacherous, rash, conceited, lovers of pleasure rather than lovers of God— having a form of godliness but denying its power." (2 Timothy 3:1-5 NIV)*

People who do not know Jesus can tell themselves all day that they are enough and they are worthy, but their roots will rot so long as the source of their value is self. Truth is not truth unless it is connected to Jesus who is all truth. The source of our value is God himself. We are because He is. Deep roots come from connecting our identity to our Heavenly Father's identity. On our own we are certainly not enough, but we are not on our own anymore! If we want to live a transformed life, we must refuse to see ourselves any longer in our pre-saved state. When the enemy lies to us and says we are not enough, we can simply say, "Yes, but God. As He is, so am I. I am only because He is."

Viewing ourselves as sinners predisposes us to live as sinners. What we focus on we move towards.

The teaching of some denominations says we are positionally righteous but not practically righteous. I believed this for years until I realized I had not encountered the full gospel. We are righteous now, not because we become sinless at salvation (that certainly is not the case), but because the righteousness of Christ now lives in us! Do you not believe the power of Jesus in us is greater than the works of the flesh?

> *"You are of God, little children, and have overcome them, because He who is in you is greater than he who is in the world." (1 John 4:4)*

Viewing ourselves as sinners predisposes us to *live* as sinners. What we focus on we move towards. The more we remain conscious of our own sinfulness, the more we perpetuate cycles of sin. The proper view of sin is to believe that we *were* sinners saved by grace, but we are *now* new creations in Christ!

Being a sinner falls under our old nature. That does not mean that we never sin, but that when we sin this is a reflection of our false selves, not our truest selves. Sinner is not an identity God gives us. It is a religious label the enemy uses to keep us powerless. When we identify more with the label "sinner saved by grace" than "redeemed child of God," we have an identity problem. If God sees us covered in the blood of Jesus, how would it please Him for us to see ourselves as still tainted and dirty? Since we are to have the mind of Christ (1 Corinthians 2:16), do we not think that includes seeing ourselves the way Jesus sees us? Since Jesus died so we could be the righteousness of God, do we think it pleases the Lord that we view ourselves as unrighteous?

> *"For our sake he made him to be sin who knew no sin, so that in him we might become the righteousness of God." (2 Corinthians 5:21 ESV)*
>
> *"If you know that He is righteous, you know that everyone who practices righteousness is born of Him." (1 John 2:29)*
>
> *"And do not present your members as instruments of unrighteousness to sin, but present yourselves to God as being alive from the dead, and your members as instruments of righteousness to God." (Romans 6:13)*

Seeing ourselves as sinners after we have received forgiveness for our sin is the same as having a form of godliness but denying its power. Is righteousness something that can be earned through good behavior and a mostly sinless life? Certainly not! Righteousness is a gift of grace that cannot be earned. Jesus had to pay for it whether or not we choose to accept His gift.

I am righteous not because I sin less than other people, but because I have accepted righteousness as a gift that I cannot earn. Righteousness means right standing with God. When God looks at me He sees Jesus. If my Creator judges me by this standard, who am I to judge myself by man-made measurements?

But doesn't Paul call himself the chiefest of sinners? Religion loves to preach this message to us. Let's look at the scripture through the correct lens and see if that's what Paul is actually saying.

> *"This is a faithful saying and worthy of all acceptance, that Christ Jesus came into the world to save sinners, of whom I am chief. However, for this reason I obtained mercy, that in me first Jesus Christ might show all longsuffering, as a pattern to those who are going to believe on Him for everlasting life. Now to the King eternal, immortal, invisible, to God who alone is wise, be honor and glory forever and ever. Amen." (1 Timothy 1: 15-17)*

Bible translators translated "I am chief" in present tense but the next verse switches to past tense, "I obtained mercy." When you read this scripture in context it is very clear that Paul is testifying of his past conversion, something he does five times in the New Testament. The message of Paul is that God used his conversion from the chiefest of sinners, someone who brutally persecuted Jews and Christians, into a faithful follower of Jesus.

If Paul was converted from a wretched sinner to a saint for God's glory, then he certainly is not implying that he still sees Himself as the chiefest of sinners. So too, we also, at the point of our salvation, were converted from wretched sinners into saints. When we still see ourselves as wretched sinners we remain powerless in this false identity. I believe it grieves the Holy Spirit when we take this scripture out of context and identify presently as the chiefest of sinners.

This does not mean that we are better than anyone who is still bound in sin. We must simultaneously remain aware of who we are without Jesus, and view ourselves currently with Jesus in our redeemed state. It is possible to remain sober about the fallibility of our old fallen nature and focus on our new nature and security in Christ.

Reflecting on the sin we have been saved from and our utter dependance on our Savior is an important part of our spiritual growth. Our conversion is not something we have to work for, it comes through faith. Paul directly addresses the wrong belief that we have to work for our spiritual conversion in the book of Galatians.

> *"Did you receive the Spirit by works of the law or by hearing with faith? Are you so foolish? Having begun by the Spirit, are you now being perfected by the flesh?" (Galatians 3:2-3 ESV)*

It is not our job to measure and assess our own sinfulness. It is the Holy Spirit's job to convict us when there is sin in our life. The Holy Spirit's conviction calls us up and out of sin. When the Holy Spirit convicts us, He always provides us with grace, which is supernatural empowerment, to turn away from our old nature. One of the ways we do this is by confessing the lies we are believing and exchanging them with truth.

Confession means to tell the truth. We cannot repent without telling God the truth. He is the Truth and he only deals with us in truth. We cannot turn from something that we have created as an identity. He will not address us in our false identities, but He will pursue us in His kindness to lead us to repentance. Repentance follows truth telling because it is the truth that sets us free.

> *"Then you will know the truth, and the truth will set you free."*
> *(John 8:32 NIV)*

I used to proudly proclaim, "I am the chiefest of sinners!" and it felt humble. Identifying with our old nature and claiming it as a label is not humble, it's heretical. False humility happens as a result of relying on our own religious striving and behavior modification and coming up short. All of our self-dependency is at its core pride. When we are truly relying on God and not ourselves we do not believe we are not enough, because we are actively depending on God's strength which makes us more than conquerors in Christ Jesus (Romans 8:37).

Just as with toxic thoughts, we do not focus on what is toxic. Instead, we identify the toxin, or the sin in this case, so we can apply the antidote. Our antidote for our sin is the blood of Jesus, and it has already been applied to all of our past, present and future sins.

The belief that our sin separated us from God is a fallacy. We separate ourselves from God in our shame when we measure our own sinfulness. My pastor, Ben Rose, boldly shares his testimony of overcoming sexual sin. He says, "When we feel shame, we engage in behaviors that confirm our shame." David writes in the psalms that he cannot escape God's presence.

> *"Where can I go from Your Spirit? Or where can I flee from Your presence? If I ascend into heaven, You are there; If I make my bed in hell, behold, You are there. If I take the wings of the morning,*

And dwell in the uttermost parts of the sea, Even there Your hand shall lead me, And Your right hand shall hold me. If I say, "Surely the darkness shall fall on me,"

Even the night shall be light about me; Indeed, the darkness shall not hide from You, But the night shines as the day; The darkness and the light are both alike to You." (Psalm 139: 7-12)

God does not withdraw His presence from us in our sinfulness; we separate ourselves. It is the nature of our false identity to separate. Just like Adam and Eve hid in their nakedness, our guilt and shame make us hide as well. Guilt is not a punishment for our sin, but it does often follow unaddressed conviction. Guilt is a deception that traps us in false identity until we come to a place of real repentance. God responds to us the same way He responded to Adam and Eve in Genesis 3 by calling out, "Where are you?" Where are you hiding, my precious daughter? Where are you hiding, my beloved son? When we respond truthfully as Adam did, God asks us the same question He asked Adam, "Who told you that you were naked?"

Who told you that you were naked? Who told you that you are the shame of your sin? Who told you that you are just a sinner saved by grace? Who told you that you are not worthy? Who told you that you are a filthy wretch?

The Holy Spirit's conviction never sounds like accusation. These statements come from Satan, the Accuser of the brethren (Revelation 12:10). Sadly, many well-meaning pastors are unknowingly giving voice to the Accuser from the pulpit. Instead of teaching their congregants humility as intended, they are reinforcing a powerless false identity of the Church.

Behind every demonic agenda is a lie, and behind every lie is a root of fear. Let's look at pride as an example. The spirit of pride whispers lies like, "You need to prove yourself," and "You cannot trust anyone but yourself," "You can do this on your own," and "You'll never measure up." Behind these lies are three of the most common fears. These fears are the fear of being alone, the fear of having no one to help us and the fear of not being enough.

Pride is deadly. Andrew Murray said, "Pride must die in you, or nothing of heaven can live in you."[31] True humility is the great comfort of the Christian life. It's where we, in our best efforts, end and Christ becomes all in us. Humility compels us to get over ourselves and get out of God's way.

Humility is rooted in love and truth. Walking in humility requires us to take up our God-given space in His strength, not our own. C.S. Lewis says, "Humility is not thinking less of yourself, but thinking of yourself less." Thinking less of ourselves is the definition of false humility.

"Here is the path to the higher life: down, lower down! Just as water always seeks and fills the lowest place, so the moment God finds men abased and empty, His glory and power flow in to exalt and to bless. Humility is nothing but the disappearance of self in the vision that God is all. The root of all virtue and grace, of all faith and acceptable worship, is that we know that we have nothing but what we receive, and bow in deepest humility to wait upon God for it." —Andrew Murray, *Humility: The Journey Toward Holiness*.

All judgment of others is a reflection of our own self judgment. We naturally see the same weakness in others that we are struggling with. Our desire to expose others' faults is a self-protective mechanism attempting to deflect our own self judgment. This is why Jesus says that we should not talk to someone about the speck in their eye when we have a plank in our own.

> *"Do not judge, or you too will be judged. For in the same way you judge others, you will be judged, and with the measure you use, it will be measured to you. "Why do you look at the speck of sawdust in your brother's eye and pay no attention to the plank in your own eye? How can you say to your brother, 'Let me take the speck out of your eye,' when all the time there is a plank in your own eye? You hypocrite, first take the plank out of your own eye, and then you will see clearly to remove the speck from your brother's eye."*
> *(Matthew 7:1-5 NIV)*

Unrighteous judgment is a human assessment based on our own understanding. Judgment assigns motives to people and is often void of compassion. Our judgment reveals areas of our life that we are still trying

---

31. Murray, *Humility: The Journey Toward Holiness*.

to be God. It is our human nature to look at the outward appearance, but only God can see the true intent of a heart (1 Samuel 16:7). To decide right and wrong, fair and unfair, just and unjust is too heavy a job for us.

Comparison is a common metric of measurement we fall into. One of the greatest gifts God has given to me is my sisters. Sadly, siblings are often our first source of comparison. My older sister, Natalie, is one of the sweetest people you will ever meet. My younger sister and I were more of the salty variety.

In high school, I had the same conversation with people about my sister over and over again. She was one grade ahead of me in school, and when I met people that knew her first, they would say, "Wow, you guys are like opposites! She's so sweet!" I used to jokingly say I was having déjà vu because this statement was repeated to me so often. I laughed it off, but deep down I always wondered: since Natalie is sweet and I'm the opposite of her, what does that make me?

Comparing myself to my sister and desperately trying to fit a sweet, quiet mold stole my passion and fire, all the things that make me potent! It took me years to realize that God made me salty on purpose! Jesus calls us to be the salt of the earth (Matthew 5:13). And being salty does not mean I'm not also sweet. Likewise with my sister, being sweet does not mean she is not also potent! Sweet and salty is a great flavor combo, like truth and love.

Our comparisons are foolish because they are almost always derived from incomplete data. We draw conclusions based on one comment, one news article, one instagram post or one conversation. This type of comparison steals our joy and robs us of gratitude. Other people were never meant to be the standard of comparison for our personal growth, happiness, talents and livelihood. We must run our own race. When we look to the right or the left, we fall right into the ditch of comparison. Paul says that those who measure themselves through the metric of comparison are not wise.

> *"Not that we dare to classify or compare ourselves with some of those who are commending themselves. But when they measure themselves by one another and compare themselves with one another, they are without understanding." (2 Corinthians 10:12 ESV)*

Opinions are formed in the same manner on incomplete data. The enemy lies to us and tells us that we know enough to form a strong opinion, but the reality is that the opinions we hold so tightly to are usually formed from less than one-tenth of the complete story. When we esteem our pride-filled opinions as better than the perspective of others, we subconsciously esteem ourselves as better than others. This is exactly what Paul warns the Church of Philippi not to do!

*"Let nothing be done through selfish ambition or conceit, but in lowliness of mind **let each esteem others better than himself**. Let each of you look out not only for his own interests, but also for the interests of others. Let this mind be in you which was also in Christ Jesus."* (Philippians 2:3-5, bold text mine)

I remember the first time I heard my good friend and mentor, Shawna Danberg, teach on perspective at a marriage retreat. The illustration has stuck with me for years. She held up a beach ball and asked a woman sitting in the front what color she saw. "Blue" she said definitively. Shawna then turned to a man sitting on her right side and asked what color he saw. "Yellow!" He insisted. She asked one more person. "Red!" With three different conclusions, who do you think was wrong? No one! The beach ball is blue, yellow and red. Some beach balls have three colors while others have six, but what color you see always depends on your vantage point.

Remember, we are talking about opinions here, not truth. Truth is not subjective to perspective. For example, the beach ball is a beach ball no matter your point of view. A partially blind person could think the beach ball is a flying saucer, and it is still a beach ball. Truth needs to be held firmly, while opinions need to be held loosely. Both must be held humbly.

Opinions that are not held humbly lead to judgements and those judgements lead to punishments. In our false identities we are addicted to retaliation. We punish people in our lives by withholding love when they wrong us. We guilt and shame others and ourselves, not understanding that these are the primary cause of our perpetuated cycles of brokeness. We punish ourselves by remaining in a pit of guilt instead of accepting our pardon. We believe God is punishing us when things do not turn out the way we hoped and prayed for. All desire for punishment comes from our own measurements of good and bad. When we surrender our false assessments, we no longer desire vengeance and punishment, but instead cry for mercy.

Have you ever noticed how quick we are to make identity statements out of bad behaviors? If a person acts in a way that is unloving the Accuser says, "They are a selfish and rude person!" rather than the truth that they likely *acted* selfishly or rudely. My daughter who easily gets her feelings hurt by her brothers is prone to yell, "He's a meany-head!" Anytime my children call each other names or use negative labels I jump in with a necessary correction, "He made a mean choice, and he is responsible for his actions, but he is not a meany-head."

Why is the distinction between behavior and identity so important? If we agree with judgment about others, it will inevitably yield bad fruit. Remember, what we believe about ourselves, we become. What we believe about others, we pull out of them. When we believe a person to be rude, we will speak to that false identity and that false identity will respond. Mike Murdock says it this way, "Every man has a king and a fool in him and the one you talk to reacts."

Instead of partnering with the Accuser, we can ask the Holy Spirit what lies a person is believing when they are not acting in a way that reflects their true identity. In this change of perspective we are now able to respond to the unloving person with compassion and speak truth to water their roots of love, rather than speaking condemnation and judgment that water their roots of fear.

If I believe I am not doing enough, then I will punish my husband for his inaction. I will judge, guilt trip, and withhold love. The root of punishment is my own unresolved guilt. This is a tactic of the enemy.

> *"Fear not; for you will no longer live in shame. Don't be afraid; there is no more disgrace for you." (Isaiah 54:4 NLT)*

Because Jesus defeated death with resurrection and ascended into Heaven, those responsible for his death now go free! Jesus took our punishment once and for all. When our judgment includes punishment it shows we are not properly extending grace and forgiveness to ourselves.

> *"For if you forgive men their trespasses, your heavenly Father will also forgive you. But if you do not forgive men their trespasses, neither will your Father forgive your trespasses." (Matthew 6:14-15)*

In case you are wondering if I still believe we need judicial systems, I do. Assigning judges who have authority over us was God's idea. There is an entire book of the Bible titled Judges, after all. Righteous judges do not measure a person's merit, they discern truth from lies.

God disciplines those He loves (Hebrews 12:6), but New Covenant discipline is not the same as punishment. To discipline means to teach, not to punish. Teaching involves both positive and negative consequences. Leah Martin explains it this way: "Discipline says, 'I'll teach you how to do it right,' while punishment says, 'I'll make you regret doing it wrong.'"

Too often we take off our belt of truth (Ephesians 6:14) and use it like a whip, leaving ourselves exposed to the enemy. The belt was considered the most crucial piece of armor, covering the most vulnerable part of a warrior and required to be worn at all times. Truth, like a belt, is meant to hold us together and carry our spiritual weapons.[32] The belt of truth was never intended to be used to whip people. It breaks my heart that truth is used as a whip by Christians often in theological, political and personal debates. We love to give the lashings of argumentative proof, sharp comebacks, harsh judgements, ungodly justifications, and prideful defensiveness. The more we use our belt like a whip the more shamefully exposed we become. Instead of taking off our belt of truth to harshly prove our point, we can help others put on their own belt of truth by coming alongside them with love, truth and encouragement.

My husband is a dentist and a few years ago he felt God leading him away from private practice to work in the prison system. I get asked often if I worry about him working at a prison. The truth is I do not because I truly believe the places God calls us are the safest place we can be.

The revelation of our identity in Christ has helped Michael minister to the prisoners in a way that he otherwise would not be able to. When you know a person's record there is a temptation to treat them on a scale from bad to horrible depending on what crimes they committed. My husband gets regular push back for treating the prisoners with kindness.

---

32. Joseph, "The Whole Armor of God - Carl Joseph Ministries."

"You don't know what he did!" is a common justification for their judgment to which he responds, "We have all done something bad; his crimes are just public. He is already receiving justice, but my job is to show him love, grace and respect." Michael's understanding is that God has not appointed him as judge. When we are judging ourselves by our actions, we will always judge others by their actions, thus perpetuating the cycles of our false identities. Judgment is merciless. By showing mercy we take dominion over judgment.

> *"For judgment is without mercy to one who has shown no mercy. Mercy triumphs over judgment." (James 2:13 ESV)*

One prisoner Michael treated had hateful tattoos all over his knuckles, face and body. At first Michael was intimidated by this man, but after talking to him for a while he gained the courage to ask about his tattoos. He said, "You seem like a really nice guy and these tattoos do not match the person I've been interacting with." The inmate explained that he was desperate to have the tattoos removed. He said he has been working to change his mindset and it is very hard to do with hateful writing all over his body. Sadly, his tattoos reinforced a negative spiritual identity and led many to judge and mistreat him. By the grace of God, Michael was able to see past his skin to speak to his heart and this man was eventually able to have the tattoos removed.

I lived in a holding pattern, waiting for Jesus to return so I could experience the tangible presence and glory I was so hungry for.

There are all sorts of societal metrics that we use to judge ourselves and others. There are family metrics created by our upbringing and the expectations of family members. There are cultural metrics created by the expectations of teachers, friends and society. There are religious metrics created by the expectations of our pastors and leaders of the church. The most destructive metric in my own life has been religion.

Religious Roots

Religion was the measuring stick that the enemy taught me to beat myself up with. This metric blinded me from seeing myself as a new creation in Christ, until the day God told me I was spiritually blind and He was going to open my eyes.

In scripture Jesus accused the Pharisees of this same thing and they were terribly offended. The Pharisees knew the Word of God intellectually better than anyone at the time and yet God called them out, essentially saying that when the blind lead the blind, everyone falls into a pit (Matthew 15:14).

When God confronted me about my own blindness, I could have easily been offended and defensive. Instead, when the Holy Spirit spoke I felt peace and great anticipation. God, in His great grace, reached down and set me free from the veil that was blinding me and the cage that was binding me. I was a prisoner of war and I was not even aware of it. Over time, religion had become my prison cell.

In so many ways, it looked like I was doing everything right from middle school through college. I got straight As. I didn't drink or party. I waited until the end of high school to start dating. I was not living a worldly lifestyle like many of my peers, but my time spent outside of my God box was just as disconnected from God. My sin was self-dependance, behavior modification, people pleasing, judgment and pride. No better than promiscuity, addiction or theft, just more acceptable in the Church.

Gradually, religion became more and more like a prison cell. I was taught that it was dangerous to consider different theological views on the workings of the Holy Spirit. I became fearful of being deceived, so I accepted interpretations of scripture that were rooted in fear and human understanding. I allowed myself to stay locked up because I believed it was the humble, good Christian thing to do. I lived in a holding pattern, waiting for Jesus to return so I could experience the tangible presence and glory I was so hungry for.

The religious spirit does not just show up like a prison cell, but also as a prosecuting attorney and judge to make sure we never escape. It wore me down with lies, telling me I was not worthy and paralyzing me with fear of rejection. Ultimately, it silenced my voice. Although Romans 8 says that the case is closed and there remains no more accusing voice against us, the religious spirit deceives us, convincing us that he still has power as our prosecutor and judge. He is constantly accusing the sons and daughters of God to keep us bound up in fear, guilt, shame and trauma.

To deflect this overwhelming weight of judgment, we become judgemental of others. The religious spirit deceives us into believing that anyone who believes something different than us is a threat to us.

Religion is like a cage over the Church. It captures Christians who have been adopted into the family of God and keeps them living like orphans rather than sons and daughters. This same cage keeps the orphans in the world, who desperately need to be adopted into the family of God, out. They see our prison cell and refuse to trade their version of bondage for our version. Why would they? Only free people free people.

I praise the Lord that I did not have to spend my entire life locked up by the religious spirit. Jesus had a jailbreak planned for me and radically set me free.

Up until my moment of freedom, religion had me in a choke hold. I could only experience God in short shallow breaths. I was unable to fully breath in the presence of God for which I was created. This shortness of breath led to a constant low level anxiety that I could not escape.

My spiritual blindness was a veil over my eyes. When Jesus rose from the dead, the curtain in the temple that separated people from being able to access the presence of God was torn in two. Through this prophetic sign God was declaring that there is no longer any separation between God and man. Religion attempts to reconstruct the veil of separation so that we cannot utilize the full access to the throne of God Christ died to pay for. This veil keeps us living separated from God, our true identity, our community and our purpose.

The religious spirit does not care if we go to church to learn about God, but it will fight relentlessly to keep us from knowing God experientially. Religion does not mind us studying biblical truths, but it blocks us from personally encountering the man whose name is Truth, Jesus. 2 Timothy 3 goes on to teach that another form of godliness without power is, "always learning but never able to come to a knowledge of the truth" (2 Timothy 3:7 NIV). Remember the Greek word for knowledge is relational knowing, not intellectually understanding. The enemy knows that intellectual knowledge about God will just puff us up and make us prideful.

Ask yourself why do you go to church? Do you go to learn about the Bible and receive some encouragement? These are not bad things, but they are not the purpose of the gathering of the saints. The purpose of our Sunday celebrations must be to spend time with the Father as the family of God. Jesus is the guest of honor. Without His presence, church is just an empty religious tradition.

Most evangelists focus on conversion, but I do not believe conversion is really what the world needs. Conversion means "The fact of changing one's religion or beliefs or the action of persuading someone else to change theirs." We do not need to convince people to think and act just like we think and act. Unity does not come from conformity. God forbid we make the goal of evangelism to change people into our image and likeness instead of God's.

Instead of conversion, I believe we need *emergence*. Emergence means "the process of coming into view or becoming exposed after being concealed." Every sinner was predestined for adoption to become a child of God if they will accept God as their Father. Every person who has committed murder was created in the image of God. Is that a hard truth for you to swallow?

Our problem with sin is not one that can be solved by conversion. Our problem with sin can only be solved by the emergence of God to us and through us.

Rooted In Truth

The gift of discernment is given to help us separate truth from lies and distinguish spiritual forces, not measure good and bad. In Romans, Paul says that God's judgment is based on truth.

> *"You, therefore, have no excuse, you who pass judgment on someone else, for at whatever point you judge another, you are condemning yourself, because you who pass judgment do the same things. Now we know that God's judgment against those who do such things is based on truth. So when you, a mere human being, pass judgment on them and yet do the same things, do you think you will escape God's judgment? (Romans 2:1-3 NIV)*

Discernment is different from the type of judgment we have discussed. Discernment is a spiritual assessment revealed to us through the Holy Spirit. Discernment recognizes spirits and the battle that is not flesh and blood.

"For our struggle is not against flesh and blood, but against the rulers, against the authorities, against the powers of this dark world and against the spiritual forces of evil in the heavenly realms." *(Ephesians 6:12 NIV)*

Massive freedom comes when we learn that all conflict we face is not with people, it is with the evil one. As we grow in discernment, we will be able to recognize what spiritual forces we are fighting and take authority against the schemes of the enemy.

Satan would love nothing more than to make us believe that our problems are because of us, other people, or our circumstances. This is never the truth. Our battle is not with flesh and blood. If we cannot discern this truth, we are powerless to rise above the warfare.

The enemy is called the Father of lies in John 8:44. Behind every lie is a demonic agenda. Sometimes these are weeds that have taken root in our soil, corrupting our souls. This deception has to be uprooted and unwound from the roots of truth. This is how we tear down strongholds and every thought that exalts itself against the knowledge of God (2 Corinthians 10:5). We will go more in depth into this idea as we journey on together.

According to Hebrews 14:5, the spiritually mature are those who have trained their senses to discern good from evil. The word for discernment in the Greek also means distinguishing and deciding. We are all called to grow in discernment and test spirits to see if something is rooted in truth and love, or lies and fear.

"Dear friends, do not believe every spirit, but test the spirits to see whether they are from God." *(1 John 4:1 NIV)*

When I have a check or a red flag about something, there are three questions that I like to ask the Holy Spirit.

1. Is this red flag at all about my own self-judgment or unresolved offense?

If the answer is yes, good questions to ask the Holy Spirit are: What do you want me to know? And what do you want me to do? We must always address what's being exposed in our own hearts before we do anything else. We can pray like David did in Psalm 139:23-24. "Search me, God, and know my heart; test me and know my anxious thoughts. See if there is any offensive way in me, and lead me in the way everlasting."

My favorite definition of wickedness is warped thinking. When we pray to see if there is any wickedness in us, we are asking God to reveal any warped thinking and lies we are believing. Woundedness is a warped filter that makes us wrongly see the world until we heal. When we allow God to search and know us, we will not judge others so easily. Remember, God's voice never sounds like the voice of the Accuser.

2. Is this red flag an attack from the Accuser?

If the answer is yes, we know the truth is the opposite of what we are hearing. For example, if we hear, "They are just so selfish!" about our spouse, then we want to speak the opposite as a blessing and turn it around. This could look something like, "Thank you God for my selfless husband! I bless him to abound in love. Thank you that your Spirit is in him to empower him to prefer others over himself! Help me to overlook his faults, keep no record of wrongs and find whatever is praiseworthy about his actions and attitudes today."

Essentially, we see the accusation of the enemy and instead of partnering with him, we intentionally partner with Jesus who is continually interceding for us. The Accuser is making accusations around the throne day and night (Revelation 12:10), but Jesus is there making intercession for us (Hebrews 7:25). Each day we have to choose to partner with the spirit of intercession or we will default to partnership with the Accuser. The fruit of this choice is always evident in our lives.

When we know our true identity, we know not to listen to the Accuser. We have authority to swat away the lies, guilt and shame the enemy attacks us with like we would an unwanted fly hovering over our head.

While we do not want to be trapped by the enemy's condemnation, we need to be aware that sometimes personal accusation of the enemy comes after a legitimate conviction of the Holy Spirit. Conviction that we do not respond to can become an open door for condemnation. Guilt and shame should be rejected outright as from the enemy. Condemnation is never from God. When the enemy attacks us we do not need to defend ourselves, and we certainly do not need to listen to any voice other than the voice of Love.

However, the voice of Love is not the voice of tolerance that our culture preaches. One of the primary functions of the voice of Love is to call us to repentance. The Holy Spirit is continually beckoning us to lay down anything that hinders real transformative love. His invitation is costly and always involves sacrifice. We need a spirit of repentance to surrender our sinfulness and offenses.

To grow we must learn to welcome the sweet conviction of the Holy Spirit and walk in quick repentance. When the enemy makes a case against us, instead of defending ourselves, we can make a case for God. When he says, "You are so prideful" we can respond, "My prideful nature is under the blood and Jesus my Savior is humility personified. His meekness now lives in me."

Although we do not yet exhibit all the characteristics of Christ, we are growing up to be just like our Father. Sin consciousness brings further bondage but God consciousness produces freedom.

"Therefore be imitators of God as dear children. And walk in love, as Christ also has loved us and given Himself for us." (Ephesians 5:1-2)

Sometimes, when we are conscious of God's holy presence, He leads us to have godly sorrow about our sins. This could be mistaken as guilt and sin consciousness, but it has one primary difference. In these moments of repentance we do not focus on our sin, we focus on our great need for our Savior and His exceedingly great forgiveness. When we realize how much we have been forgiven, we are much quicker to forgive others (Luke 7:47). Since He paid our debt in full, the case is closed. Instead of making a case for ourselves, we get to plead the case of Christ. This is the gospel!

3. Is this red flag here to help me discern a lie and replace it with truth?

If the answer is yes, we can ask the Lord to uproot the lie and trust the Holy Spirit to guide us into all truth (John 16:13).

We must be careful to not label judgment as discernment. Many believers use the word discernment to justify man-made theologies that keep us comfortable and limit God. Discernment is not an intellectual pursuit; it is a gift of the Spirit. Ironically, the Holy Spirit is often quenched in the name of "discernment." There is no true discernment without the full operation of the Spirit of Truth. We must surrender completely to the Holy Spirit if we are going to be able to discern truth from lies in the days ahead as the enemy's deception gets thicker and thicker.

> *"But God has revealed them to us through His Spirit. For the Spirit searches all things, yes, the deep things of God. For what man knows the things of a man except the spirit of the man which is in him? Even so no one knows the things of God except the Spirit of God. Now we have received, not the spirit of the world, but the Spirit who is from God, that we might know the things that have been freely given to us by God. These things we also speak, not in words which man's wisdom teaches but which the Holy Spirit teaches, comparing spiritual things with spiritual. But the natural man does not receive the things of the Spirit of God, for they are foolishness to him; nor can he know them, because they are spiritually discerned. But he who is spiritual judges all things, yet he himself is rightly judged by no one. For "who has known the mind of the LORD that he may instruct Him?" But we have the mind of Christ." (1 Corinthians 2:10-16)*

We have the opportunity to grow in discernment when we practice distinguishing truth and lies (Hebrews 5:14) and approve what is excellent so as to be pure and blameless (Philippians 1:9-10).

Identity revelation helped Jamie Winship excel as a cop, get handpicked by the CIA for peace mediation in high-conflict zones, and share Jesus to Muslim extremists in Southeast Asia and the Middle East. He teaches extensively on identity and walks people through a life-changing process called identity exchange. This technique exchanges the lies of the world for the liberating truths of God.

In his book, *Living Fearless*, Jamie says, "Be Released! Please! There are ideas inside your mind, heart, and spirit that no one has ever thought of before. And the beauty is that these ideas want to come out of you. The sad part is that for most of you, it's not going to happen because your false self—your fear, guilt, and shame—will shut down your creative and imaginative true self. But there's good news! It can happen, and it can start today. You could say no to it today as well; you have that freedom.

But I hope you will not. I hope you will not dare to say no to what is within you. The world needs what you have. The world needs the real you."[33]

When I began my own journey of identity, God showed me many false identities that I have carried throughout my life. One of these came from the nickname I received in third grade, Miss Mary Motor Mouth. The enemy told me that I am too loud, that I talk too much, and that I'm just too much! Soon I lost my confidence and my voice. When I confessed these lies, God called me His Mouthpiece! The enemy's lies are always the opposite of our true identity. God then led me to Isaiah 59.

> *"As for Me," says the Lord, "this is My covenant with them: My Spirit who is upon you, and My words which I have put in your mouth, shall not depart from your mouth, nor from the mouth of your descendants, nor from the mouth of your descendants' descendants," says the Lord, "from this time and forevermore." (Isaiah 59: 21)*

Our believing informs our being, which informs our doing. When we do the deep work of discerning the truth and lies of our inner beings, we pioneer the path to our destiny that God has laid out for each of us.

> *"For this reason I bow my knees to the Father of our Lord Jesus Christ, **from whom the whole family in heaven and earth is named**, that He would grant you, according to the riches of His glory, to **be strengthened with might through His Spirit in the inner man**, that Christ may dwell in your hearts through faith; that you, **being rooted and grounded in love**, may be able to comprehend with all the saints what is the width and length and depth and height— to know the love of Christ which passes knowledge; that you may be filled with all the fullness of God." (Ephesians 2:14-19, bold mine)*

---

33. Winship, *Living Fearless: Exchanging the Lies of the World for the Liberating Truth of God*.

ROOT FIELD NOTES
Identify who you are in your true identity

Find a quiet place and start by breathing in God's love for four seconds. Hold that breath for four seconds, imagining His presence filling you up like a balloon. Now, for four seconds breathe out whatever negative emotion is weighing you down. Repeat this exercise until you feel settled and present. Ask the Holy Spirit the following questions. Then journal the free flow of thoughts that come to your mind as you fix your eyes on Jesus.

Questions:

Holy Spirit, who has been lying to me about my identity? What lies am I believing about myself?

_____
_____
_____

Who do I need to forgive for this lie?

_____
_____
_____

Who do you call me?

_____

_____

_____

Activation:

Take some time to go on a treasure hunt to unpack different facets of your true identity with the Holy Spirit. Ask Him for scriptures that reveal pieces of your identity. Co-creating with the Holy Spirit, craft two to three identity statements that you can use as mantras to stay rooted in truth.

Examples:

I am an encourager and co-creator who prophesies Heaven's solutions.

I am a shepherded shepherd, gently led and gently leading.

I am an awakener, exhorter, and equipper of abiding action.

Encounter:

On a piece of paper and write down the lies you are believing about yourself.

Imagine yourself handing those lies over to Jesus, the image of the invisible God.

What does He do with your list?

Look into the eyes of Jesus and ask Him, "Who do I need to forgive for these lies?"

Imagine taking every person that comes to mind to the cross and leaving them at the feet of Jesus.

Say out loud "I forgive ___ for ___," in faith.

Now look again at Jesus and ask Him, "What's the truth? What names do you call me?"

Recommended Resource:

I recommend investing in personal identity coaching if you want to grow in your true identity. Jamie Winship's team offers coaching at Identityexchange.com.

My family also offers identity coaching at Fieldguideforfamilies.com

GROW V

Figure 15: Grafted in Olive Branch
Figure 16: Tree Trunk Full of Sap   Figure 17: Tree Rings of Growth

GROW
Chapter Five

How do you remain connected with your true source of growth?
Identifying God's presence

Identifying the Sap

JUST LIKE SAP IS the vitality of a tree, the supernatural Spirit is our life source. Sap provides nutrients to new leaves enabling them to grow. Without the sap of the Holy Spirit, we cannot experience true life.

The sap of the Spirit is truly revolutionary. It is a fuel far greater than any other source we have encountered. Tree sap carries energy out into the branches and the sap of the Spirit is the energy source our bodies were created to run on. We have not experienced true life until we have connected ourselves to this heavenly fuel.

"The trees of the Lord are full of sap." (Psalm 104:16)

Once we have learned to flow in the supernatural empowerment of God, we will not want to live apart from this divine connection for a moment. Few know how to tap into this life source and fewer still know how to flow in it. This chapter we will learn how to identify, connect and flow in the sap of the Spirit providing us with everything we need to thrive.

The sap of the Spirit flows through us when we become a living sacrifice. Everything that we do can be done as an act of worship. Eric Gilmour says it like this, "What many people do not understand is that the soul was made to do all things while looking at Jesus so that everything done—whether eating or drinking, cleaning or working, preaching or praying, teaching or counseling — is done unto the glory of God."[34]

The writer of Romans put it this way, "I beseech you therefore, brethren, by the mercies of God, that you present your bodies a living sacrifice, holy, acceptable to God, which is your reasonable service" (Romans 12:1).

The word *present* used in this text has multiple meaningful definitions. The Greek word is parístēmi and it means: to place a person or thing at one's disposal; to bring into one's fellowship or intimacy; be present (of time); to stand by or near; to present (show) by argument, to prove.[35]

When we present *(place a person or thing at one's disposal)* ourselves before God's presence, *(to bring into one's fellowship or intimacy)*, presently *(of time)*, and continually *(to stand by or near)*, we effortlessly present *(to show by argument, to prove)* His love to the world.

This is our highest purpose: to experience the love of God empowering us to love Him back and love others. We present ourselves to God as a living sacrifice; He transforms us and presents us to the world as carriers of His glory.

To be a living sacrifice, we must continually surrender our thoughts for His thoughts, our desires for His desires, our passions for His passions. When we live with an awareness of God's presence, mundane moments are transformed into extraordinary encounters. We serve a living God that we were created to experience!

Allow me to illustrate this point with a recurring scene from my life. I am standing at the kitchen sink attempting to get through stacks of dirty dishes. A child is crying at my feet. Another is on the toilet yelling for assistance. I glimpse the piles of laundry on the couch that need to be folded and spot fresh dog pee on the carpet. Overwhelm tempts me, but gratitude rescues me. The Holy Spirit whispers the reminder I need to shift me from stress to praise, "This moment is holy." My spirit leaps in agreement. And so it becomes exactly what I believe it to be. One moment of surrender shifts my daily tasks done out of duty to worship done before my King.

---

34. Gilmour, *Into The Cloud: Becoming God's Spokesman*.
35. G3936 - Parístēmi - Strong's Greek Lexicon (Kjv).

Simple intentionality frees us from feeling like a slave to our circumstances. Instead, we get to make the powerful choice to become a willing servant. When our circumstances are less than ideal, we have the power to control our response. Will we complain or will we worship? I want to respond like Mary the mother of Jesus, when she received her divine and equally painful assignment: "And Mary said, "Behold, I am the servant of the Lord; let it be to me according to your word" (Luke 1:38 ESV).

Encounters with God give us context for our faith. While we never create theology based on emotional moments, the Lord is meant to be experienced. He is, after all, the God that created all of our emotions. We are emotional beings made in the image of our emotional God. Many of us have been taught that emotions come with instability. While this is often the case with emotions that are not surrendered to God, emotional does not have to mean unstable.

Jesus is the Word made manifest dwelling among us (John 1:14). When we encounter the Holy Spirit, the Holy Scriptures come alive to us. We really can live the Word of God. The reality of Emmanuel, God with us, does stir our emotions. This is not hype; this is an outward expression of our innermost beliefs. The Bible is filled with stories of people experiencing the tangible presence of God. He is described in terms meant to be felt like a consuming fire, wind and living water. All of these elements are felt. I pray the Lord will always keep my heart tender towards Him.

Our hunger for God leads us to experience Him in community, but gatherings cannot be the highest point of encounter for us. Alone in the secret place, saints from every time period in history testify of the most profound touches from God. The deepest and richest encounters I have had with Jesus have not been at conferences or retreats but when I am alone with Him.

Somewhere between sweeping the floors and making lunch, the Holy Spirit makes Jesus' presence known to me in a way that marks me forever. Some of these moments I never even speak about to anyone because they are so holy and so intimate.

Wherever we look for God, we will find Him and when we find Him, that is to become aware of His omnipresence, we are given the grace to do everything from divine love. To do so we must, as Johann Wolfgang von Goethe beautifully states, "Cease endlessly striving for what you would like to do and learn to love what must be done."

Of Brother Lawrence (who wrote *Practicing the Presence of God*), it was said, "The most excellent method he had found of going to God, was that of doing our common business without any view of pleasing men, and (as far as we are capable) purely for the love of God."

God's presence is found in the present. We've all heard it said, the present is a present. It's a gift that must be received. God's grace is only available to us in this current moment. Fear is cultivated when we imagine future circumstances without God's empowering grace available to us in the moment.

I am a visionary and part of the expression of my true identity is spending time rising up on the clouds with Jesus to take in a 10,000-foot view of life. There are certainly appropriate times where the Holy Spirit will lead us to dream of our future, but we cannot live in that space. Focusing on yesterday or tomorrow can prevent us from fully living in the present moment before us.

When my thoughts are being pulled by the past or to the future, one of the ways I ground myself in the present is by narrating my life to myself as though I was a character in a novel. It may sound funny, but it increases my awareness and gratitude dramatically. Other times, I center myself through the activation of my five senses by acknowledging something I can see, feel, taste, smell and touch.

Another way I ground myself in the present when I feel myself drifting is through intentional breathing. When we become aware of God's presence we find He is closer than the air we breathe. If we dig a little deeper we will find that He is our very breath. God's name in the Hebrew, YHWH, is made up of consonants that creatively model the sound of breathing.

Let's practice becoming present right now. Unclench your jaw, unfurrow your brow and release any tension you are holding in your body. Take a deep breath and inhale "Yah" then slowly exhale "Weh." Let's do it again, this time breathing in "Yah" for four seconds, holding it for four seconds, and then breathing out "Weh" for four seconds. Do you feel more aware of the presence of God all around you? The name of our Lord is the sound of our breathing. He is in our every breath. Incredible, right?

At any moment we can breathe in peace and breathe out anxiety. Breathe in acceptance and breathe out rejection. Breathe in honor and breathe out shame.

Connecting to the Sap

Disconnection is the biggest threat to our spiritual growth. When we live disconnected from God we live disconnected from our true identity, from others and from our purpose. God wired us with supernatural sap of the Spirit to keep us connected.

In John 15, Jesus says that unless we abide and remain in life union with Him, we cannot bear fruit. This is one of my favorite passages in all of scripture. Take a minute and read it slowly, imagine yourself tasting, chewing, and swallowing the truth in this passage like we learned to do in previous chapters.

> *"Abide in me, and I in you. As the branch cannot bear fruit by itself, unless it abides in the vine, neither can you, unless you abide in me. I am the vine; you are the branches. Whoever abides in me and I in him, he it is that bears much fruit, for apart from me you can do nothing." (John 15:4-5 ESV)*

Separate from God we can do nothing that produces eternal fruit. As soon as we disconnect from the Spirit we have to run on false fuel that's dependent on ourselves and anything other than God. This is religious striving, and it leads to death. It scares me to think of all the things I thought I did for God, but because I did them separate from God, they have no eternal value.

Religion was meant to die with Christ. Judaism (the Law of the Old Covenant) is a religion, but Christianity (New Covenant) is a relationship. There is nothing for us to work for, nothing that can be earned. Jesus paid it all for us! The veil was torn in the temple to signify that Jesus finished the work so there is no longer any separation between us and God. Paul says that the law brings death but the Spirit brings life (2 Corinthians 3:6). It's complete; the law has been fulfilled! In a moment Jesus put an end to religion!

So why, then, do we still struggle with religious striving? The enemy is a master of deception and his goal is to deceive us. If he can get us into self-dependency, religious striving, and relying on our own best effort, he can nullify the power of the cross in our lives.

Matthew 7:21-23 is a very important warning in scripture that highlights the importance of doing things with God rather than merely for

God. Speaking of the day of judgment Jesus says, "On that day many will say to me, 'Lord, Lord, did we not prophesy in your name, and cast out demons in your name, and do many mighty works in your name?' And then will I declare to them, 'I never knew you; depart from me, you workers of lawlessness'" (ESV).

Jesus is teaching us that we can run thriving ministries, preach, share the gospel, cast out demons, prophesy, even do miracles, signs and wonders, all disconnected from God. This is a sobering reality that will put a healthy fear of the Lord in us.

"This is the heart of the spirit of religion: 'Give them everything but His presence.' Why? Because only His presence gives life. This is why some hate religion and why others die under it, because it only gives a picture of Jesus but never introduces the person of Jesus." —Eric Gilmour, *Enjoying The Gospel*[36]

I hope that we have well established that knowing about God and knowing God are not the same thing. To truly know someone we have to spend time in their presence. Having a personal relationship with the Lord is not an option, it's a requirement for salvation.

Daily, even minute by minute at times, we have a choice: are we going to live in life-union, connected to our true source or are we going to live separate and disconnected? Separation is the greatest deception and results in powerlessness.

Because of technology, we are likely the most disconnected people group ever to live. Wherever we look we are tempted with counterfeit connection. Social media, while not inherently bad, is a huge trap for counterfeit connection. Television shows and movies hook us with counterfeit connection. Addictions to drugs, alcohol, food and other substanceless substances are at an all-time high. Behind every addiction is disconnection. Behind all dysregulation and negative behaviors is also disconnection.

Connection is the opposite of addiction and the antidote for religion. Connection does not just happen; it requires intentionality.

Family traditions are wonderful for cultivating connection. Growing up, one of my favorite days of the year was our annual Christmas tree hunt. My aunts, uncles, cousins and grandparents would all gather

---

36. Gilmour, *Enjoying the Gospel*.

in a giant caravan to drive up Mt. Ashland and search for Christmas trees. One walkie talkie was distributed to each vehicle and we had a blast talking to each other on our way up the snowy mountain. All the kids took turns practicing radio etiquette, "Roger, Roger! Over and out!"

Much like walkie talkies, there is effort required to achieve and maintain communication with the Holy Spirit. First, walkie talkies require charged batteries. It is absolutely essential that we spend time set apart in the presence of God to recharge. We cannot give what we have not received. In order to keep our attention on the Lord throughout the day amidst all of life's distractions we need times where we give God our undivided attention. In these moments face to face with God, He deposits within us everything we need for the day.

Jesus Himself said, "But when you pray, go into your room and shut the door and pray to your Father who is in secret. And your Father who sees in secret will reward you" (Matthew 6:6 ESV).

In his book, *Sit, Walk, Stand*, Watchman Nee says, "Only those who sit can stand. Our power for standing, as for walking, lies in our having first been made to sit together with Christ. The Christian's walk and warfare alike derive their strength from his position there. If he is not sitting before God he cannot hope to stand before the enemy."

Our Bridegroom King beckons us to come away and sit with Him. Imagine Jesus calling to you personally as He does in Song of Songs, "My beloved spoke and said to me, 'Arise, my darling, my beautiful one, come with me'" (Song of Songs 2:10 NIV).

There is no formula to our time in the secret place. The goal is simply to prioritize connection to God away from all of life's distractions and there hold our mind and heart as an offering before Him.

Waiting on the Lord is one of the most important, and sadly neglected, spiritual disciplines.

We have made prayer into a duty when it was created to be the place of purest delight. In its simplest form, prayer is communing with God. Our minds might desire to bring the Lord our list of requests, but our soul is yearning for unhindered fellowship. Our gracious Lord will fulfill *both*. A relationship that involves nothing more than petitions is not one of true love. We can certainly ask our good Father to act on our behalf and on others, but these requests must only take a small fraction of our time spent with Him.

A date with my husband involves listening as much as talking. There are times that we are just quietly content in each other's presence. We plan date nights to give each other our full attention. Few things make me feel more loved than having my husband's unbroken eye contact and full focus. And so it is also with our Lord.

David W. Augsburger makes an excellent observation in his book *Caring Enough to Hear and Be Heard*. "Being heard is so close to being loved that for the average person, they are almost indistinguishable."[37] Intimacy means into-me-see. It's being fully seen, known and loved. This is the longing of every soul, creating a void that can only be filled by God.

It is in the secret place that we intentionally hold our hearts open before the Lord, waiting in stillness and solitude with our eyes fixed on Jesus. As often as our minds wander, we bring them back to behold the beauty of the Lord. As we do, our Beloved becomes the one desire of our hearts positioned far above all others. It is here that we give Him His first and rightful place.

> "One thing I have desired of the LORD, That will I seek: That I may dwell in the house of the LORD All the days of my life, To behold the beauty of the LORD, And to inquire in His temple." (Psalm 27:4)

"Our devotional life with God is more like the planting of a garden. When we arise from sowing into the secret place, we will not usually be able to point to immediate results or benefits. What we sow today will require an entire season of growth before the results are manifest. The wisest thing you'll ever do in this life is to draw close to God and to seek Him with all your heart. I never consider time invested in the secret place to be wasteful; and even if it is, I gladly waste it upon my Lord! When you neglect the secret place, He's not disappointed *in* you, He's disappointed *for* you. One day of exhilaration in the Holy Spirit is worth a thousand days of struggle! The greatest things in life—those things that carry eternal value—always come at the steepest price. The closer you get to God, the more you realize He's in no hurry. No one can mentor

---

37. Augsburger, *Caring Enough to Hear and Be Heard: How to Hear and How to Be Heard in Equal Communication*.

you into an abiding relationship with Christ. We all have to find our own way to abiding in Christ. When all is said and done, we must shut the door, get into the secret place with God, and discover what an abiding relationship with Christ will look like for ourselves." - *Bob Sorge, Secrets of the Secret Place*[38]

Just like a battery must be tethered to an outlet for a time to be able to hold the power needed to sustain it for the day's use, we need time tethered to the feet of Jesus.

Additionally, walkie talkies have to all be set to the same communication channel. One twist of a dial and a once clear communication can turn into blaring static noise. We have a real enemy who is trying to divert us from the channel of the Spirit. He works overtime to get us to lose our signal so he can overwhelm us with static noise. In war time this interference with communication is a legitimate tactic called electronic warfare. We must be as aggressive about combating distractions as we would about obvious psychological warfare.

Walkie talkies also require a close proximity to work. As we drove up the mountain, our cars had to remain within a certain radius of each other in order to maintain the connection. When we catch ourselves disconnected, distracted or deceived we must immediately check our reception.

In other translations of John 15, we are instructed to abide in truth and abide in love. Our connection is maintained through communication and reception.

We are invited to live connected to the voice of God and meditate on the truth of His Word day and night. This communication with the ever-present Spirit keeps us connected as we abide in truth. To remain in truth, we have to believe the truth that is revealed to us in relationship with the Holy Spirit.

To abide in love, we must continually receive the love of God as our supernatural empowerment. To remain, we have to choose connection over production. This looks like focusing more on being who we were made to *be* rather than on doing whatever it is we are called to *do*.

Sap can only flow when we are rooted in our true identity and allow God to produce the fruit through our lives. All our doing flows from our being. When we choose to focus on connection and *being* over *doing*,

---

38. Sorge, *Secrets of the Secret Place: Keys to Igniting Your Personal Time With God.*

production is supernatural, without effort. Striving is the curse; enjoyment is our covenant.

Are we receiving everything we need from the indwelling Spirit within us? In Matthew 10, Jesus instructs us to freely receive and freely give. We cannot give that which we have not received.

> "As you go, proclaim this message:'The kingdom of heaven has come near.' Heal the sick, raise the dead, cleanse those who have leprosy, drive out demons. Freely you have received; freely give." (Matthew 10:7)

When God is our true source we lack nothing. James 4:2 says we have not because we ask not. We freely receive and freely give. If we are in need of grace to deal with a difficult situation, we simply and freely receive His grace and give it away in faith. If we need wisdom, we do the same. James 1:5 instructs us to ask, believe, and receive.

> "Wisdom is a tree of life to those who embrace her; happy are those who hold her tightly." (Proverbs 3:18 NLT)

If we recognize the diversion tactics of the enemy to keep us from receiving everything we need, we can intentionally change the dial back to the Holy Spirit living within us. When I hear static noise and feel myself disconnecting, I like to ask the Lord two simple questions: What do you want me to know? And what do you want me to do?

As we resync up with the channel of the Spirit, we will again be able to hear the voice of truth and flow in sync with our loving leader.

Flowing in the Sap

There is a rhythm we tap into in the Spirit when we remain connected that is far more powerful than any false fuel we are tempted to depend on. A rhythm is a strong and weak element in a flow that creates forward movement.[39] We are the weak element and the Spirit is the strong element. In 2 Corinthians 12, Paul describes weakness as our super power. Acknowledging our weakness moment to moment invites God's strength to manifest in our lives.

---

39. "Rhythm," in *Merriam-Webster Dictionary*.

"But he said to me, 'My grace is sufficient for you, for my power is made perfect in weakness.' Therefore I will boast all the more gladly about my weaknesses, so that Christ's power may rest on me. That is why, for Christ's sake, I delight in weaknesses, in insults, in hardships, in persecutions, in difficulties. For when I am weak, then I am strong." (2 Corinthians 12:9-10 NIV)

This verse became my lifeline when I moved to China my senior year of high school. I lived with my aunt, uncle and cousins and attended an international school where my uncle worked. God allowed a few supernatural things to happen to assure me that He was with me.

I flew out of one of the busiest international airports in the U.S., having never flown by myself before. I remember being in a line that wrapped around an entire terminal, completely unsure of how I was going to get through it and get on my plane in time. A lady came up to me out of nowhere, singling me out in the massive line, and asked to see my boarding ticket. She then led me to the other side of the airport and escorted me straight onto my plane without saying another word. I was the last passenger to board my plane to Seoul, Korea where I would go on to my connection to Qingdao. It took off minutes after I was seated. To this day I am convinced that lady was an angel.

During my first week in China, my passport slipped out of the folder my uncle was carrying on his way to the embassy. When we noticed it was missing, we retraced his steps along the dirt road but had no success locating it. Without a passport, I would have been unable to obtain a longer visa, or travel home, so I would be stuck in the country illegally. We prayed and a week later it was turned into the embassy to the shock of the staff. These are just two examples of numerous miracles I experienced. These miracles gave me the assurance that I needed to keep the faith when things got extremely hard a couple of months later.

One day after a volleyball match, I had excruciating pain suddenly shoot down my back and legs and I collapsed. This began a painful journey of me not being able to walk without support. We lived in a sixth floor apartment and the international school also had six flights of stairs, making getting around in a wheelchair impossible. Nothing could get me to surrender control quicker than living in a foreign country with doctors who speak a language I could neither speak nor understand. The utter reliance on the support of others was humbling to say the least. It was during this time that 2 Corinthians 12:9 became my favorite verse.

Once we have the revelation of this truth, weakness becomes our superpower. Rejoicing in weakness as Paul instructs does not mean we deny the reality of our pain. We rejoice because of the grace available to us in our pain. Grace can be defined as unmerited favor and supernatural empowerment. Because of grace, our weakness and Christ's strength creates the rhythm we flow in.

Accepting our weakness and flowing in grace is the essence of abiding. Continual surrender releases us to flow in the sap of the Spirit, giving us supernatural momentum.

In his book, *Surrender to Love*, David Benner describes surrender as a release of effort, tension and fear through trust. It requires us to let go of self-dependence and transfer our full weight onto someone or something. He says, "Floating is a good illustration of this, because you cannot float until you let go. Floating is putting your full weight on the water and trusting that you will be supported. It is letting go of your natural instincts to fight against sinking. Only then do you discover that you are supported."[40]

Brenner continues to illustrate this point by saying, "Surrender is the discovery that we are in a river of love and that we float without having to do anything. Apart from such surrender, we always are in the grip of some degree of fear. Apart from such surrender, we will always thrash about, trying to stay afloat by our own efforts. And apart from such surrender, we remain self-preoccupied as our willful attempts to stay in control cut us off from life itself."[41]

Anyone else guilty of willful attempts to stay in control? Control is an illusion. It is only when we lose it that we realize we never had it to begin with. "I'm about to lose it!" is a phrase I've caught myself saying to my children in moments of weakness. When I say this, it carries a negative and desperate connotation, but Jesus flips the script and says whoever loses his life will find it (Matthew 10:39). We can lose our tempers and fight for control or we can lay down our lives and lose ourselves. When we choose the latter, we find the grace we need to rejoice in our

---

40. Benner, *Surrender to Love: Discovering the Heart of Christian Spirituality*, 61.
41. Benner, *Surrender to Love: Discovering the Heart of Christian Spirituality*, 63.

weaknesses and crucify our flesh. "Losing it" can become something we celebrate rather than fight against.

It is only when we enjoy intimate fellowship with the Lord that we can willingly surrender to His love. In his book, *Absolute Surrender*, Andrew Murray says, "Being filled with the Spirit is simply this - having my whole nature yielded to His power. When the whole soul is yielded to the Holy Spirit, God Himself will fill it."

We cannot flow in the sap of the spirit and experience the supernatural momentum apart from surrender. The flow is released by letting go.

Another way to view yieldedness is rest. The Bible repeatedly refers to rest not as the action of resting (like taking a nap, laying on the beach, etc), but the refuge of the soul. Isaiah 30:15 says, "In returning and rest you shall be saved; In quietness and confidence shall be your strength."

> *Accepting our weakness and flowing in grace is the essence of abiding.*

This type of deep trust and sure confidence is the rest that we can experience right in the middle of life's craziest storms. Rest is the promised land we can access whenever we choose. There are, however, giants that try to prevent us from experiencing this rest. This is why the writer of Hebrews describes a striving into this rest. There is only one kind of godly striving: Striving towards full surrender, full trust and full faith.

> *"God's promise of entering his rest still stands, so we ought to tremble with fear that some of you might fail to experience it. For this good news—that God has prepared this rest—has been announced to us just as it was to them. But it did them no good because they didn't share the faith of those who listened to God. For only we who believe can enter his rest."* (Hebrews 4: 1-2 NLT)

Throughout scripture we are told not to fear, but in this passage we are told we ought to fear not experiencing rest. This is meant to get our full attention. When we experience this glorious realm of rest, we never want to go back to our old stress and anxiety inducing ways!

We are commanded in the Word of God to not be anxious and to not worry. Yet sadly, most of us are worried, stressed, anxious and overwhelmed on a regular basis. In order to overcome these dominant emotions, we have to come out from under their grip. We have to reject overwhelm and stress. Our brains need the reminder that we have the power to choose whether or not we will submit to anxiety.

Like we have established in previous chapters, we cannot always control our circumstances but we can control our reactions. This is why self-control is a fruit of the Spirit. It is our reactions, not our circumstances, that create our experience. We can control ourselves. How? By controlling our thoughts and surrendering to the love of Jesus. Paul tells us in 2 Corinthians that it is the love of Christ that controls us.

> *"For the love of Christ controls us, because we have concluded this: that one has died for all, therefore all have died; and he died for all, that those who live might no longer live for themselves but for him who for their sake died and was raised."* (2 Corinthians 5:14-15 ESV)

Do you consider worrying about your family a normal expression of your love for them? You must determine in your heart that you are not going to fall into the trap of worry anymore. Worry is the enemy's prayer language. It is harming you and the person you are worried about.

Stress is a trauma response that points to an unmet need (emotional, physical or spiritual) or unhealed places in our hearts. Learning to better cope with stress is not the solution, working to eliminate the root of our stress responses is. Our bodies were never meant to live in a continued state of stress.

My pastor, Jenny Donnelly describes rest as the pocket in the eye of the storm. In her book, *Still: 7 Ways To Find Calm In Chaos*, she uses a powerful acronym for how we can experience rest.

R- Release
E- Every
S- Single
T- Thing

There is no rest without surrender. Jenny says, "Rest means that we are resting in what is happening right this second with a complete trust that God will meet us in our next moment."

Judgments and pride-filled opinions steal our rest faster than anything else.

When the Lord first started teaching me about a posture of rest that can be maintained through the most chaotic of moments, I was determined to test this theory. Prior to this, I had become accustomed to motivating myself to get things done by getting into what my husband refers to as "hurricane mode." I used stress as a false fuel source that created a lot of negative momentum. It was both effective and destructive. I knew I needed to learn how to tap into another fuel source.

God first started teaching me about the glorious rest realm that I could live in 24/7 around Christmas time. I was so amazed that I could get through my long list of holiday preparations with two children under two in total peace and not give into the temptation to be fueled by stress. I remember feeling like I was floating on a cloud and I could not believe I didn't know about this glorious rest realm before.

Step by step, Jesus was teaching me to walk in the Spirit. I didn't do it perfectly then and I still do not, but the principles God taught me changed my life. This new found rest realm was put to the test on Christmas morning. I woke up early to prepare breakfast for fifteen people. Once breakfast was in the oven baking, the kids started opening their Christmas gifts. As I took the hundredth picture of my son playing with his new train table the smoke detectors went off. The sweet smell of cinnamon bread had been replaced with the strong smell of smoke.

I rushed to the kitchen to discover a flaming fire in my oven. We had just installed a security system that automatically notified the fire department. Before I even had time to call them myself, the fire department showed up at our doorstep. Within seconds we went from peacefully opening gifts to putting out a fire, testing my new found rest revelation. Is rest really available in the middle of chaos? My first response was to laugh. My second was to pray.

My dad asked me for flour to throw on the fire and I accidentally handed him sugar. Thank goodness he realized my mistake before throwing sugar on the fire and was able to have the fire out just as the fire fighters arrived. As it turns out, meeting firefighters and getting to see their firetruck was even more exciting to my two-year-old than his new train table.

Rest is indeed available right in the middle of chaos, but we have to choose it. One of the ways we choose the lifestyle of rest every week is by taking a sabbath. Doing so revealed to me that I was addicted to busyness. Seeking nothing but connection with my family and God for a day proves to be a weekly challenge for me. Halfway through the day, I'm dying to work on a project and produce something. When I surrender this urge, I am always met with joy and deep gratitude for the present moment before me. God says he made the sabbath for us (Mark 2:27). Sabbath is a gift from God to center us. It is a built-in reset. It is a weekly test to see if we believe that more can be accomplished when we practice resting.

In John Mark Comer's book, *The Ruthless Elimination of Hurry*, he says, "The Hebrew word Shabbat means 'to stop.' But it can also be translated 'to delight.' It has this dual idea of stopping and also of joying in God and our lives in His world. The Sabbath is an entire day set aside to follow God's example, to stop and delight."[42]

Corrie ten Boom said, "If the devil can't make you sin, he'll make you busy." There is an acronym for busy that has always been sobering to me: Being Under Satan's Yoke. Jesus' yoke is easy. He says in Matthew 11:28-30, "Come to me, all who labor and are heavy laden, and I will give you rest. Take my yoke upon you, and learn from me, for I am gentle and lowly in heart, and you will find rest for your souls. For my yoke is easy, and my burden is light."

The second that our to-do list "for God" steals our margin to love His people well, we have lost touch with our true purpose.

Notice that He does not say no burden, but a light one. Rest is not the absence of labor, it is a state of the soul. Busy is not just keeping occupied, it is a state of the soul being preoccupied. I become preoccupied when I try to solve things on my own and rely on my own strength. I remain in a prayerful state when I am in a posture of receiving and releasing by faith. This is how we pray without ceasing and remain in communion with the Father.

In these moments where my soul feels busy, cluttered or heavy I declare out loud, "I am prayerful and present, not preoccupied." The state of being busy, or preoccupied almost always leads to overwhelm. Anytime our yoke is heavy we are carrying something Jesus didn't ask us to carry.

It is important to note that some of the most steady and centered

---

42. Comer, *The Ruthless Elimination of Hurry: How to Stay Emotionally Healthy and Spiritually Alive in the Chaos of the Modern World.*

people I know are the ones with the fullest schedule. God often grows our capacity supernaturally when we are in alignment with our destiny. Having a calendar full of things God has asked us to do doesn't make us busy.

Busy is a state of mind. Busy is a choice. Jesus was not preoccupied with the needs of the multitudes; He was occupied by the will of the Father. He declared that He must be about His Father's business. Jesus was about God's business, not earthly busy-ness. He cared for the multitude and served them without becoming preoccupied by their needs. The second that our to-do list "for God" steals our margin to love His people well, we have lost touch with our true purpose.

The story of Mary and Martha is a classic illustration of this truth. This passage found in Luke 10:38 is one that I go back to time and time again.

> *"As Jesus and his disciples were on their way, he came to a village where a woman named Martha opened her home to him. She had a sister called Mary, who sat at the Lord's feet listening to what he said. But Martha was distracted by all the preparations that had to be made. She came to him and asked, "Lord, don't you care that my sister has left me to do the work by myself? Tell her to help me!" "Martha, Martha," the Lord answered, "you are worried and upset about many things, but few things are needed—or indeed only one. Mary has chosen what is better, and it will not be taken away from her." (Luke 10:38-42 NIV)*

I am willing to bet that Martha expressed and received love through acts of service. She was not corrected by Jesus because serving Him is bad, but because she was preoccupied with her serving. Jesus desired her attention. Martha was doing what was culturally expected, while Mary broke all cultural norms as a woman, sitting at the feet of a rabbi. No doubt everyone in the room thought Mary was the one who would be reprimanded, but in one moment Jesus changed the storyline for women everywhere. He did not just make the bold allowance to have a woman sit at His feet, He commended it! While religion still tries to exclude women, everything Jesus did empowered women.

When we wrestle into rest and spend time set apart in God's presence, we can serve the Lord without the worry, stress and distraction.

When we apply Mary's heart posture to Martha's to-do list, our service becomes a true act of love.

Delight is the pathway to His presence. John Piper says, "God is most glorified in me when I am most satisfied in Him." We cannot fulfill our purpose on the earth apart from connection to our Creator which leads to delight in His goodness.

All of nature has three primary parts that point to the triune God. Trees have roots, a trunk and branches. Blossoms have petals, stems and pollen. Fruit have seeds, a nutritious inner layer and a protective outer layer. All of creation testifies to the beauty of our Creator and invites us to continually connect to His love.

> *"For since the creation of the world God's invisible qualities—his eternal power and divine nature—have been clearly seen, being understood from what has been made, so that people are without excuse." (Romans 1:20 NIV)*

GROW FIELD NOTES

Identify how to abide in the presence of God

Find a quiet place and start by breathing in God's love for four seconds. Hold that breath for four seconds, imagining His presence filling you up like a balloon. Now, for four seconds breathe out whatever negative emotion is weighing you down. Repeat this exercise until you feel settled and present. Ask the Holy Spirit the following questions. Then journal the free flow of thoughts that come to your mind as you fix your eyes on Jesus.

Questions:

Holy Spirit, how do I disconnect from you throughout my day?

_____
_____
_____

How can I prioritize time to get away with you in the secret place?

_____
_____
_____

How do I have a tendency to live more in the past or future?
_____
_____
_____

How do you anchor and ground me in the present?
_____
_____
_____

How do I rely on false fuel instead of connecting to you, my true source?
_____
_____
_____

How can I get rid of these false fuels?
_____
_____
_____

Activation:

This week when you feel disconnected or dysregulated, pick one of the following tools. Take a picture of the five grounding techniques and the acronym for ABIDE. Upload the picture to a note in your phone so you have quick access when you need it.

<u>Five Senses:</u> Name five things you can see, four things you can touch, three things you can hear, two things you can smell, and one thing you can taste. Savor your senses in the present moment.

<u>Body Scan:</u> As you take deep breaths slowly scan your body to release tension in every spot you notice it being held. Start with your head, release your furrow brow, unclench your jaw, and continue down your body. Repeat body scans until you have released all tension.

<u>Shake it Off</u>: Move your body for one minute shaking, jumping, stretching, dancing and/or crossing your arms and tapping your hands on your shoulders rhythmically.

<u>Narrate:</u> Let the voice of love narrate your present moment to you as though you were a character in a novel. Receive His compassionate narrative and allow yourself to be reminded of the larger storyline of His faithfulness to you.

<u>Deep Breathing:</u> Breathe in God's love for four seconds. Hold that breath for four seconds, imagining His presence filling you up like a balloon. Now, for four seconds breathe out whatever negative emotion is weighing you down. Repeat a few times until you feel centered.

Now take a minute to go through this acronym for ABIDE.

A | ADORE

Give your attention and affection to God.

B | BELIEVE

Call to mind scripture, promises of God, prophetic encouragement and your true identity.

I | IDENTIFY

Confess to the Lord lies you are believing and fears that are stopping you.

D | DELIVER

Repent, change your mind and hand over all doubt, worry, anxiety, toil, control.

E | ENJOY

Delight in the present moment in the flow of surrender to Love.

Repeat as often as you feel disconnected.

Encounter:

Lay flat on your back. Imagine yourself in a river. Relying on your own strength is like walking upstream against the current. Ask the Holy Spirit, "In what areas am I doing this in my life and relying on my own strength instead of you?"

Now imagine yourself jumping into the deep water and surrendering to the current. How does that feel? As you float down the river, the temptation is to lift your head and look around each river bend. But in doing so your whole body tenses up and soon you are resisting the flow. You do not have to know what is ahead. You can trust Him. Lay back and find the flow of surrender.

Recommended Resources:

The Still Experience by Jenny Donnelly Tetelestaiministries.com/courses/the-still-experience.

Rest Training - Tetelestaiministries.com/courses/rest-training.

POLLINATE VI

Fig 18
olive grove

Figure 18: The Kingdom Grove

POLLINATE

Chapter Six

How were we created to flourish in community?
Identifying your kingdom family and legacy

"Those who are planted in the house of the LORD Shall flourish in the courts of our God." (Psalm 92:13)

Cross Pollinating

Have you noticed that the tallest trees are the ones planted in a healthy grove? Trees that are planted in isolation will often fall over without the support of the underground root system of other trees planted near it when storms come. Like trees, we are created to flourish in groves.

We do not just need the support of other tree roots, we also need proximity to healthy trees for pollination. When the wind of the Spirit blows, cross pollination takes place that is needed to produce good fruit and continue to multiply. Connecting with a kingdom family enables us to receive and release seeds of revival and participate in bringing Heaven to Earth.

From the very beginning of the creation of humankind, God stated it is not good for man to be alone (Genesis 2:18). The enemy will always try to isolate us and keep us separated because he knows that without community we will be powerless and ineffective Christians. Proverbs 18 teaches that when we isolate ourselves we are seeking our own desires and keeping ourselves from wisdom. Isolation is foolishness.

> *"Whoever isolates himself seeks his own desire; he breaks out against all sound judgment." (Proverbs 18:1 ESV)*

People are our legacy and loving them is our purpose. We were created to grow under relational pressure, and we need a tribe to thrive. Proverbs 27:17 says, "As iron sharpens iron, so one person sharpens another" (NIV).

For centuries, discipleship has happened around tables, with shared meals and intentional fellowship. We do not graduate from a student to a rabbi once we have obtained enough knowledge. God calls us all to be students and teachers simultaneously. We are to serve and to be served, to lead and to be led, to love and be loved. This is the picture of New Testament discipleship: as we are poured into, we pour into others.

When God woke me up to my true identity, the inheritance I carried and intimacy available to me, I began experiencing the supernatural life. I was baptized in fire alone one day without anyone laying hands on me. I experienced a second in-filling of the Holy Spirit like the disciples did in the upper room on the day of Pentecost. I began praying in a heavenly language having never heard anyone speak in tongues before. I was not seeking the gift of tongues, I was seeking Jesus, the gift giver. The more I pursued Him, the more I began experiencing the supernatural.

The hunger I had for the presence of God led me to daily radical encounters. I was no longer a spiritual orphan, but I still felt very alone since my friends and family thought I was crazy. I knew that I needed to experience collectively what I had only experienced individually in my most intimate times with the Lord.

In answer to my prayer for community, God told me to google the word, "collective." To my surprise, I found a church called The Collective only ten minutes from my house that had a women's event coming up. I immediately knew that God wanted me to attend. That night, I encountered the heart of the Father and received inner healing for the first time. I found a safe, transparent group of people equipped with the full gospel that were able to walk with me on this journey of inner healing and personal transformation. I came alone, but I left with a spiritual family.

At The Collective, I experienced what it means to be "individually valuable and collectively powerful." A few weeks later I brought my sister with me, soon after her own spiritual awakening. The message on confession catalyzed transformation in her marriage. One after another, God has encountered every member of my family and is leading them into their true identity.

What I discovered is that a culture built on safety, transparency, vulnerability and honor is like a greenhouse for spiritual growth. No church is perfect, but I truly believe God wants to use the Church to heal the Church from wounds inflicted by the Church.

There are many parts of our spiritual formation that require community. Confession and the sharing of testimony are two essential components of our growth that happen when the wind of the Spirit moves through a group of people. Our testimony is the key to unlock the freedom of others. Our story is God's story; it's not about us. We have a choice whether or not we will release pollen when the wind of the Spirit moves. There is an impartation in each of us that when we release, it multiplies the work of the Spirit. Cross pollination requires our participation and proximity to others.

> *"And they overcame him by the blood of the Lamb and by the word of their testimony, and they did not love their lives to the death." (Revelation 12:11)*

One of the ways we can love not our lives is by dying to our reputation to vulnerably and boldly share our testimony. Transformation happens in the specific. Have you ever heard the raw testimony of a believer who did not hold back parts of their story in self-protection? If you have heard someone share who has died to their reputation, I guarantee you remember the specific occasions of raw transparency because it is one of the most powerful invitations for transformation that you can receive. Healed people heal people just like freed people free people.

Personally, I had never encountered this type of vulnerability in the Church until the day I stepped into a Her Voice event. I was shocked and captivated as I listened to a panel of women, now some of my close friends, speak on topics taboo in most churches. Abortions, affairs, homosexual relationships, identity confusions, abuse, pornography, drugs, alcohol, promiscuity, child loss, miscarriage, rape and molestation. While some of these testimonies were B.C. (before they met Christ) many happened after. Some did the sinning and others had been sinned against. The devil does not fight fair. People who have been horrifically sinned against suffer the punishment of shame just as much, if not more than those who have done the offending. Nothing portrays the gospel message, *come as you are* like raw confessions from ministry leaders free of shame.

Each one of the women testifying who had been set free had something in common: confession and prayer. They also had *someone* in common: Jesus. Community is only beneficial in so much as they lead us to Jesus. We can confess and pray for God's forgiveness, but if we do not have someone to hand over that which has bound us, we will stay bound. Jesus is the only one who can carry the weight of our sin and shame.

> *"Surely he took up our pain and bore our suffering, yet we considered him punished by God, stricken by him, and afflicted. But he was pierced for our transgressions, he was crushed for our iniquities; the punishment that brought us peace was on him, and by his wounds we are healed." (Isaiah 53:4-5 NIV)*

Healthy communities never elicit confession to judge or shame. Spirit-filled ministers bridge the gap between our shame and Jesus. We are all called to be ministers of the gospel. This means we need to receive this type of ministry, and we need to minister this way to others. This ministry of confession and freedom happens when we walk in direct contrast to shame and condemnation and walk instead in the spirit of honor with people on the path of repentance. When we do this, we negate shame. "Let's take it to Jesus," is my heart posture when I am ministering to people. I only know the way down the path of confession and repentance because I have walked it many times myself. Confession followed by prayer is always the first step of healing.

> *"Instead of your shame you shall have double honor, And instead of confusion they shall rejoice in their portion. Therefore in their land they shall possess double; Everlasting joy shall be theirs." (Isaiah 61:7)*

Confession is a catalyst to transformation. Confession is simply telling the truth and scripture says truth is what sets us free (John 8:32). It has been said that whatever we cannot talk about the enemy owns. Some people are so familiar with their dysfunction that they cannot even comprehend what freedom feels like. What is kept secret grows in the dark. To be healed, we must bring things to the light. When we hear the testimony of others, our soul lights up with hope; *If He did it for them, He can do it for me!*

> *"Whoever conceals their sins does not prosper, but the one who confesses and renounces them finds mercy." (Proverbs 28:13 NIV)*

When we conceal our sins from others we begin to become blind to the effect of sin in our lives. Maybe you are bound with a secret that you know is destroying you or maybe you have lied to yourself for so long that you actually believe your own lies. You may be using minimizing language like, "I have it under control," "Everyone does it," "At least I don't X,Y or Z," "This is just between me and God," "It's in the past." Lying to ourselves and minimizing our sin and trauma is self-sabotage.

Secrets we carry, big or small, are often the root of sickness and disease, not just in our soul, but in our physical body as well. Unhealed generational trauma and unconfessed generational sin in our family lineage can turn into generational sickness. Our children will either inherit our healing or they will inherit our brokenness. The work of soul healing that we refuse to do will chase down our children. Time does not heal all wounds, Jesus does.

> *"Therefore confess your sins to each other and pray for each other so that you may be healed. The prayer of a righteous person is powerful and effective." (James 5:16 NIV)*

Some say, "God forgives me," and they are right. Confession to others is not a requirement for forgiveness from God, but it is a requirement for healing. James 5:16 states this unequivocally. Sadly, many Christians have never experienced a safe place to confess. Partial confession can bring temporary alleviation of guilt but will cause more harm than good in the long run. Tip of the iceberg confessions must be avoided. You will feel a physical weight lift off you when you give a full disclosure to someone you trust.

If your heart is beating a little faster as you read this and you know there is something you need to get off your chest, I encourage you to ask the Holy Spirit right now to bring to mind one or two safe people you can confess to. Maybe you need to call them right now or text them to set up a meeting. Take at least one action step immediately before the enemy talks you out of it. Let the Holy Spirit guide your disclosure. He will bring to mind the necessary details to confess without causing more harm. Remember, the enemy wins by keeping us in bondage! It's time to tell on the devil! When we expose his wicked schemes, we escape secret suffering.

Destructive Pollination

Caution is advised, however, because not all cross pollination happens by the wind of the Spirit. Insects, specifically flies, beetles and moths are also agents of cross pollination. We do not want this type of pollination in our lives! Insects in the Bible are often agents of destruction and symbolize the demonic. It is so important that we plant ourselves around believers that are led by the Spirit. When we get around people who have the fruit of the Spirit in their lives, we are nourished by their sweet fruit.

A foundation of psychological safety is essential for healthy vulnerability. Healthy vulnerability is never used as a weapon to attempt to control a desired outcome. Honor is only honor when praise is genuine and selfless. By contrast, flattery is manipulative and fake. Transparency does not need to be demanded, just humbly invited.

We must forgive leaders who use toxic, controlling and manipulative tactics and call it vulnerability. They will be held accountable, and these leaders are not to be trusted. I do not know anyone who has matured in their faith who has not experienced some degree of betrayal. One of the most common places Christians experience betrayal is with church leaders. It is understandable that many have put up walls of self-protection to avoid vulnerability, but it is detrimental to our growth. These walls stand in the way of our healing if they are not taken down.

Jesus was betrayed and abandoned by His disciples, the first fruits of the first Church, and yet He still died for them. How then can we abandon what Jesus sacrificed His life to redeem? The writer of the book of Hebrews gives clear instructions to not forsake gathering with other believers. It does not say, "Do not give up meeting together unless… you are persecuted for it, or you are hurt by the Church and need space to heal, or there is no church in your area that fits your preferences or until the technology is developed so you can watch church online."

> *"And let us consider how we may spur one another on toward love and good deeds, not giving up meeting together, as some are in the*

habit of doing, but encouraging one another—and all the more as you see the Day approaching" (Hebrews 10:24-25 NIV).

I do not believe mass gatherings where we can sneak in and out without being truly seen and known is what the writer of Hebrews intended. Jesus promises us, "For where two or three gather in my name, there am I with them" (Matthew 18:20 NIV). Sunday services as we have become accustomed to in the American Church often do not fulfill our need for community. Stewarding authentic relationships and each individual's heart-felt participation is the biblical model for our gatherings. I am convinced that there are depths of Jesus that we can only encounter in community. Satan fights hard to keep Christians from gathering together because he knows our power comes through unity.

> *Transparency does not need to be demanded, just humbly invited.*

If you have ever tried to get your family ready for church on a Sunday morning, or out the door on a Friday night for a conference, or host a small group in your house, you know what it is like to experience the enemy's resistance. A typical Sunday morning may look like you overslept, you are out of milk, your toddler is having a continual meltdown (and if you are honest, so are you), the baby has a blowout on the way out the door, you are baited into a pointless argument with your spouse, the car is out of gas… etc. Just my family? I doubt it because I know the degree of difficulty we face is often connected to the degree of importance. Gathering with other believers is hard because it matters.

Each of us is just one part of the Body of Christ, and we were not created to be able to function without connection to the other parts. Comparison to others prevents us from belonging and operating as the body part others need us to be.

> *"For the body does not consist of one member but of many. If the foot should say, "Because I am not a hand, I do not belong to the body," that would not make it any less a part of the body. And if the ear should say, "Because I am not an eye, I do not belong to the body," that would not make it any less a part of the body. If the whole body were an eye, where would be the sense of hearing? If the whole body were an ear, where would be the sense of smell? But as it is, God arranged the members in the body, each one of them,*

as he chose. If all were a single member, where would the body be? As it is, there are many parts, yet one body. The eye cannot say to the hand, "I have no need of you," nor again the head to the feet, "I have no need of you." On the contrary, the parts of the body that seem to be weaker are indispensable, and on those parts of the body that we think less honorable we bestow the greater honor, and our unpresentable parts are treated with greater modesty, which our more presentable parts do not require. But God has so composed the body, giving greater honor to the part that lacked it, that there may be no division in the body, but that the members may have the same care for one another. If one member suffers, all suffer together; if one member is honored, all rejoice together." (1 Corinthians 12:14-26 ESV)

Tragically, the Church has an autoimmune disease. We attack others, not understanding that we are attacking ourselves. We do not have to agree with someone in order to show honor. We do not have to be treated the way we want to in order to show respect. Even validation does not require agreement. When we validate others we simply communicate, "I see you, I hear you, and you matter." We can communicate all of these messages even when we disagree with someone's opinions, world views or life choices.

I am so grateful that I have people in my life who hold different beliefs than I do. Too often churches become echo chambers of our own understanding. Churches that do not allow members to be critical thinkers with differing opinions more resemble cults than church as God intended. I would never expect you to agree with 100% of my conclusions on every topic. Disagreements are not just okay with me, they are encouraged! Maybe now is a good time for a heart check: Are you okay receiving from someone you do not 100% agree with?

The rejection many experience in the Church comes from people who feel rejected themselves. Hurt people, hurt people and wounded people, wound people. The test when we inevitably experience church hurt in the form of judgment, rejection, and even betrayals, is to guard our heart from bitterness and offense. This command in scripture begins with, "above all else" implying the utmost importance.

> "Guard your heart above all else, for it determines the course of your life. Avoid all perverse talk; stay away from corrupt speech." (Proverbs 4:23 -24 NLT)

The NKJV says, "Out of the abundance of the heart the mouth speaks." Meaning, what is in our heart will come out in the words we speak. Whether we like it or not, our mouth will reveal our heart.

Proverbs 18:21 says, "The tongue has the power of life and death, and those who love it will eat its fruit" (NIV). We will see fruit, whether good or bad, from what we speak into the lives of others and what we allow them to speak into ours.

Lisa Bevere says it like this, "What you're saying, you are sowing." God used the spoken word to create the universe. As children of God, we have been given the same authority to fashion our environment with our spoken words.

It reminds me of the famous Spider-man line, "With great power comes great responsibility." I cannot think of Spider-man without thinking of my little brother who was obsessed with the character when he was little. One day my mom panicked as she discovered the screen popped out of a window in her second story bedroom and the window wide open. She called for Sam, my three-year-old little brother, and found him safely inside the house. When asked if he had been on the roof, Sam replied, "Don't worry mom, I stick!" With his child-like faith he truly believed he was Spider-man. Because of the authority we have been given in Christ, our words have the same superpower, they stick.

Our words are seeds of pollination that can bring cursing or blessing.

> "Likewise, the tongue is a small part of the body, but it makes great boasts. Consider what a great forest is set on fire by a small spark. The tongue also is a fire, a world of evil among the parts of the body. It corrupts the whole body, sets the whole course of one's life on fire, and is itself set on fire by hell. All kinds of animals, birds, reptiles and sea creatures are being tamed and have been tamed by mankind, but no human being can tame the tongue. It is a restless evil, full of deadly poison." With the tongue we praise our Lord and Father, and with it we curse human beings, who have been made in God's likeness. Out of the same mouth come praise and cursing.

My brothers and sisters, this should not be. Can both fresh water and salt water flow from the same spring? My brothers and sisters, can a fig tree bear olives, or a grapevine bear figs? Neither can a salt spring produce fresh water." (James 3: 5-12 NIV)

James concludes chapter three by saying words of blessing are words of wisdom. He compels us to sow words that are pure, peace-loving, considerate, submissive, full of mercy and good fruit, impartial and sincere. He concludes in verse 18 saying, "Peacemakers who sow in peace reap a harvest of righteousness."

We are instructed to be *peacemakers* as Jesus was, not peacekeepers. Peacekeepers avoid confrontation. Plagued by fear of man, peacekeepers appease people and keep the peace at all costs. This could not be further from the way of Jesus who, in Matthew 5:9 says, "Blessed are the peacemakers for they will be called children of God" (NIV). Peacemakers carry an inner peace even in times of exterior conflict. A peacemaker will confront others in love with the motivation of restoration of peace.[43]

To remain in our true identity as children of God we have to sow our words in peace. How we start a conversation matters. If we come into a discussion in our false identity, offended, angry, defensive or argumentative, we will pull out the false identity of others like an agent of destruction. Instead, if we approach a conversation in our true identity as a peacemaker, we will pull the true identity out of others and become agents of reconciliation. This is one of the most underutilized superpowers of spirit-filled believers! When we possess inner peace, we pull peace out of others like a magnet. In the same way, when we possess inner conflict, we pull conflict out of others. We attract what we carry.

Jesus makes it clear that the motivation of our heart matters when we speak. In Luke 6:45 He says, "A good man out of the good treasure of his heart brings forth good; and an evil man out of the evil treasure of his heart brings forth evil. For out of the abundance of the heart his mouth speaks." When our motivation is pure, desiring connection and restoration instead of retaliation and revenge, we will sow words of peace that reap a harvest of righteousness.

God strategically positions us around people to be ministers of grace

---

43. Erickson and Erickson, *The Flourishing Family: A Jesus-Centered Guide to Parenting with Peace and Purpose.*

and healing. We are called to be thermostats that change the temperature of every room we step into, not thermometers that simply measure the temperature. We are atmosphere shifters who have been given authority over all toxic negativity.

If we repeatedly find ourselves affected by the negativity of others, we need to establish clear boundaries in those relationships. The right to speak directly into our lives should only be given to those who have fruit on their tree that we desire. Sadly, not everyone has pure intentions and our best interest in mind. Word curses, especially from other believers, can have a physical effect in our lives.

Gossip is a disease that can poison our fruit more quickly than anything else. Slander is a trap, much like quicksand. We can step into it by accident and without a plan for a way of escape, it will suddenly consume us. Eleanor Roosevelt said, "Great minds discuss ideas; average minds discuss events; small minds discuss people." I do not know about you, but I want to surround myself with great minds!

What we hear affects our souls. When we spend time with people who continually talk about other people we are left feeling drained and empty. These negative seeds are sown into the soil of our hearts and will affect what comes out of our own mouths. If we want pure ears that hear the voice of the Lord clearly we need to be vigilant about what we are listening to. Saying, "I'm not comfortable talking about other people who aren't here with us", simply walking away, or speaking something honoring to shift the conversation like, "Isn't it great that they…" or "I love that they are…" are three strategies I recommend when someone around us is beginning to speak poisonous words or non-edifying opinions of others.

Take a minute and say this prayer out loud if you, like me, know you are guilty of speaking poisonous words.

Jesus, I repent for speaking negatively about myself and others. Thank you for forgiving me! I pray the prayer of David (Psalm 141) and ask you to set a guard on my mouth so I would not sin against you! I plead the blood of Jesus over the words I've spoken rooted in evil. I call a crop failure of every negative word I have sown and release seeds of blessing now in their place. I ask for your help to sow words of life. May the words of my mouth and the meditations of my heart be pleasing in your sight, Lord my Rock and my Redeemer (Psalm 19:14). In Jesus' name I pray, amen.

Those of us who put a guard on our mouths and ears will grow into steadfast trees. This is what it means to guard our hearts above all else.

Another way we guard our hearts is by having courageous conversations. When we avoid conflict, we feed it. John Delony says it like this, "If you are about to say something important but you stop yourself and think, 'If I say this, it could mess things up.' You can rest assured, things are already a mess. Conflict deferred is conflict amplified. Say your important things. Speak your needs out loud. Be honest and get them out in the open. Silence can be a lie too."

Guarding our mouths and choosing silence out of fear or convenience are two very different things. James 1:19 tells us, "You must all be quick to listen, slow to speak, and slow to get angry." Learning to listen to understand rather than listening to respond is one of the most important things we can do for our relationships. When we listen to understand, we are much more likely to have a healthy response. Silence has its own message that most often communicates our lack of value. While there are times to take a pause or hold our tongue, silence is not the answer. In a moment of conflict, silence may feel safer, but trust me, silence is not safe.

> *"If your brother sins against you, go and tell him his fault, between you and him alone. If he listens to you, you have gained your brother. But if he does not listen, take one or two others along with you, that every charge may be established by the evidence of two or three witnesses." (Matthew 18:15- 16 ESV)*

The goal of healthy conflict is the preservation of connection. Jim and Lynne Jackson teach a connected parenting framework that is so effective that I utilize it in all of my relationships, not just with my children.

The Connected Families framework for connection in conflict is:

1. You Are Safe With Me
2. You Are Loved No Matter What
3. You Are Called and Capable
4. You Are Responsible For Your Actions[44]

---

44. Jackson and Jackson, *Discipline That Connects With Your Child's Heart: Building Faith, Wisdom, and Character in the Messes of Daily Life.*

Bad communication is like throwing gasoline on the fire of a conflict. As we have established, simply guarding our words is not enough, we have to guard our hearts. Communication is not just what we say but *how* we say it. Our tone of voice and body language are communicating for us whether we want them to or not. Rather than coming into a conflict fast, loud and large, we can approach it low and slow. We guard our hearts and control our tone by accessing, "What is going on with me?" and focusing on our own emotional regulation before we bring confrontation to someone else. All behavior is communication. Instead of criticizing others, we can become curious and find the unmet need or the gift gone awry. A foundation of safety, love and belief helps us hold others accountable for their actions through the invitation for connection even in conflict.

The Pollination of Power

If I knew I was leaving this earth I would choose my last words to my loved ones carefully. Do you know the last words Jesus spoke? They are found in Acts 1:4-8. Let's read this passage understanding the weight and importance of these last words our Savior spoke on this earth.

> *"And being assembled together with them, He commanded them not to depart from Jerusalem, but to wait for the Promise of the Father, "which," He said, "you have heard from Me; for John truly baptized with water, but you shall be baptized with the Holy Spirit not many days from now." Therefore, when they had come together, they asked Him, saying, "Lord, will You at this time restore the kingdom to Israel?" And He said to them, "It is not for you to know times or seasons which the Father has put in His own authority. But you shall receive power when the Holy Spirit has come upon you; and you shall be witnesses to Me in Jerusalem, and in all Judea and Samaria, and to the end of the earth." (Acts 1:4-8)*

Did you notice how the disciples repeatedly interrupted Jesus' last word asking Him the wrong question? Without the infilling of the Holy Spirit, we too get stuck asking Jesus the wrong questions. They sound like: *"Why?"* and *"When will you?"* and *"What if..."* Without the Holy Spirit, we try to grasp for understanding rather than receiving revelation.

The last message of Jesus is that we need the empowerment of the

Holy Spirit to become His witnesses throughout the earth. The word witness in the Greek is the same word used for martyr.[45] Jesus gave clear instructions to the disciples to not go out into the world *until* they receive power from the baptism of the Holy Spirit.

When the person of Jesus was removed from the earth, the person of the Holy Spirit was sent to us as a gift to multiply the presence of Jesus throughout the entire world. The presence of God is with us always, but it is the Holy Spirit that fills us with His power. The Holy Spirit is the third person of the trinity. He is not a force or an "it." The Holy Spirit is a person and He is God, just as Jesus is God; they are three in one. This is the beautiful mystery of the trinity.

> *And Jesus came and spoke to them, saying, "All authority has been given to Me in heaven and on earth. Go therefore and make disciples of all the nations, baptizing them in the name of the Father and of the Son and of the Holy Spirit, teaching them to observe all things that I have commanded you; and lo, I am with you always, even to the end of the age." (Matthew 28:18-20)*

When the wind of the Spirit blows, the person of Jesus and power of God is revealed to us and in us. Just as Jesus promised, this was the case as the mighty wind of the Spirit blew into the meeting of believers on the day of Pentecost.

> *"On the day of Pentecost all the believers were meeting together in one place. Suddenly, there was a sound from heaven like the roaring of a mighty windstorm, and it filled the house where they were sitting. Then, what looked like flames or tongues of fire appeared and settled on each of them. And everyone present was filled with the Holy Spirit and began speaking in other languages, as the Holy Spirit gave them this ability." (Acts 2:1-4 NIV)*

Jesus knew that His disciples needed the baptism of the Holy Spirit to be sent into the world as witnesses and martyrs. Most of the disciples were brutally martyred. The apostle Peter, who denied Jesus right before His crucifixion, became one of the most bold witnesses to ever live because of the supernatural empowerment of the Holy Spirit.

---

45. Strong's Greek: 3144. Μάρτυς (Martus) -- a Witness.

We can whitewash our lives with our own religious striving and determination, but it is absolutely impossible to experience true transformation without the power of the Holy Spirit.

Attempting to do ministry without the baptism of the Holy Spirit is ineffective at best and down right destructive in many cases. The Holy Spirit's power transformed twelve scared, tired, doubting, grieving, and broken men into the twelve pillars of the New Testament Church. These men went into the world with boldness and authority, refusing to deny Christ even when they were tortured and eventually killed for the gospel.

God wants to empower us to be His witnesses. The authority of our witness comes from our willingness to die for Christ. And not just in one moment of intense persecution, but to die daily, laying down our lives to follow Jesus. We cannot be a witness if we are not willing to be a martyr. The words are synonymous.

With the empowerment of the Holy Spirit, we are sent into the world as witnesses, sharing the testimony of Jesus as those who have not just heard the message, but have become it. We are to be walking dead men and women boldly proclaiming the good news. God calls us to be prophets, messengers and mouthpieces who speak the word of the Lord as empty vessels.

The testimony of how the gospel has changed our life is one of the most powerful seeds of cross pollination that our trees were created to release. The word "impartation" best illustrates this concept of cross pollination in scripture.

In the New Testament, the Greek word for impartation is *metadidómi,* and it means to give, to share or to bestow.[46] In scripture, we are taught that the gospel message is imparted. We also see an example of wisdom being imparted in Deuteronomy 34:9 when Moses, at the end of his life, lays hands on Joshua to impart wisdom to him. Paul teaches us that spiritual gifts are imparted (Romans 1:11) and noted that he needed to be present with them to do so, implying that this type of impartation requires proximity. Paul writes to his spiritual son Timothy, "Do not neglect the gift that is in you, which was given to you by prophecy with the laying on of the hands of the eldership" (1 Timothy 4:14).[47]

What we never see in scripture being imparted is righteousness. In-

---

46. Strong's Greek: 3330. Μεταδίδωμι (Metadidómi) -- to Give a Share Of.
47. "What is impartation?" GotQuestions.org.

stead we are taught that righteousness is imputed. Imputed means to be credited to another's account. Romans 4:3 says, "Abraham believed God and it was credited to him as righteousness." Righteousness is not imparted to us, it is credited to us and manifests in us the more we believe what we have received. Remember, we withdraw in faith only what has already been deposited into our account. We only have access to what we believe we have.

According to Paul, our imputed righteousness is not the only thing we have to have faith to release. Paul also instructs Timothy to, by faith, stir up the gifts that were given to him through impartation.

> *"Therefore I remind you to stir up the gift of God which is in you through the laying on of my hands. For God has not given us a spirit of fear, but of power and of love and of a sound mind. Therefore do not be ashamed of the testimony of our Lord, nor of me His prisoner, but share with me in the sufferings for the gospel according to the power of God, who has saved us and called us with a holy calling, not according to our works, but according to His own purpose and grace which was given to us in Christ Jesus before time began." (2 Timothy 1:6-9)*

Faith has to be cultivated, activated and released. "Fan into flame the gifts of God," is how the NIV translates the beginning of verse 6. There is a big difference between faith and hype. When we stir up our faith we focus on God's greatness and our emotions often reflect our sincere faith. In contrast, when we try to hype up a spiritual experience our focus is on ourselves and our emotions.

I had no frame of reference for the supernatural power of the Holy Spirit until I began experiencing His presence alone in my house, just me and Jesus. Subconsciously, growing up I believed that tangible displays of God's power were for Bible times, not for today. I shared earlier in this chapter that listening to the voice of the Lord led me to a women's event at The Collective Church. At this point in my journey, I had begun to experience spiritual gifts, but the manifest power of God was still brand new to me.

I remember being wrapped up in worship with my eyes closed and hands raised, not even noticing when a minister came up to me and very gently laid hands on my head. You can imagine my shock when I immediately fell to the ground under the power of God. Before I even opened my eyes someone behind me graciously caught me and prevented me from hitting the floor with a thud. I had truly never seen this happen until it happened to me for the first time. I went home that night and asked God to show me if my experience was biblically supported or not.

I grew up in the Church, but I consider myself to have been unintentionally sheltered from the supernatural workings of the Holy Spirit. We did not have cable TV in our home so I never caught a glimpse of healing crusades on TBN. I also never saw the gifts of the Spirit in operation. I never witnessed miraculous healings, demons cast out, or other signs and wonders.

I had read the Bible cover to cover, but somehow missed the numerous accounts of people falling over under the power of God. Abram (Genesis 17:3), Joshua (Joshua 5:14), Ezekiel (Ezekiel 1:28, 3:23), Daniel (Daniel 8:17, 10:15), Peter, James, John (Matthew 17:6), and Paul (Acts 9:4, 26:14) are all recorded collapsing in God's presence.

When John collapsed at the feet of Jesus in a vision in Revelation 1:17, the Greek word for "fell" used is *pipto* which means to fall from an upright position. As a word used to describe men in battle, it can imply falling forward or backward. While sometimes people fall in the manifest presence of God and get right back up, other times people fall like John did, "as one dead."[48]

Now, I have been in countless gatherings in many different churches across the country where people fall under the power of God. I have experienced this even when no one lays hands on me. I have had times when I got right back up and times when I was unable to move under the power of God for over an hour. Apparently, on one particular occasion I looked like John did, "as one dead," because my husband confessed to me later that he watched over me, taking my pulse and checking my breathing every few minutes. I have no recollection of him doing this, but the visual makes me laugh every time I think about it.

Impartation that I have received through the laying on of hands and the pollination of the power of God has been a critical part of my spiritual growth. And while I believe the power of God is essential, we must be cautious about counterfeit experiences.

---

48. "Why Do People Sometimes Collapse in the Presence of God?"

Sadly, I have also seen ungodly things done while being labeled, "the power of God." I have been in gatherings where ministers too aggressively lay their hands on people, pushing them over. I have seen miracles exaggerated, as if God needs us to lie for Him to get the glory. I could not move on without a warning because too many times I have seen desire for the power of God become idolatry. Ministers that are known for certain manifestations are put on pedestals and before we know it, our focus is on a person instead of God.

Caution with *charisma* (the Greek word for spiritual gifts) is wise while skepticism is destructive. Skepticism weakens our faith, but discernment strengthens it. Biblically, we have all the evidence we need to believe the Holy Spirit moves in our midst supernaturally and powerfully. Throughout scripture, we read of moves of God's Spirit that are wild but never weird. There is no place for skepticism about these things in the life of a Spirit-filled believer, only discernment.

Since my first encounter with a Spirit-filled church, I have discovered that all denominations fall somewhere on a spectrum between Spirit and Truth. One extreme side of the Church is all about the things of the Spirit and has forsaken Truth, making it all about their experiences. Another extreme side of the Church is all about Truth and has forsaken the things of the Spirit, because it is foolishness to their natural minds (1 Corinthians 2:14). The three parts of the Trinity are not God the Father, God the Son and God the Holy Scriptures. Though never explicitly stated, this is the emphasis of many denominations who err on the side of Truth.

Jesus taught us that the two pillars of His kingdom are Spirit and Truth. God is Spirit *and* Truth. Division in the Church comes when we forsake the Spirit in pursuit of Truth or forsake Truth in pursuit of the Spirit. Spirit and Truth cannot be separated without destruction. Jesus is both Spirit and Truth.

> *"But the hour is coming, and now is, when the true worshipers will worship the Father in spirit and truth; for the Father is seeking such to worship Him. God is Spirit, and those who worship Him must worship in **spirit and truth**." (John 4:23-24, emphasis mine)*

Impartation was one of the foundational practices of the new testament church. In Hebrews 6:2, the laying on of hands is listed as one of the six elementary teachings of Christ. When we experience victory in an area of our lives, we are given authority that we can impart to others. The spiritual gifts we have been given can be activated in others through impartation. We will dive deeper into spiritual gifts when we discuss the blossoms on our tree.

Cross pollination happens through impartation and yields multiplication. Good fruit leads to the multiplication of more good seeds. Bad fruit leads to the multiplication of more bad seeds. Perhaps this is why Paul instructs Timothy to not be hasty laying his hands on people and warns that if he does, sharing the consequence of the sins of others may be the result (1 Timothy 5:22). We must use discernment. The enemy is a copycat and he uses impartation to further his kingdom as well. Each piece of fruit on our tree carries seed with further potential for multiplication, whether good or bad.

Perfect trees do not exist, but purpose-driven ones thrive. When we allow God to plant us around other flourishing trees, we grow. The wind of the Spirit blows and the pure pollination produces life in us. We receive the support from others with deeper roots than ours and provide support for believers whose roots are not yet fully established.

POLLINATE FIELD NOTES
Identify how to connect to your kingdom family and legacy

Find a quiet place and start by breathing in God's love for four seconds. Hold that breath for four seconds, imagining His presence filling you up like a balloon. Now, for four seconds breathe out whatever negative emotion is weighing you down. Repeat this exercise until you feel settled and present. Ask the Holy Spirit the following questions. Then journal the free flow of thoughts that come to your mind as you fix your eyes on Jesus.

Questions:

Holy Spirit, how have I been lying to myself about sin patterns in my life?

_____
_____

How can I partner with a spirit of confession?

_____
_____

How have I resisted the power of the Holy Spirit?

How would you like me to serve at my church in this season?

_____
_____

How can I be fully planted in a kingdom grove? What hurt or fear is keeping me from being seen and known in healthy relationships?

_____
_____

How can I receive impartation in this season?

_____
_____

How would you like me to impart what you have given to me, to others?

_____
_____

How would you like me to share my testimony this week?

_____
_____

Activation:

Invite someone you have had conflict with to a table for a courageous conversation. Own your part. Apologize even if it is 99% their fault. Listen to understand and practice using a couple of the following validating phrases.

Thank you for telling me.

I believe you.

I can understand why you felt that.

I would have felt the same way.

I would imagine that might make you feel ____, is that right?

Is there more?

I never thought about it that way.

I am committed to our relationship.

I'm not sure what to say, but I want you to know I care.

Do you want me to just listen or help with solutions?

Encounter:

Ask the Holy Spirit to lead you to a safe, spirit-filled community where you can encounter Him collectively this week. Enter into the presence of God respectfully and full of faith, suspending all thoughts of suspicion and doubt. Engage as an active participant of the service, not a spectator. Be surrendered and grateful for however God chooses to move.

Recommended Resource:

Confront sin patterns that you have been circumnavigating and get support to cross the island at CrosstheIsland.com.

BRANCH VII

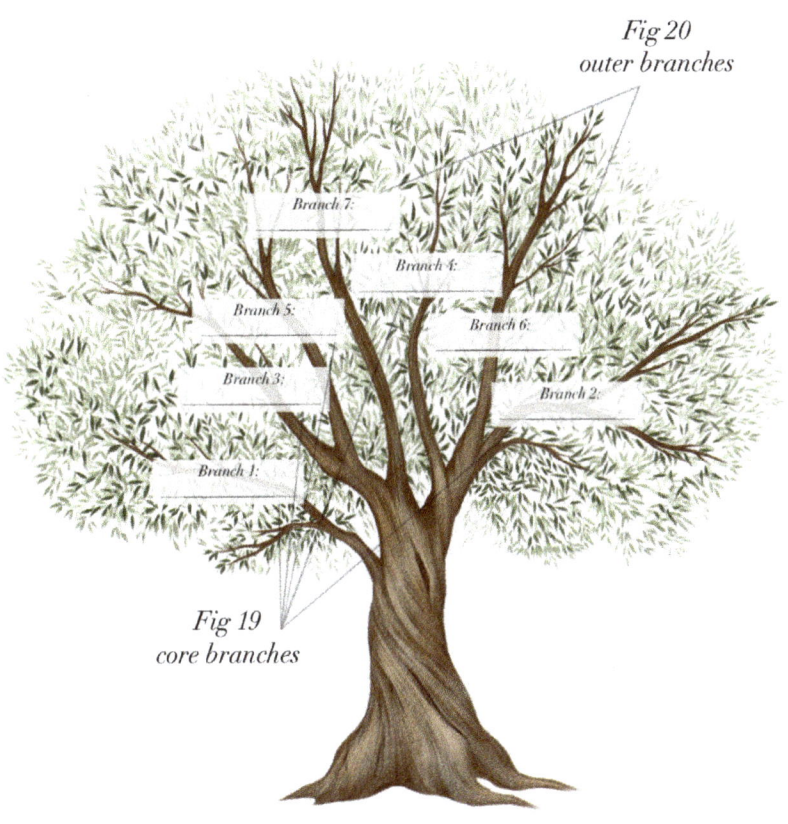

Figure 19: Five Core Branches of Calling
Figure 20: Outer Two Branches of Calling

BRANCH

Chapter Seven

*Where are you called to serve?
Identifying your burden and reach*

IMAGINE YOURSELF AS A thriving tree reaching into every space God has destined you to occupy. Our branches represent our callings. They are the *where* of our story and the key to identifying our *when*, *what*, and *why*.

In a previous chapter, we established that the trunk of the tree is our union with Jesus. From the foundation of our true identity in Christ, and grown out of dependency on the Spirit, our branches are the callings God has designed for us to grow into.

Some of our branches have to be spiritually discerned while others are laid out for us in scripture as biblical priorities for every believer. When properly applied, these kingdom principles produce massive fruit in our lives.

Before we dive into some kingdom principles that must be applied in order for us to step fully into the call of God for our lives, we need to address counterfeit formulas. Spiritual orphans use formulas to manipulate their desired outcomes. Sons and daughters of God apply principles out of love for Father God and obedience to His ways. A formula is an equation with a predictable input and output. It is rooted in control and constricts the works of God. Religious formulas use God transactionally, but kingdom principles are applied in relationship with the Father.

Identifying Our Core Branches

If we were to cut the trunk of a healthy tree, we would see rings that have developed one on top of another, signifying the growth of the tree. Imagine this picture as we discuss the topic of biblical priorities. These tree rings also look like targets (*Refer to figure 17*). Kingdom growth only happens when we target the areas God has directed us to and nourish our branches in proper order.

The main priorities of a Christian are:

1. Spouse
2. Children and Grandchildren
3. Family (parents, siblings, grandparents, etc)
4. Local Church + Close Friends
5. Vocation + Community (outside the church)

I intentionally did not include God on the list of priorities because He is not just a branch, He is our whole tree. Certainly, prioritizing the cultivation of our relationship with Jesus through proper daily nourishment must come before everything else, but there is no God box to be checked. God's rightful place is in all and through all.

You might be asking, what about a single person? If a single person desires to be married and have children they nourish their spouse and children branch in prayer. These branches can be prioritized in prayer even before they are fully grown. For those who feel they are not called to be married or to have children, their first branch would be family.

It's important to note that our core branches are composed of people God has put in our path that we have some level of relational proximity to. God also calls us to reach people we may never know personally, and we will identify these branches later on in this chapter.

When we carry God's heart for the people He has positioned in our core, we will continually prioritize them in prayer. We are anointed to pray for the people in our lives and the places we live. God has given us authority over specific territory in the kingdom of God! Our prayers posture our heart towards the people and places God has called us. Without prayer, it is impossible to maintain biblical priorities. Ask yourself, if I am not praying for my spouse, children and family regularly, who is?

While we must always prioritize our core branches through prayer, proximity and time are not always the way we show we are prioritizing a relationship. Sometimes the best way we can demonstrate love is through strong boundaries. I am grateful that some healthy boundary teaching has made its way into the Church, but I am cautious of our tendency to over correct. The principle of boundaries can be wrongly applied to putting up walls with people. Many use the term, "guard your heart" from Proverbs 4:23 out of context as an excuse to withhold love. This could not be further from the teachings of Jesus.

Healthy boundaries should protect our priorities often by limiting the access people have to us. We can be welcoming to everyone while still holding firm boundaries. I am a pretty open person, and I love to include people in anything and everything. I have had to learn the hard way that it is not always "the more the merrier" with close relationships. Trust needs to be given in the right time to the right people.

Another lesson I have had to learn the hard way is knowing how and when to help people. In the name of being a "good Christian" we can easily do things out of obligation, trying to help anyone and everyone. In reality, this is the quickest way to burn out. In Galatians 6, Paul outlines boundaries for us by differentiating between the term "burden" and "load."

> "***Bear one another's burdens***, *and so fulfill the law of Christ. For if anyone thinks he is something, when he is nothing, he deceives himself. But let each one test his own work, and then his reason to boast will be in himself alone and not in his neighbor. For **each will have to bear his own load**.*" *(Galatians 6:2-5 ESV, emphasis mine)*

The original Greek word for burden refers to an excessive and crushing weight. The original word for load means cargo or daily toil. Scripture is clear that we are to carry each other's burdens, but not each other's loads. In her book *I Do Boundaries*, Havilah Cunnington uses the illustration of a huge boulder for a burden versus a backpack for a load. Paul instructs us to help each other when we have burdens in our life that are crushing. It is our responsibility to carry each other's burdens but not each other's loads.

Hard work and daily toil is a part of God's plan for each of us. We are not responsible for other people's daily loads or emotions. Understanding the difference between a burden and a load can help us stay focused on our assignments rather than being driven by needs.

Paul instructs us to not think we are too important to carry the burdens of others. This type of self-importance is full of deception. I love how the amplified version translates verse 4: "But each one must carefully scrutinize his own work [examining his actions, attitudes, and behavior], and then he can have the personal satisfaction and inner joy of doing something commendable without comparing himself to another."

The work we do serving and loving the people God puts in our path is commendable before God but is not to be compared to the work God calls others to. When our motives are not pure, we may desire to be compared to others and deemed better than them. The motivation of those with a pure heart is to be commended by God alone.

Prioritizing Our Core Branches

When God puts people in our path, we need to spiritually discern the level of access we give them to our personal lives. For example, we may spend more time with a friend than a sibling for a season of our life, and still rightfully prioritize our family. Proximity does not dictate our priorities, our heart posture does.

When it comes to the branches of my own tree, I still struggle regularly to nourish them in proper order. I am a person who craves purpose and impact. I am easily deceived into believing that significance is found outside the walls of my home rather than in the service of my husband and children.

2 Corinthians 9:10 is a passage that speaks of kingdom multiplication that people most often apply to finances. The verse says, "He who supplies seed to the sower and bread for food will supply and multiply your seed for sowing and increase the harvest of your righteousness." Paul is indeed speaking of generosity in this passage, but financial generosity is not the only application of this principle of multiplication. This illustration was first used by the prophet Isaiah.

> *"For my thoughts are not your thoughts, neither are your ways my ways, declares the LORD. For as the heavens are higher than the earth, so are my ways higher than your way and my thoughts than your thoughts. "For as the rain and the snow come down*

from heaven and do not return there but water the earth, making it bring forth and sprout, giving seed to the sower and bread to the eater, so shall my word be that goes out from my mouth; it shall not return to me empty, but it shall accomplish that which I purpose, and shall succeed in the thing for which I sent it." (Isaiah 55: 8-11 ESV)

Our seed can be time, talents, resources, finances or even relational influence. The kingdom principle of multiplication applies to all of the above. We are called to a life of generosity not just with our finances, but with our time, talents, resources and relationships as well. When we freely give of ourselves to the people and places God has assigned us, our seed multiplies.

The seed accomplishes what God purposes for it, not what we purpose for it. His thoughts are higher than our thoughts. Religious formulas apply the concept of sowing seed by promising a specific outcome. Kingdom principles produce growth that is non-specific and non-linear. A harvest is guaranteed whenever a kingdom principle is applied, but the harvest can come in many forms. It could be spiritual, physical, psychological, financial or relational. The form of the seed is not always the form of the harvest. For example, you can sow a financial seed and that investment will not return void, but it may return to you in the form of relational blessing rather than financial. Wealth is so much more than money. When kingdom principles are applied, the principle investment always grows, but we do not get to decide the outcome of our blessing.

When we give away our time, our talents, and our finances, God multiplies them. In the Parable of the Talents in Matthew 5:29 Jesus says, "To those who use well what they are given, even more will be given, and they will have an abundance" (NLT). In order to branch into every sphere of influence God has called us to, we must apply these biblical principles.

God has put a destiny in each of us that is completely beyond our own ability to reach. To prepare us, the Lord takes us through seasons of stretching, pruning and testing to expand our capacity. He will not trust us with more influence if we have not been faithful to steward the influence He has already given us. Many people crave a stage in public places to share the Word of God, but they are not being faithful to teach the Word of God to their own children.

Then there are others who are faithfully serving their family and they do not believe they have the capacity to serve outside of the home. Out of false humility they reject the platforms God has called them to. Admittedly, I have done both.

I almost broke up with my husband when we first started dating because he believes women can be leaders in the Church, and, at the time, I was adamant that we could not. God told me that this was not a salvation issue, and we agreed to disagree for eight years of marriage until God started to reveal to me scripture that I had always applied out of context. For years I believed the lie that my ministry is only to my family. I was deceived into thinking that because I am a woman I cannot serve as a minister of the gospel and that my only assignment is to raise my children and love my husband.

The first person that Jesus told He was the Messiah was a woman at the well, who became the first evangelist. Being a woman did not disqualify her from sharing the gospel with any and everyone. Throughout His ministry, Jesus went against cultural norms to empower women. Matthew, Mark and Luke all record a group of women who followed Jesus and were present at His crucifixion and burial. After His resurrection, Jesus appeared first to Mary Magdalene and other women disciples. The testimony of women is recorded and honored throughout the Bible in a time when the testimony of women was not accepted culturally. Mary Magdalene was considered an "apostle to the apostles" by the early church. Priscilla, Chloe, Lydia, Apphia, Nympha, the mother of John Mark are just some of the names recorded in scripture of female leaders of the early church. Junia is specifically given the title of an apostle and Phoebe called a deaconess and overseer. Even in the Old Testament, God gave women authority. Deborah was a judge, a leader of Israel and a prophetess. Miriam, Huldah and the wife of Isaiah are also referred to as prophetesses.[49]

When we share the fragrance of Christ with our family first, the impact spreads to our neighborhood, to our church and to the other spheres of influence God has called us to.

---

49. The Neglected History of Women in the Early Church | Christian History Magazine.

Prophets and prophetesses had authority to speak the word of the Lord. So, if Paul's command in 1 Timothy 2:12 to not permit *a woman* to speak is interpreted to be applied to *all women*, not just a specific woman in a specific situation in the church that Paul was addressing, is that not a direct contradiction of the rest of scripture?

I have written an appendix to provide guided prayer to ask the Lord to open the eyes of our understanding on this topic and other doctrinal differences that tear apart the Church. If women leading and serving pastorally triggers you like it did me, I urge you to humbly examine the original context and utilize the scripture guide I have provided. I am so grateful I married a man who champions my voice and does not believe being female disqualifies me from ministry.

The reality is, I allowed destructive doctrine to keep me from stepping into the sphere of influence that God has called me to. Then, when God opened my eyes to my wrong beliefs and called me to serve outside of my home, I wrestled with properly prioritizing my family and seeing my ministry at home as more important than any other ministry task.

Through my spiritual growth journey I have found that the devil exists in extremes. He works overtime to keep some of us from doing anything other than serving our family. And for those who accept other assignments to spread the gospel, He wages war on our desire to serve our family first.

Serving my family first does not mean that I have a perfectly clean home all the time. It is futile to maintain self-imposed standards that God does not call us to. He is not looking for perfect homes; He is looking for humble hearts willing to serve the needs of others above our own. However, I have found my home often reflects the priorities in my heart. When my heart is postured towards loving service, my home is usually in order. When my heart is cluttered with my own ambition and desires, my home reflects the disorder of my heart. Disorder simply means lacking order. Serving my family first means that I must reject the pressures of the world, (and sometimes the Church) to find fulfillment outside of my home. I cannot be present and fulfilled in the service of my family when my heart is cluttered with the expectations of others, even those that come in the name of ministry.

I prioritize my family rightly when I see the mundane moments as invitations into the presence of God. Our service to our family is an act of worship, a fragrant offering that we are privileged to pour out. When we share the fragrance of Christ with our family first, the impact spreads to our neighborhood, to our church and to the other spheres of influence God has called us to.

There is an essential kingdom principle of time multiplication that is vital to understand if we are going to branch into every space God has destined us to. God miraculously multiplies our time when we first serve our families and the people He puts in front of us. If I jump to tasks outside of my home without prioritizing my family, the grace of God does not empower me. I will feel overwhelmed and behind all day. The good news is, I do not have to decide between ministering to my family and ministering to the rest of the world. It is not either/or. It is both when done in proper order. If we want the wind of God behind us, we have to submit to His ways. Family is the first church. It is the birthplace of revival. Children are God's gifts that we have the honor and responsibility of stewarding.

I prioritize my family by choosing to believe that the impact I make in the heart of my children is far greater than any external impact I will ever make. The home is the creator of culture. I serve my family rightly when I believe in the significance of this call and reject worldly significance that calls for my attention every time I open social media.

When there are unfulfilled places in our hearts, it is easy to be tempted to pursue significance rather than pursuing Christ alone. Jesus is the All Sufficient One. Every pursuit of significance that does not keep Jesus at the center is idolatry.

I had no idea how much self-worth I derived from the success of my wedding photography business until God asked me to lay it down completely. The Holy Spirit had to detox me from my addiction to accomplishments that provided a quick return on investment. Our children and our marriages do not use the same metrics for success. My desire for instant gratification still tempts me to invest in tasks that yield a quick return rather than the long-term investment into my family that can take years to see a return on.

The truth is, relational investments take time. Sometimes, they take *all* of our time. But, when the posture of our hearts reflects the priorities laid out in the Word of God, the Spirit of the Lord works miracles in our everyday life by multiplying our time beyond what is naturally possible.

Just like when Jesus fed the five thousand with five loaves and two fish, I find that as I pour myself out for my husband, my children, my family, my church, and my community, there is not just supernatural multiplication, there are leftovers. But first, just like the loaves and fishes, we must be broken. My selfish ambition has to break. My pride has to break. My laziness has to break. My fear of man has to break. My impatience has to break. My opinions have to break. My fleshly desires have to break. Ultimately, my will has to break so His will can be done.

God is honored with our sacrificial offering like He was when Mary broke the jar of costly perfume at His feet (John 12). Sacrifice is meant to be hard. It is not a sacrifice if it costs us nothing. It is hard to lay our lives down even for those we love most, but the sweet aroma of worship comes from sacrifice. We cannot become the hands and feet of Jesus without full surrender to Jesus.

> Every pursuit of significance that does not keep Jesus at the center is idolatry.

With Jesus there is always resurrection after death. This resurrection looks different each day, but there is always revival, dead things coming to life, when we surrender to the way of Jesus.

Sometimes resurrection looks like a defiance of all natural timing when we prioritize our families and serve in the order that God has ordained for us. Other times, resurrection looks like joy when nothing of instant gratification was produced or the ability to be present and experience God in between the wiping of a bum and washing dishes. We do not decide the miracle, but miracles follow kingdom principles.

Just as God led the Israelites in the wilderness with a cloud by day and a pillar of fire by night, God wants to lead us out of our home to encounter the lost world. He does not hide us away forever, but I have had to learn that there are days when the cloud does not leave the camp. And on those days, our faithful obedience to serve our families is vital. Our obedience to the principles of God leads to experiencing the favor of God.

Let us not neglect the ones who are right in front of us who carry the greatest invitation for significance. Family is our legacy and our most worthy investment. Jesus' greatest miracles happened in the form of interruptions. Are you interruptible? We must reject the deception that the extraordinary works of God happen outside our home and instead embrace our call to serve in ordinary ways. The Lord invites us daily to see the transformation of the ordinary to the extraordinary when we apply faith as we sweep the floors. While we teach our children multiplication tables, God works miracles in the multiplication of our time.

When God multiplies our times, finances, and talents it's always for His purposes. Even our rewards for faithfulness must be surrendered to Him. When Christians think of a woman flourishing in and out of her home they most often think of "the Proverbs 31 woman."

This might shock you, but Proverb 31 was not written for women. The first nine verses of this proverb are the wisdom of a mother given to King Lemuel intended to instill value for women. Prophetically, it depicts Israel and the Church.[50] This passage of scripture is not meant to be a list of qualifications that women should strive to live up to. Proverbs 31:10-31 illustrates the potential God has put in all of us to grow and flourish in our roles. When we are faithful stewards, we serve our family as well as our community. God calls many to run businesses and be in marketplace ministry. He calls others to positions in government.

It breaks my heart when Christians do not feel that their presence is needed in other spheres of influence beyond the home. I believe much of the problems we see in the world today are because Christians have abdicated their roles. We did not step into legislation, so the enemy did. We did not get on the school board, so the enemy did. We did not prioritize discipling our children, so the enemy did.

Even still, it breaks my heart more when believers use their voice to influence those outside of their home more than they do those in it. This is not an either/or extreme that we have become addicted to. God does not call us to find middle ground, He calls us to higher ground.

> *"For God is not a God of disorder but of peace, as in all the meetings of God's holy people." (1 Corinthians 14:33 NLT)*

Identifying Our Burden

God created the Church to reach into every sphere of influence. It has been observed that every culture has seven areas of influence: family, religion, education, media, arts and entertainment, government and business. One or more of these categories will relate to our outer branches.

---

50. Searl, "What Is the Meaning of Proverbs 31 and Why Is It Popular?"

We discern our calling by asking God to give us His heart for people. Lou Engle says, "Pay attention to your tears, they will lead you to your destiny." By praying a simple prayer, "God break my heart for what breaks yours," God can reveal to us our calling. Some people's hearts break over poverty because they are called to be a solution for the poor and needy. Others hearts break for specific nations or cultures because that is who they are called to serve. When we do not understand where God has called us to reach, we will be overwhelmed by the injustices, tragedies and needs of the world.

Overwhelm can prevent us from action. If we do not have a specific target from God and understanding of where we are called to serve, we will spin around in circles our whole life responding to immediate needs and making very little impact. Need and injustice abound. While we are not driven by need, the needs we notice can be clues to our calling and assignments.

I remember the first time I prayed the scary prayer, "God break my heart for what breaks yours." It was a few months after the birth of my daughter, and my heart for vulnerable children was bursting. Most of my life, I had looked away from the reality of the horror of human trafficking and its prevalence in our own neighborhoods. I had no idea how harmful this denial was until God gave me courage to face this issue head on. When God gives us His heart for something, we are never the same, and we can never look away from the issues that break His heart again. I discovered that the U.S. is among the top three nations of origin for sex trafficking victims with 300,000 children are at risk of commercial sexual exploitation every year.[51]

Discovering these statistics left me feeling helpless. What could I possibly do to make a difference in the fastest growing criminal enterprise in the world that generates over 150 billion dollars a year in revenue globally?[52] God's answer to me was unexpected, "Foster Care."

A quick google search revealed the correlation between trafficking and foster care. Children in foster care are much more vulnerable to

---

51. Department of State, United States of America, *Trafficking In Persons Report*.
52. International Labour Office, Special Action Programme to Combat Forced Labour (SAP-FL), and Fundamental Principles and Rights at Work Branch (FPRW), *Profits and Poverty: The Economics of Forced Labour*.

child trafficking. 60% of child sex trafficking victims have been in the child welfare system.[53]

If one family in one third of U.S. churches adopted, there would be no children waiting to be adopted in the foster care system (currently there are over 122,000 foster care children waiting to be adopted and 380,000 U.S. churches).[54]

In response to human trafficking, foster care is both restorative and preventative. It is restorative for children in the welfare system who have already been abused sexually, physically and/or through neglect. Foster homes provide a place of refuge for these children while their parents are offered the support they need to heal.

Foster care is also preventative for the children who are adopted out of the system. More than 23,000 children age out of the foster system every year with no family, no home and no support system. The majority of these young adults end up homeless, in jail, or forced prostitution. These kids are extremely vulnerable to becoming victims of human trafficking.

I already identified a branch on my tree as adoption and knew I was called to serve different parts of the adoption triad: birth families, adoptive families and adoptees. The day I learned about the realities of human trafficking I identified another branch on my tree. I am called to serve those who have been affected by, or are vulnerable to, human trafficking. These two branches cross specifically with foster care.

When God first spoke to me about foster care, I was ready to sign up immediately, but my husband was not. In fact he was adamantly against the idea of fostering. Because I understood biblical priorities, I knew my job was not to convince my husband. A desire to appease a spouse is never a sufficient enough reason to step into something as strenuous as foster care. I knew God Himself would have to call Michael, and I was full of faith that He would in His timing. My foster care branch was identified, but all assignments beyond prayer were not yet in season.

When the time was right God gripped my husband's heart and connected the same burden: human trafficking, with the same solution: foster care, exactly like He had done for me two years prior. Tears filled

---

53. Miller, "Foster Care and Human Trafficking."
54. U.S. Department of Health and Human Services, "The AFCARS Report Preliminary FY2019 Estimates as of June 23, 2020 - No. 27."; Brauer, "How Many Congregations Are There? Updating a Survey-Based Estimate."

carry the kingdom with us in our speaking, loving, working and living in such a way that others want to discover this most precious treasure for themselves.

Our outer branches consist of specific people groups and places God has appointed us to reach. Who God has given us a burden for leads us to where He wants to position us to serve.

partnership with us, He most often leaves the last step of gathering the harvest to us. We expect God to reposition people so they walk right into the doors of our churches, when Jesus gave us the command to, "Go!" God prepares the harvest and positions us to gather. How can we expect to gather the harvest if we are not faithful to go?

> "Go into all the world and preach the gospel to all creation." (Matthew 16:15 NIV)

Just like Boaz, a picture of Christ, gives Ruth access to a specific field to glean in, God has prepared a field for each of us.

> "Boaz went over and said to Ruth, 'Listen, my daughter. Stay right here with us when you gather grain; don't go to any other fields. Stay right behind the young women working in my field.'" (Ruth 2:8 NLT)

> "Don't you have a saying, 'It's still four months until harvest'? I tell you, open your eyes and look at the fields! They are ripe for harvest." (John 4:35 NIV)

The field God has prepared for us is full of His favor. The harvest field that is ripe to us is not ripe to everyone because each of us have our own places and people attached to our callings. If we have been working in a field that is not fruitful, it may be that we are laboring in the wrong field. Staying in our lane to harvest within the boundaries of our unique calling is required for a fruitful harvest. Loyalty to the people God has put in our path, like Ruth to Naomi, will lead us to the places God desires to position us to receive His favor. The protection and provision of the Lord accompanies the places He calls us to. God wants to set us up in fields ripe for harvest!

> "The kingdom of heaven is like treasure hidden in a field. When a man found it, he hid it again, and then in his joy went and sold all he had and bought that field." (Matthew 13:44 NIV)

The value of the kingdom of God is worth any cost. It must become our highest treasure and most earnest pursuit. We have a mandate to uncover the treasure of Christ in the fields He has appointed us to. We

Michael's eyes as we listened to Nicole Fitzpatrick share stories about personally rescuing children from the horrors of sex trafficking in Mexico. Because of one woman's "Yes" to Jesus, more than 2490 children and counting have been rescued. Nicole, her husband Jason, and the Village Global Team do not just rescue these children from unimaginable evil, they are also committed to raise and restore them. The Village Global has two homes where they house over 100 children.

Britt Hancock, the founder of the mission organization Mountain Gateway, says fighting human trafficking is like holding up a bucket to collect water in the middle of a monsoon. Understanding this, I once again had the thought: *what can we possibly do here in the U.S.? Maybe we have to move to Mexico and work with The Village Global to make a difference.* It was very evident the Holy Spirit had touched my husband during the service. As soon as it ended I asked, "What did the Lord speak to you?" I'll admit I was not expecting his answer. He said the Lord asked him to open up his heart to fostering. After receiving a burden from the Lord, Michael underwent a radical transformation from saying, "I will never foster" to leading the way for our family to get our foster license.

Identifying Our Outer Reach

If we do not know the people and places we are called to, we most likely are not asking the Holy Spirit the right questions. I am convinced that God longs to talk to us about how He has created our unique destiny seed. Remember James 1:5-6 says, "If any of you lacks wisdom, let him ask of God, who gives to all liberally and without reproach, and it will be given to him. But let him ask in faith, with no doubting, for he who doubts is like a wave of the sea driven and tossed by the wind." To be deeply rooted and abundantly fruitful we must seek the Lord for the blueprint embedded inside the DNA of our destiny seed.

Each of us has our own mission field that God has prepared for us. Jesus tells us in Matthew 9:38, "So pray to the Lord who is in charge of the harvest; ask him to send more workers into his fields" (NLT). God never tells us to pray for revival, He tells us to pray for Him to send workers to go into the harvest fields. Have you ever prayed for God to send you into your own field?

I believe that when we pray for souls to be saved, healed, and delivered, God faithfully prepares people, but because of His commitment to

BRANCH FIELD NOTES
Identify where you are called to serve

Find a quiet place and start by breathing in God's love for four seconds. Hold that breath for four seconds, imagining His presence filling you up like a balloon. Now, for four seconds breathe out whatever negative emotion is weighing you down. Repeat this exercise until you feel settled and present. Ask the Holy Spirit the following questions. Then journal the free flow of thoughts that come to your mind as you fix your eyes on Jesus.

Questions:

Holy Spirit, where do I first invest my time? What are my biblical priorities?

_____

_____

_____

Where do I need to implement healthy boundaries in my relationships?

_____

_____

_____

Where in the area(s) of influence are you directing me? (Government, Education, Business, Family, Religion, Media, and Arts & Entertainment)

_____
_____
_____

Where have you given me a burden? (Clues: What angers me? What do I hate? What makes me cry? What world issues bother me the most?)

_____
_____
_____

Where would I most like to leave an impact with my life?

_____
_____
_____

Where have you anointed me to reach beyond my current sphere of relationships?

_____
_____
_____

Where is the mission field you have prepared for me?

_____
_____
_____

Encounter:

Imagine looking at Jesus. He has tears in His eyes. Ask Him, "Jesus, break my heart for what breaks yours." Wait a minute to hear a word, see a picture or feel an emotion. Cup your hand on His cheek and catch a single tear. Did you know tears have unique compositions? This tear represents the burden the Holy Spirit is giving to you. As you examine the tear in your hand using your sanctified imagination, ask the Holy Spirit for supernatural vision. Watch as the tear is magnified as though it was under a microscope. What is inside your tear drop? Continue to dialog with Jesus and accept the burden, and any emotions that come with it, as a gift from Him. Ask Him, what do you want me to know about this burden and what do you want me to do?

Activation:

Refer to Figure 19 and list your core branches in order of biblical priorities. If you are not married and wish to be, and/or do not have children but wish to have children, you may label a marriage and children branch understanding your assignment to nourish the branch in prayer before it's fully grown. The most common core branches are: 1. Spouse 2. Children and Grandchildren 3. Family (parents, siblings, grandparents,... etc.) 4. Local Church & Close friends 5. Vocation & Community (outside the church). Refer to Figure 20 and list your outer branches. The outer branches may include the burden and field God has called you to harvest. Remember, these are people God has appointed you to reach beyond those you have relational proximity to.

Recommended Resources:

Get involved in the fight against human trafficking at Thevillageglobal.org. Read One More Rescue by Nicole Fitzpatrick.

WEED VIII

Figure 20: Weed - Trauma, Demonic Oppression, Lies, Sin or Offense
Figure 21: Counterfeit Blossoms   Figure 22: Entangled Fear Roots

WEED
Chapter Eight

*How does the enemy entangle you?
Identifying hindrances to your freedom*

"There are a thousand hacking at the branches of evil to one who is striking at the root." -Henry David Thoreau

The Invasion

Ever since Adam and Eve were kicked out of the garden, bad fruit has become a part of the world we were born into. Behind all bad fruit like anger, control, bitterness, anxiety, and stress, is a bad root. These roots are weeds that are invading our soil.

Rotten fruit that pops up is intended to warn us about what's growing in our root system underground. Those of us who desire to grow spiritually and experience true life cannot be apathetic or passive towards weeds in our soil and bad fruit trying to alert us to deeper issues. Behind all bad fruit is a fear root kept alive by a false belief.

Weeds are plants that harbor disease. They can produce chemicals that are toxic to the surrounding growth. By reducing crop growth and inhibiting harvest, weeds are the greatest threat to our spiritual growth. Weeds are the result of demonic deception and thrive off of lies and fear. They spread toxins and disease, quickly choking our nourishment needed to sustain true life.

We are commanded in the Word of God to watch out for and actively resist the schemes of the enemy. James 4:7 says, "Submit yourselves therefore to God. Resist the devil, and he will flee from you" (ESV).

I have observed three primary mistakes we as Christians make that keep us from uprooting the weeds that are preventing our spiritual growth.

1. Ignoring the negative fruit that is weighing down our trees.

An invasion of pride will keep us from being able to see the negative cycles we are in. The enemy deceives many into focusing on everyone else's bad fruit while remaining blind to our own. Meanwhile, our tree is clustered with the rotten fruit of our flesh that is killing us. Some of us have accepted rotten fruit in false humility, which is another form of pride. It can sound like, "This is just my personality" or "God's grace will cover it" or "I'm just a sinner." An unwillingness to face the reality of the bad fruit on our tree that is weighing us down will result in spiritual death.

> *Behind all bad fruit is a fear root kept alive by a false belief.*

2. Managing bad fruit by hacking at branches.

Others of us are obsessed with assessing ourselves and trying to clean up our spiritual life on our own. This was me. Anytime a piece of rotten fruit of my flesh showed up on my tree, I immediately tried to cut down the branch it was growing on. I cut these branches off by suppressing my emotions and managing my behavior. Striving to protect my image in this way resulted in an invasion of weeds in the soil of my soul. From the outside it looked like my tree was not producing much bad fruit, but underground the negative root systems continued to cause destruction.

3. Picking at weeds.

Some of us have a basic understanding of spiritual warfare and attempt to address the weeds behind bad fruit in our lives, but instead of uprooting the weeds we simply pick at them. Anyone who has picked at a weed and pulled it up by its leaves rather than its root, knows this causes the weed to spread even more. When we obsess over the schemes of the enemy and spend all of our time rebuking the devil, we are essentially picking at weeds. Rather than using our authority to uproot them, we unknowingly cause them to spread.

In our spiritual root system there are four primary causes of weeds with roots of fear. These weeds negatively affect what we believe and how we see the world.

1. Trauma & Emotional Wounds
2. Demons & Lies
3. Our Flesh & Sin
4. Unforgiveness & Offense

In this chapter we will discuss the different tools God has given us to uproot anything growing in the soil of our souls that is causing destruction.

My Weeds

One of the weeds that invaded the soil of my soul was abandonment. I lacked the tools and understanding I needed to identify and address this root so it continued to spread as I tried to suppress the fruit of unwanted negative emotions.

We have discussed the two primary root systems growing in each of us, fear and love. These root systems connect clusters of negative and positive roots. The bad fruit that surfaces is always connected to an unseen weed and fear root. Often we experience secondary emotions or unwanted behavior that can seem completely unrelated to the primary root causing them.

For example, the fruit of anger that surfaced for me was connected to a weed of abandonment. Bad fruit like anger are meant to signify to us that something is not right under the surface. Anger is a secondary emotion. When I suppressed and stomped on this emotion, I only increased the problem.

It is worth noting that anger is not a sin. Jesus experienced anger and never sinned. However, anger that is unaddressed, suppressed, or given into, often leads to sin.

Ephesians 4:26 says, "Be angry **and** do not sin" (ESV, bold mine). The Bible has a lot to say about anger. Proverbs 12:16 says, "The [arrogant] fool's anger is quickly known [because he lacks self-control and common sense], but a prudent man ignores an insult" (AMP).

Righteous anger arises in us when we are outraged by things that oppose God and His ways. Paying attention to things that upset us most like trafficking, addiction, poverty or violence will help lead us into our calling.

However, the majority of anger we experience is not righteous anger. Most often we get angry because of perceived injustices towards ourselves. Rather than turning the other cheek like Jesus instructs us to in Matthew 5:39, our flesh wants to fight back. James 1:19-20 says,"Let every person be quick to hear, slow to speak, slow to anger; for the anger of man does not produce the righteousness of God" (ESV).

Growing up, religion taught me to conceal my emotions and manage the bad fruit on my own. I picked rotten fruit as quickly as I could off my tree, but I never addressed the weeds growing in my soil. Jesus confronts the Pharisees for doing the exact same thing. In Matthew 23:25 He says, "Hypocrites! For you are so careful to clean the outside of the cup and the dish, but inside you are filthy" (NLT).

All my attempts to become a professional fruit manager failed when I met my husband. To put it simply, Michael does not possess the skill or desire for emotional suppression. Growing up, I felt like Elsa in the movie *Frozen*, "Conceal, don't feel; don't let it show!" Michael's expression of negative emotions felt very unsafe to me. Taking on his emotions, I found that I was no longer able to suppress the emotions that I thought I had mastered. This led us into years of explosive arguments and cycles fueled by fear, guilt, shame and trauma.

Then we had two children just a year apart that brought on another level of testing. I found myself angry at their emotional expressions, unaware of the connection to my own childhood trauma. Feelings of anger produced deep shame within me.

I need you to know I had a wonderful childhood with incredibly loving parents. Trauma is simply the lasting emotional response that often results from living through a distressing event. What one person perceives as traumatic can be completely different than someone else. Trauma can happen in the womb or before a person starts to develop memories. We can have lasting emotional responses to things that seem insignificant, but our body recorded as traumatic. Trauma responses can even be passed down generationally.

We do not have to understand the reason our body is holding onto trauma to recognize the common stress responses: fight, flight, freeze and fawn. The fight response says, *"I won't,"* and controls by any means.

The flight response says, *"I'm out,"* and will escape by any means. The freeze response says, *"I can't,"* and avoids by any means. The fawn response says *"I will,"* and pleases by any means.[55] My husband and I reacted most commonly with "fight," hence the explosive arguments.

As I share parts of my story and you reflect on your own, please know that honor and honesty can coexist. We do not bring up the past to dwell on it, but the Holy Spirit can lead us to uproot that which is causing us pain and stealing from us. He does this by revealing, healing and sealing these memories. The Holy Spirit will bring up a memory to reveal the lie we believed in that moment usually accompanied by an offense we began to harbor, often subconsciously.

When we do not heal, we see everything through the distorted lens of our wounds. This leads to cycles of heartache and broken relationships. If we do not get to the root of these demonic cycles we will pass them down to our children. What we are unwilling to fight becomes our children's battles.

My dad's own generational trauma, battles with drug and alcohol abuse and mental instability, led to him leaving my mom, older sister and me when I was one. A marriage and two children was too much for him. I have no memories from these first years of my life. Sometimes trauma comes from what did not happen to you rather than what did. In my case, it was the lack of secure attachment with my biological father.

Dr. Karyn Purvis, a developmental psychologist specializing in the area of attachment said, "Attachment refers to the emotional bond between caregiver and child. Caregivers respond to their child's needs repeatedly over time, forming a pattern of interaction called attachment style. These early experiences form the foundation of how their child understands and engages in relationships throughout life. Through intentional work, people can understand how their past has impacted them and determine what they need to do to move towards healing."[56]

Dr. Purvis, co-author of The Connected Child and the co-creator of Trust-Based Relational Intervention®, taught tens of thousands around the world about the need for trauma-informed care and trust-based

---

55. Empowered to Connect, *Cultivate Connection Course: Empowering Parents to Empower Children*, 70.
56. Empowered to Connect, *Cultivate Connection Course: Empowering Parents to Empower Children*, 36.

interventions for vulnerable children. Her research and teachings have helped me immensely to heal my story and become equipped to work with vulnerable families.

"If we are willing to piece together our stories and see the relationship between what happened then and what's happening now, we get to make choices about what happens next." - Scott McClellan contributor to Cultivate Connection Course.[57]

My passion to care for vulnerable children came out of my experience as an adoptee. My mom remarried a wonderful man who adopted me when I was four. He chose to take on all financial responsibility for my older sister and me and gave us his last name. I consider my biological dad's willingness to release us for adoption a selfless and loving act.

We maintained an open relationship with my biological dad throughout my childhood. Doing so was not always easy, but I am grateful my parents encouraged us to preserve our connection with him. I credit my parents for the positive relationship I have with my bio dad today. They chose to honor him in every situation. Had they held offense, judgment or animosity towards him, I believe our relationship would be very different today.

In my earliest memories I understood the gift of adoption. It was the picture of redemption. God used adoption to take a broken family and make us whole again. Adopting one day myself became my dream at a very young age.

Growing up, I became a mini adoption advocate, proudly telling everyone that I had two dads. I believed that my situation had turned out better than my biological parents remaining married and raising us. My heart to testify of God's redemption through adoption was great, but my denial of the loss that comes with every adoption story was not.

Instead of running into the arms of Jesus who heals and transforms, I ran to religion and settled for a band-aid to cover over my abandonment wound. Despite experiencing literal adoption as well as spiritual, being adopted into the family of God, I lived like a spiritual orphan. I was caught in the cycle of endlessly trying to do better, work harder and prove myself valuable.

---

57. Empowered to Connect, *Cultivate Connection Course: Empowering Parents to Empower Children*, 34.

Growing up, my bio dad benefited from some counseling and would occasionally check in with my sister and me regarding what he called our "father wound." Each time he did I was offended by the suggestion that there was some part of me that was negatively affected by him leaving us. I insisted that I was not hurt or bitter and there was nothing to heal.

The day God supernaturally removed the scales from my eyes, I began to see Father God rightly and in His reflection see myself rightly. This was the first time I had a real encounter with the Spirit of adoption (Romans 8:15), and it marked the beginning of a detox from performing for love. God had a plan to get to the deep roots of abandonment and the orphan spirit that I still carried.

After months of gently unraveling lie after lie that I believed and setting me free with the truth, the Lord told me that it was time to deal with my father wound and root of abandonment. Once again I thought to myself, "What father wound?" I truly felt nothing.

The Holy Spirit asked me to imagine my husband leaving my daughter who was two at the time. Emotions flooded me immediately, and I wept. Anger, betrayal, hurt, guilt and shame hit me like stormy waves. I could imagine how devastated my daughter would be, how she would ask about him all the time and how she would blame herself no matter what assurance I gave her that it was not her fault. I knew this is how I must have felt, and I wept not out of self-pity but surrender.

For the first time, I acknowledged the loss that is part of every adoption story. As an adult woman, I finally let myself grieve the loss of not having my biological dad raise me. In that moment I discovered something unexpected: grief is holy.

Once I acknowledged the reality of my story, it was time to forgive my dad again. In so doing, God freed me from a spirit of abandonment. Forgiveness is the gateway to freedom. This time when I encountered the Spirit of adoption, I gained a new confidence to boldly approach Father God trusting completely in His goodness.

One of the biggest things that came out of this encounter was an ability to accept my emotions and extend grace to myself. Before, I was so hard on myself. Anytime I experienced negative emotions I would spiral into guilt and shame. "Get it together, Mary," and "What's wrong with you?" were common thoughts that tormented me.

I was unhealthily obsessed with self-improvement and striving to fix myself which led to pride when I felt I was doing good, and crushing defeat when I felt I was not. I was caught in a cycle of condemnation and self-criticism. Because I was judgemental of myself, I was also judgemental of others. Healing in this area freed me to be compassionate and curious towards myself and those I love. This was truly life changing!

It was incredibly hard for me to validate my husband and my children's emotions when I was unable to validate my own. This kept me from being the grace-filled, confident parent I so desired to be. The most significant transformation that came from this encounter was in the area of marriage and parenting.

Garden Tools

There are a number of tools available to help us uproot the weeds in our life. Each tool has an important purpose in our garden and knowing how to use them will bring greater victory. The Holy Spirit, our Master Gardener, always leads us to the right tool at the right time. To say there is only one way to deal with weeds would be foolish. To deny the existence of weeds would be even more foolish. Yet sadly this is the response of many Christians.

There is a demonic agenda behind every weed in our soil. Remember, we wrestle not against flesh and blood, but principalities and powers (Ephesians 6:12).

Before I present any of my conclusions to you on the topic of demons, I encourage you to flip to the appendix and read through the scripture guide I have provided on deliverance. Allow the Holy Spirit space to guide you through passages that are often skipped over in our Bible studies. I will offer you a brief overview of my perspective, but it is much better to see God's perspective directly in the Bible.

In other countries, the veil is thinner between the spiritual and physical realm. You do not have to convince anyone of the existence of demons or their ability to manipulate everyone, including Christians. This is not the case for the American Church, slumbering under a satanic lullaby and held captive by lies such as, "Christians can't have a demon!" "Demonic oppression is only in foreign nations," or worse still "Demons don't exist." All of these statements are based on false doctrines founded on the lies of demons themselves.

Could it be possible that the American Church is missing the authority and power that we need to experience the full gospel? I believe the answer is yes. The Bible speaks repeatedly about people having unclean or evil spirits (Matt. 11:18; Mark 7:25; 9:17; Luke 4:33; 8:27; 13:11; John 7:20; 8:48–49, 52; 10:20–21).

As Christians we cannot be *possessed* by demons, but we can be *oppressed* by them. Demonic weeds are invaders of our soil, not the primary possessors of it. In the same way, squatters are invaders of a property, not the owners. If we have truly made Jesus Lord of our life, God possesses the title deed to our soul. The problem is not with who possesses, but rather who trespasses on our property.

Demons do not have the legal right to be on our land, but purchasing the land does not automatically remove them. If we have squatters on our property, it is our responsibility to tell them to get off or to notify the authorities to forcefully remove them. Jesus' death and resurrection gave us authority over the enemy. He took back the keys of death and Hades for us (Revelation 1:18), but it is our choice if we are going to use this authority or live in bondage. I have never heard of a property owner befriending a squatter on their property and handing them keys to their house. Yet this is what Christians do all the time, becoming friendly and familiar with demons sent to destroy us. Under the disguise of "quirks" or "weaknesses" demons hide in plain sight.

> *Healing in this area freed me to be compassionate and curious towards myself and those I love. This was truly life changing!*

When speaking to the Canaanite woman in Matthew 15:21-28, Jesus refers to healing through deliverance as the "children's bread." In Matthew 12:43-45, Jesus warns of the dangers of casting demons out of someone who is not desiring to be filled with the Holy Spirit or the demons will come back seven times worse. For those who believe Christians are fully delivered at the moment of salvation, I pose the question: why is Simon saved and baptized in Acts 8:13, but Acts 8:23 makes it clear that Simon was still bound and poisoned by bitterness? Simon's story is a great example of this process of progressive freedom. Acts 8:13 says that Simon believed and was baptized, but Acts 8:23 makes it clear that his heart was still bound and says he was poisoned by bitterness.

In my experience, those who believe Christians can not have demons have never cast out a demon themselves. In Matthew 10:8, Jesus gives the direct command, "Heal the sick, cleanse the lepers, raise the dead, cast out demons. Freely you have received, freely give." Much of the American Church has not seen the sick healed, the dead raised or demons cast out. I went to biweekly Bible studies most of my life but until God removed the veil from my eyes, I skimmed over these verses as though Jesus' commands did not apply to me.

Most Christians play hide and seek with demons. Some are the hiders, some are the seekers. Hiders are like toddlers who put their hands over their eyes and think they are now invisible. They believe that because they cannot see demons, that they also cannot be seen or manipulated by demons. "I don't see you, you don't see me," is a cute game with a loving parent but terrifying if played with a hungry lion. 1 Peter 5:8 says, "Your adversary the devil prowls around like a roaring lion, seeking someone to devour" (ESV).

Focusing only on what is seen in the physical realm is carnal Christianity. Professing to believe in an unseen God but denying the existence of an unseen enemy are non-congruent beliefs. Romans 8:6 says, "For to be carnally minded *is* death, but to be spiritually minded *is* life and peace." Paul says that those who are carnally or naturally minded believe the things of the spirit are foolish.

> *"But the natural man does not receive the things of the Spirit of God, for they are foolishness to him; nor can he know them, because they are spiritually discerned." (1 Corinthians 2:14)*

Seekers, on the other hand, are constantly looking for a demon behind every door. This belief system increases demonic activity in a person's life. There are Christians who believe everything is the devil's fault and take no personal responsibility.

I love what Dr. Jack Hayford says, "You cannot cast out the flesh and you cannot disciple a demon." We have to be able to recognize the difference between a battle with our flesh where we need to deny ourselves, and a battle with a demonic stronghold that we need to use our authority to cast out.

We must become Christians who refuse to play the devil's games. We are no longer interested in hide and seek because we have matured. We know we are seated with Christ in heavenly places, and we've been given all authority under Heaven. We rule and reign with Christ and use our authority as the Holy Spirit instructs us to. We fight from a place of rest because we know the battle is already won. We do not let the enemy get us on the defense; we live on the offense.

Ephesians 1:19-22 says:

> *"I also pray that you will understand the incredible greatness of God's power for us who believe him. This is the same mighty power that raised Christ from the dead and seated him in the place of honor at God's right hand in the heavenly realms. Now he is far above any ruler or authority or power or leader or anything else—not only in this world but also in the world to come. God has put all things under the authority of Christ and has made him head over all things for the benefit of the church."* (NLT)

Jesus is seated far above all power or leaders of this world. Guess where we are seated? With Him! "And God raised us up **with Christ** and seated us **with him** in the heavenly realms in Christ Jesus" (Ephesians 2:6 NIV, bold mine). Jesus has been given all authority. Since He lives in us, how much authority do we have? All authority. "Look, I have given you authority over **all** the power of the enemy, and you can walk among snakes and scorpions and crush them. Nothing will injure you" (Luke 10:19 NLT, bold mine).

Perhaps you are wondering, if we have *all* authority, why are Christians still tormented? Using authority and having authority are not the same thing. The enemy only has authority that we give him by forfeiting our own authority.

A good example of this is a recurring fight my son and daughter had when they were two and three. Finn would tell Lucy she could not have something and then she would cry. Then Lucy would tell Finn he's a bad guy and that he could not have something. Then he would cry. This is just like it is with the enemy. Finn and Lucy do not have the authority to say what each other can and cannot have. As their mother, I do not take into consideration their empty threats. Forfeiting my authority and letting my children make all the decisions would be ridiculous. Yet this is exactly what we do with the enemy. We believe the deception that he has more power over situations than we do and in so doing we hand our authority over to him. We only give him power when we believe he has power over us.

Like a snake or a scorpion, the enemy is beneath us. He crawls around on the earth while we are seated far above him in heavenly places. We do not freak out when we discern a snake or a scorpion in our lives, but we do need to exercise the position and authority we have been given and intentionally step on them. Some die immediately with one stomp, others need to be stepped on a few times.

While we do not go searching for the enemy under every rock, we must be watchful for his schemes in our lives and ready to crush him when the Holy Spirit helps us discern his activity. Every recurring negative cycle in our lives has demonic activity behind it. Back to the original illustration: we do not allow weeds to overtake our garden, but we do not pick at them either. Understanding how to properly uproot these weeds is vital to our spiritual health.

Shovel

A common tool to uproot weeds is a shovel. When applied directly to the root, shovels can be very effective for removing unwanted weeds. A shovel has to be stepped on and pressure has to be applied to the weed in order to get underneath the root system. This same principle is true when we use our authority to cast out demons.

As we are led by the Spirit, we will be able to discern which spiritual forces we are fighting against. I have seen demons leave with one command, but most often it takes a persistent shoveling to get the demon to uproot completely. The shovel represents the authority we have in the name of Jesus that when applied to a spiritual root, always brings freedom. We pray and apply pressure until we feel the tangible lift of that spiritual force.

Demons love to hide in churches that do not have deliverance ministries. But once identified, demons will put on a show to try to distract and intimidate people. My experiences going through deliverance felt like I was at the back of my body watching like a bystander. I still had free will and could choose to submit to or resist the process, but I was not in control of the manifestations in my body. I had no idea that I had a demon until one threw me on the top of a couch and shrieked. I know that probably sounds alarming, but it was quite comical actually. After that experience, no one would be able to convince me or my husband who was sitting next to me, that demons are not real or that they cannot oppress Christians.

Demonic manifestations do not happen to every person experiencing deliverance. I have prayed for many people who have gotten freedom through a cough or tear. We can exercise our authority and tell the demons to leave quickly and quietly in Jesus' name, but sometimes they do not listen and leave with a shriek just like Scripture records in Acts 8:7, "Many evil spirits were cast out, screaming as they left their victims" (NLT). When we understand the authority we carry, there is no reason to be intimidated by demons in whatever form they manifest.

Demons being cast out is one of the miraculous signs that Jesus tells us in Mark 16:17 will follow those who believe. When we believe casting out demons is a part of the Christian life, the Holy Spirit will give us opportunities to experience deliverance ourselves and take others through it.

When witnessing a demonic manifestation, the enemy might try to tell you that people are acting, and it is not real. I can assure you that the average person is not that good at acting, and no one wants to become undignified in this way. Freedom on the other side of deliverance is worth our dignity! Remember, spiritual things seem foolish to our natural minds, but the spiritual realm is more real than the physical one.

In Isaiah, we are told to refute everything that rises up against us. We do not have to scream and yell, but opening our mouths and intentionally using our authority is a requirement to defeating the enemy. If we were to simply pray, "God help them," I believe God would say, "You help them!" In Matthew 17:14-21 Jesus is not happy that the disciples did not heal the boy who was oppressed by a demon themselves with the authority he had given them. After expressing His disapproval, Jesus goes on to blame the disciples' unbelief. We have been instructed to use our authority to speak to the demons and tell them to leave in Jesus' name, just like the disciples did.

> "No weapon that is fashioned against you shall succeed, and **you shall refute** every tongue that rises against you in judgment. **This is the heritage of the servants of the Lord** and their vindication from me, declares the Lord." (Isaiah 54:17 ESV, bold mine)

Behind every demon is a lie. We have already established that the enemy's power comes through deception. Once we identify a demon, it is important that we discern the lie that allowed it to operate in our lives. Breaking agreement with the lie is how we maintain our freedom. Renouncing the lies and agreeing with the truth is the primary way we take authority over spiritual strongholds.

Remember it is the truth that sets us free! Let's look at a few examples of demonic forces, the lies behind them and ways we can uproot them.

The Spirit of Legalism & Spirit of Religion

Legalism and religion are rooted in the lie that spiritual maturity has to be earned and proven. We replace this lie by declaring the truth that we are always growing in the grace of the Lord, not our own works.

> Declaration:
> *I renounce the spirit of religion and the spirit of legalism. I renounce the lie that I have to strive to follow rules to be acceptable to God. I renounce my judgment of myself and others who do not do things the way I think they should. I renounce self-righteousness and self-reliance above the workings of the Holy Spirit. Forgive me Jesus for allowing these lies to penetrate my heart.*

The Spirit of Pride

Pride is rooted in the lie that we can handle things by ourselves and through our own understanding. The truth is we can do nothing without God, and He reveals His will to us as we humble ourselves.

> Declaration:
> *I renounce the spirit of pride. I renounce the lie that I have to prove myself and rely on my own knowledge and understanding. I lay down my right to understand and instead receive child-like faith. I renounce the lie that I need to know all the answers to be able to act. Forgive me, Lord, for being proud. Forgive me, Lord, for being offended by others who disagree with me. I surrender to you, Lord, and ask you to cleanse me now of the sin of pride.*

The Spirit of Accusation & The Critical Spirit

Accusation is rooted in the lie that God will not defend us, and we need to fight for ourselves. The truth is God alone is the righteous judge, and He always vindicates those with a pure heart.

Declaration:
I renounce the spirit of accusation and the critical spirit. I renounce the lie that God cannot defend me. I take back any words of slander, accusation, and gossip I have spoken and cancel the negative harvest of these words. I renounce words I have spoken with wrongful attitudes and impure motives. Jesus, I ask you to cleanse my mouth and fill it with words of life. Forgive me for the judgment in my heart towards any person, situation or myself.

Fear of Man & Fear of Rejection

People pleasing is rooted in the lie that God cannot meet our deepest needs. The truth is that the fear of the Lord leads us into a relationship with God where He provides everything we need.

Declaration:
I renounce fear of man and fear of rejection. I pray that I would fear you alone, God. Forgive me for desiring acceptance by others more than you, Lord. What other people think about me is none of my business; forgive me for being preoccupied with the opinions of others. I renounce fear of rejection and the lie that my identity is found through the acceptance of others. Forgive me for rejecting others in my own insecurity. Thank you that I am accepted in the Beloved and will never be rejected by you.

Blowtorch

The presence of God is like a blowtorch that can burn up every destructive root growing in the soil of our souls. My favorite testimonies are the ones where people are set free from a life of bondage to addiction, sexual immorality or fear in one moment in the fiery presence of God. We serve a God who is able!

When I am experiencing spiritual warfare, getting into the presence of the Lord and worshiping Him is my favorite battle plan. Just as Paul and Silas' chains were loosened and their prison door opened when they worshiped the Lord (Acts 16), we are freed from our bondage when we do the same.

It is also the fiery love of God that burns up trauma from our past. When we experience distressing events, trauma can lodge itself in our bodies causing physical and emotional pain that can seem unrelated.

Our emotional triggers are created to reveal to us areas where we are in need of healing. When we are curious about the root of these negative emotions and remain compassionate towards ourselves, we can experience inner healing and radically transform these triggers.

We can ask the Holy Spirit questions like: *When was the first time I felt this way?* Allow your mind to take you back to that time. Ask: *Where was Jesus when this happened?* When you find Jesus in your mind's eye, pay attention to where He is, what He is doing, and His facial expressions. Ask: *What lie did I believe about you or myself in this moment?* Renounce the lie that comes to mind. Ask: *Who do I need to forgive for this lie?* After forgiving that person or multiple people, ask: *What is the truth?* If Jesus is far off, invite Him to come closer. You can also ask: *What was stolen from me in this memory?* Once identified, imagine Jesus giving you a gift. Ask: *What are you restoring to me?*

It may seem like this encounter only happens in your imagination, but I can assure you a real exchange takes place in the spirit.

The blowtorch is an effective tool when carefully applied to areas in our soil that need healing. When we pursue inner healing, it is very important that we are being guided by the Holy Spirit and we do so with safe people who will not hinder the work with condemnation and criticism. We do not want to dig up memories that the Holy Spirit is not leading us to dig up. Spirit-filled counselors can be valuable guides on our healing journeys.

Weed Killer

The third and final tool to help us uproot the weeds growing in the soil of our souls is weed killer. This tool effectively destroys the most destructive weed: offense. When offense takes root in our soil, it poisons our tree with bitterness and unforgiveness. If not dealt with, this weed will rot our good roots and completely take out our tree.

The solution to addressing the poisonous root of offense is the cross. In this illustration, our weed killer is the blood of Jesus. Without it, offense will slowly kill us. But when we apply forgiveness, we kill these weeds. Weed killer does not immediately remove the weed, but it blocks the roots from forming.

This is how it is with forgiveness. When we choose to forgive, we are not denying the injustice that happened. We are also not saying that the pain is not real. But when we apply the blood of Jesus, it blocks offense from taking root and spreading poison through our soil to our heart. The hurt does not automatically go away, but the bad roots are destroyed so they cannot cause further destruction.

In Luke 17:1 Jesus tells us offenses will come. The word for offense in the Hebrew is the word *skandalon* which means trap, specifically the part of the trap where bait is attached.[58] Offenses are the traps of the enemy that lure us into bondage. In this life, it is inevitable that traps of offense will be set for us. People will misunderstand us, mistreat us, and even some will betray us. We cannot control the hurtful actions of others, but we do have the power to choose if we are going to be taken captive by the trap of offense.

Paul says he practices forgiveness because he is not unaware of Satan's schemes and plans to outwit us. The number one scheme of the enemy to destroy us is unforgiveness.

> "I urge you, therefore, to reaffirm your love for him. Another reason I wrote you was to see if you would stand the test and be obedient in everything. Anyone you forgive, I also forgive. And what I have forgiven—if there was anything to forgive—I have forgiven in the sight of Christ for your sake, in order that Satan might not outwit us. For we are not unaware of his schemes." (2 Corinthians 2:8-11 NIV)

Weed killer almost always has to be applied repeatedly, even to the same weed. As often as an offense is remembered, forgiveness can be released. Sometimes, even after the weed has been removed we may detect a fragment of the root remaining in the soil. I have always marveled at how painful the smallest of slivers can be. The Master Gardener cares enough to tend to the tiniest slivers in our soil. Instead of being poisoned by massive or microscopic roots, we need to get to the source and address the offense in our hearts. The blood of Jesus repels the enemy and keeps the bitter roots of offense from destroying us.

The Root Behind The Root

---

58. John Bevere, *The Bait of Satan: Living Free from the Deadly Trap of Offense.*

We are all in a process of becoming love which coincides with becoming fearless. 1 John 4:18 says, "There is no fear in love. But perfect love drives out fear, because fear has to do with punishment. The one who fears is not made perfect in love" (NIV).

The first usage of the word fear in this verse means the causing of fear, panic or alarm. Timothy is saying love does not cause fear and torment. When he says, "the one who fears" a different word is used. This is the word *phobeó* and it means to "put to flight or to terrify."[59]

I believe it is significant that different words are used here. We are all going to experience the first kind of fear, but we should not be the cause of such fear. Panic, alarm, and the cause to be afraid is a normal part of life. However, if we want to be made perfect in love we cannot let fear rule us. We cannot, as the Greek word indicates, be put to flight by fear. When we are put to flight by fear we run off our destiny path. Instead, we must learn to face our fear.

Is God leading you to speak in front of people and you have a fear of public speaking? Do it afraid! Do not let the enemy use fear to put you to flight. Are you afraid of sharing your faith with people? Do it afraid! Do not let the enemy use fear to put you to flight. Rather than run, stop and pay attention to the areas you feel intimidation because it can be a clue to kingdom assignments.

Whatever area you feel fear, God's grace is present to help you face that fear. All fear that is not from God can be conquered by His perfect love. When we are afraid we can replace our fear of man, fear of rejection, fear of failure, fear of death and every other root fear with the fear of the Lord. We do not have to be rid of all other fears, we just have to make sure we fear God most of all. The fear of God is the beginning of wisdom (Psalm 111:10) and the beginning of knowledge (Proverbs 1:7). Where the Spirit of the Lord is, there is freedom (2 Corinthians 3).

Whenever people confessed their fear to Jesus in the gospels, He led them straight to confront that fear. When we confess our fear, we are given the strength to confront it. Fear is a terrible master that rules far too many Christians. Fear loses its control on us when we confess and confront our fears. It has been said that all fear boils down to the fear of death. We are afraid of the death of our reputations. We are afraid of the

---

59. G5399 - Phobeō - Strong's Greek Lexicon (KJV).

death of our dreams. We are afraid of relational death. We are afraid of pain and disease which is ultimately the fear of physical death. This is why when we willingly lay down our life, we experience true life! Jesus conquered death and the grave so that we do not have to live in fear. Our spiritual growth, our true identity, our callings, and our assignments are all found on the other side of our fears.

WEED FIELD NOTES
Identify how you live in freedom

Find a quiet place and start by breathing in God's love for four seconds. Hold that breath for four seconds, imagining His presence filling you up like a balloon. Now, for four seconds breathe out whatever negative emotion is weighing you down. Repeat this exercise until you feel settled and present. Ask the Holy Spirit the following questions. Then journal the free flow of thoughts that come to your mind as you fix your eyes on Jesus.

Questions:

Holy Spirit, how is offense hiding in my heart? Who do I need to forgive?

_____

_____

How are trauma responses like fight (control by all means), flight (escape by all means), freeze (avoid by all means) or fawn (please by all means) operating in my life?

_____

_____

How can I partner with you to heal the pain points in my story?

How have I opened doors to the enemy?

How are negative cycles affecting my life?

How does the enemy repeatedly trip me up? What is his playbook?

How has intimidation held me back? What would I do if I had no fear?

How would you like me to pursue further freedom?

Activation:

Imagine yourself carrying the same authority Jesus had when He walked the earth. Say out loud, "spirit of ___ get off me in Jesus' name. You have no more power over me. I choose to partner with a spirit of ___ (say the opposite spirit). Example: "Spirit of pride get off me now in Jesus' name. You have no more power over me. I choose to partner with a spirit of humility." Take a bottle of olive oil, or whatever oil you have in your house, and pray over it. Ask the Holy Spirit to anoint it. Pray in your prayer language if you have one or say "Jesus you are holy. You are the worthy one." Continue repeating statements about His supremacy. Remember to engage your heart or this will be an ineffective religious ritual. Apply a small amount of oil to each door post. You may be led to open the front and back door and tell every evil spirit to get out in Jesus' name. Pray until you feel a shift in the spiritual atmosphere. Take the oil around your property line, car and anywhere else the Holy Spirit leads you.

Encounter:

Imagine yourself climbing up the hill of calvary. You see Jesus nailed to the cross and lock eyes with him. His face is almost unrecognizable. Blood drips down his brow. His body is bruised and broken. Take a minute and allow the truth that He endured this torturous death for you to sink in. Now look to your left; who is there with you? You may see one or fifty people standing there that you need to forgive. You most likely will need to forgive yourself. Take time with everyone, saying out loud, "(*their name) I forgive and release you. You owe me nothing. I bless you." Once you've finished, look to the right. Is there anyone else standing at the foot of the cross you need to forgive? If so, repeat the same statement forgiving, releasing and blessing each one. Once you've finished, look to the horizon. Jesus is there wearing a white robe, clothed in glory. He defeated sin for you. Freely you have received his forgiveness, now you can freely give it away to everyone who has offended you. Imagine walking every person you forgave over to Jesus. Say, "I leave you now with my friend, Jesus. I no longer hold you hostage in my heart. He is my Protector, Defender and He alone is responsible for you now."

Recommended Resources:

If you have experienced trauma in any form, I recommend finding a trusted inner healing minister in your area that can help guide you at Bethelsozo.com/book-sozo.

If you have identified negative cycles in your life and need freedom, I recommend finding someone equipped in deliverance ministry to pray with you. Here is a global map of deliverance ministers at Isaiahsaldivar.com/deliverance.

SPROUT IX

Figure 23: Evergreen Leaves of Purpose
Figure 24: Sprouting Leaves of Seasonal Assignments

SPROUT

Chapter Nine

*When is God asking you to act?
Identifying your unchanging purpose and seasonal assignments*

Evergreen Leaves

THE PURPOSE OF LEAVES is to turn light-energy into food by breathing in carbon dioxide and breathing out oxygen. Similarly, our purpose is to breathe in the love of God and breathe out love for others. Like the tree receives light-energy and through a process of photosynthesis converts that energy into food, we breathe in the love of God, and He converts it supernaturally into love for others. Our leaves provide shade and covering for others to take refuge in.

The evergreen leaves on our tree represent our unchanging purpose. Jesus tells us our purpose is the first and greatest commandment: loving God and loving our neighbor. Who is our neighbor? Whomever God has positioned us in close proximity to.

> *"Jesus answered him, 'The first of all the commandments is: 'Hear, O Israel, the LORD our God, the LORD is one. And you shall love the LORD your God with all your heart, with all your soul, with all your mind, and with all your strength.' This is the first commandment. And the second, like it, is this: 'You shall love your neighbor*

as yourself.' There is no other commandment greater than these.'"
(Mark 12:29-31)

"If you really fulfill the royal law according to the Scripture, 'You shall love your neighbor as yourself,' you do well." (James 2:8)

Many overcomplicate their purpose. It is simply this: to receive and give God's love. We continually freely receive and simultaneously freely give (Matthew 10:8). We will either be driven by pleasure or driven by purpose. When we receive God's love, we will naturally want to say yes to His promptings. After a reminder to obey, Paul assures the Philipians, "For God is working in you, giving you the desire and the power to do what pleases him" (Philipians 2:13). Those who are driven by spiritual purpose over fleshly pleasure are given desire from God. When we are motivated by pleasure we cannot trust our desires. But when we are motivated by purpose, the desires of our heart become one with God's desires. Love is the best motivator of obedience. Doers can never outwork lovers.

"If I speak in the tongues of men or of angels, but do not have love, I am only a resounding gong or a clanging cymbal. If I have the gift of prophecy and can fathom all mysteries and all knowledge, and if I have a faith that can move mountains, but do not have love, I am nothing. If I give all I possess to the poor and give over my body to hardship that I may boast, but do not have love, I gain nothing."
(1 Corinthians 13:1-3 NIV)

When we are occupied with the love of God and consistently say yes to Him, we will find ourselves right in the middle of the assignments He has prepared for us. We say things like, "God use me!" The heart behind this statement can be good, but I am convinced God does not want to use us; He wants to *partner* with us. If I said, "I just want my husband to use me however he wants to!" You would think I was brainwashed in an abusive relationship. God does not use us like pawns; His love moves us into action.

One of my childhood pastors was chronically ill and had a near death experience where he got to experience Heaven. The way he described Heaven impacted me deeply and has become our family motto:

fun with purpose. I have never had more fun in my life than when I live aligned with my Kingdom purpose.[60]

Seasonal Leaves

Olive tree leaves are marvelously designed by our Creator with an antibacterial, antiviral and anti-inflammatory effect. Likewise, the leaves on our tree can be used to fight the viral infections our world is plagued with. The Church is God's remedy to infectious problems everywhere. Our assignments are the solutions God put inside of our DNA seed to bring to the world. Our purpose is unchanging, but our assignments often change seasonally.

The problems we notice most are almost always the ones we are created to become a solution for. What I believe to be the main problems in each sphere of influence is guaranteed to be different than what you believe, simply because we carry different solutions.

A new leaf sprouts on one of our branches when God pulls on our heart strings, and we notice a problem that we are carrying a kingdom solution for. What problems especially bother you in your family, in your church, in your community?

My husband is bothered when ministries have to charge for events and resources because some are not able to afford the cost. Michael is tempted to not engage in church activities that cost money, not because we cannot afford them, but because of the hindrance it can be to others with financial limitations. The enemy tries to get him to not participate out of principle, while the Holy Spirit repeatedly calls him to pay extra to cover the cost for someone who cannot afford it. He has learned to acknowledge that it costs money to reach people with the life-changing love of Jesus and, as a solution, he is called to be a kingdom-funder!

> *Love is the best motivator of obedience. Doers can never outwork lovers.*

My sister gets emotional when the Church condemns public schools but neglects to care for the millions of children in the system. She argues that simply pulling our own children out of public schools is not the solution. What about the children whose parents cannot afford to send

---

60. Courson, *A Glimpse of Heaven: A Vision of Eternity in a Moment of Hell*.

their children to private school or stay home to homeschool them? As the Church, we must spearhead education reform by starting alternative schools as well as affecting change within the current public school system. She realizes that this is not everyone in the Church's assignment but has answered the call herself by saying yes to substituting in public schools and serving on her school district's Community Curriculum Advisory Board. She hopes to start a school someday.

A dear friend of mine is infuriated by people who condemn abortion but do not provide any practical solutions to vulnerable women who feel they have no other option. God only hates abortion because He loves people. She carries a dream that maternity homes and resources would be available to support every woman who chooses to parent. Two of the ways she is working to bring this solution to her community is intercession and administration. She intercedes for mercy to triumph over judgment in the Church and that the Holy Spirit would overflow through us with compassion for the broken, hurting and needy. In addition to intercession, God has given her an assignment to volunteer her time to meet the practical administrative needs of organizations working towards this same goal.

I am also devastated by the Church's lack of support for vulnerable families, but most burdensome to me is the Church's lack of engagement with the foster care system. I am convinced there would not be government run orphanages worldwide or foster care systems if the Church knew who she was. We are meant to be the system because we are God's solution! God made it clear in James 1:27 that pure religion looks like caring for the vulnerable. This is our God-given responsibility. I can talk all day about the problems in the foster care system. I see these problems clearly, because I carry part of the solution as an advocate, reformer and foster parent. While many have not been given the same assignment to foster parent, everyone is called to foster *care*. No believer is exempt from the assignment to engage with the vulnerable and care for their community in some way.

One of the branches on my tree is *Foster Care and Adoption* because I have identified that this is an area that I have been called to serve with many different assignments throughout my lifetime. However, there are many leaves on my tree related to fostering that cover core branches of my tree as well. Foster parenting, for example, is an assignment on my

Children branch. Caring for my children, including my foster children, comes before everything other than my marriage. Engaging as a foster parent has also given me assignments on my local *Community* and *Church* branches with social workers, therapists, agency workers, CASAs, and other foster and adoptive parents. While foster parenting, I have had many leaves sprout on my outer branch of *Foster Care and Adoption* as well involving advocacy and training. Understanding which assignments are on core branches and which ones are on my outer branch helps me order my priorities.

One of the other main problems that I see in the Church is the lack of activation of believers in their true identity and kingdom authority through personal relationship with Jesus. True faith leads us into abiding action. The assignment to write this book came as a result of this need for discipleship that has burdened me for years. I pray that this book is a solution that activates intimacy, identity and inheritance in every reader. Intimacy is Christ *to* us; identity is Christ *in* us, and inheritance is Christ *through* us.

If God has called us to serve somewhere (our branches), He has also assigned us seasonal assignments in that area (our leaves). There is an order of priority, and there is an order to the timing. Not every assignment given to us by God is for life, in fact, most are not.

Sometimes God gives us an assignment that we are supposed to nurture in prayer for years before we act on it. These leaves on our tree must be discerned. In 1 Chronicles 12:33, the sons of Issachar are commended for understanding the times. We too must be people who know how to act based on our discernment of spiritual seasons.

> *"For everything there is a season, and a time for every matter under heaven: a time to be born, and a time to die; a time to plant, and a time to pluck up what is planted; a time to kill, and a time to heal; a time to break down, and a time to build up; a time to weep, and a time to laugh; a time to mourn, and a time to dance; a time to cast away stones, and a time to gather stones together; a time to embrace, and a time to refrain from embracing; a time to seek, and a time to lose; a time to keep, and a time to cast away; a time to tear, and a time to sew; a time to keep silence, and a time to speak; a time to love, and a time to hate; a time for war, and a time for peace. What gain has the worker from his toil? I have seen the*

business that God has given to the children of man to be busy with. He has made everything beautiful in its time. Also, he has put eternity into man's heart, yet so that he cannot find out what God has done from the beginning to the end." (Ecclesiastes 3:1-8 ESV)

Timing is an essential component to our flourishing. Jesus reprimanded the Pharisees in Matthew 16:3 for not knowing how to interpret the signs of the times. There are four Greek words for time used in the New Testament: *aion, chronos, kairos,* and *hora*. In her book *Discernment*, Jane Hamon explains it this way, "So in the overarching, eternal plan of God (aion), there is the normal passing of time (chronos), which if responded to properly sets us up for the opportune times of favor, breakthrough and refreshing (kairos). Within these kairos times are 'now' moments (hora) for miracles. We must be sensitive to the Holy Spirit so we can shift our hearts and minds and align with our 'now' seasons."[61]

When we faithfully walk with the Lord through the normal chronos of our life, we will walk right into opportune times and kairos moments that catapult us into our destiny. This is what the faith walk looks like! We stay on our timeline by obeying the Lord one step at a time, remaining in His love.

Obedience to God keeps us on our timeline, but disobedience displaces us from the timeline of our God story. The scary truth is when we do not listen to God's voice and obey Him we get off our destiny timeline, and we can miss the kairos times and hora moments of predestined miracles.

Another way we can get off of our timeline is when we take old assignments into a new season. Assignments become draining to us when the grace on that particular assignment is being lifted. This is one of the first signs that God is moving us on. However, sometimes assignments become draining not because it is time to move on, but because we are doing it with the wrong energy source. Relying on false fuel will always lead to burn out. Being able to discern between the two is essential for the Christian walk.

"Whatever you do, work heartily, as for the Lord and not for men, knowing that from the Lord you will receive the inheritance as

---

61. Hamon, *Discernment: The Essential Guide to Hearing the Voice of God.*

your reward. You are serving the Lord Christ." (Colossians 2:23-24 ESV)

Development Seasons

Throughout scripture, we see a theme of wilderness training where God leads His sons and daughters into a season of preparation, setting them apart. No one can escape their journey of spiritual formation without wilderness seasons, and we would not want to! God invites us into the wilderness to pour His love on us.

> *"Therefore, behold, I will allure her, Will bring her into the wilderness, And speak comfort to her. I will give her her vineyards from there, And the Valley of Achor as a door of hope; She shall sing there, As in the days of her youth, As in the day when she came up from the land of Egypt. "And it shall be, in that day," Says the* LORD, *"That you will call Me 'My Husband,' And no longer call Me 'My Master'" (Hosea 2:14-16)*

The Lord uses wilderness seasons to get Egypt, a picture of the world, out of our hearts. Often God will allow us to experience temporary barrenness in the wilderness so we can understand our value *is not* in what we produce. As slaves in Egypt, the children of Israel's worth was *only* in their ability to work. The world is currently experiencing the same bondage and it seeps into the Church in the form of religion.

The root of religious striving are lies that revolve around not being and doing enough. "I am not doing enough. I am not doing a good enough job. I am not enough." To get the mindset of slavery out of His children, God leads us into the wilderness where we have to trust God completely for all provision. We are no longer called slaves; we are friends of God!

> *"I have loved you even as the Father has loved me. Remain in my love. When you obey my commandments, you remain in my love, just as I obey my Father's commandments and remain in his love. I have told you these things so that you will be filled with my joy. Yes, your joy will overflow! This is my commandment: Love each other in the same way I have loved you. There is no greater love than to lay down one's life for one's friends. You are my friends if you do what I command. I no longer call you slaves, because a*

master doesn't confide in his slaves. Now you are my friends, since I have told you everything the Father told me. You didn't choose me. I chose you. I appointed you to go and produce lasting fruit, so that the Father will give you whatever you ask for, using my name. This is my command: Love each other." (John 15:9-17 NLT)

Some of us have heard from the pulpit so many times that we are not enough that it feels dangerous even to consider that the opposite is true. The narrative of the Bible is very different from the worldly narrative that says everyone is enough on their own. The truth is, without God we are *not* enough. But, when we receive Jesus, we never have to be without God again! Now, we are more than a conqueror because we belong to Christ Jesus (Romans 8:37). The one who is more than enough lives in us.

If we believe we are not enough, we are saying Jesus' sacrifice was not enough. To identify as not doing or being enough we have to identify ourselves without Jesus, a position we should never take again. Our own best righteousness is like filthy rags (Isaiah 64:6), but we are not on our own anymore!

God also uses wilderness seasons to remove our scarcity mindset around money, time and identity so we can experience His abundance. We serve the God of more than enough!

"He turned rivers into a desert, flowing springs into thirsty ground, and fruitful land into a salt waste, because of the wickedness of those who lived there. He turned the desert into pools of water and the parched ground into flowing springs." (Psalms 107:33-35 NIV)

The most marking wilderness season the Lord has led me through began the same year as the world faced a global pandemic. Before COVID, God spoke to me that I needed to be prepared for my husband to be laid off, and that He was going to transition him into something different.

This transition began as a spiritual move to new territory that eventually correlated with a literal move. In Genesis 13, God told Abram to leave behind the known, comfortable and safe territory so He could settle in the land of Hebron which means communion. Much like Abram's separation from his family before God changed his name, God asked me to leave family and friends behind to find my true identity in this new land. This spiritual move was to a land without borders, and to obey His voice I had to surrender my tightly held theology that limited Him. After Abram obeyed the Lord, he pitched his tent under the oak of Mamre which means richness, fullness and satisfaction. I was actively clinging to the promise that as I obeyed, God would provide this for me as well.

Then it happened: Michael was temporarily laid off, labeled as a non-essential worker as the first wave of global shutdowns began. Michael came to me with an opportunity to transition to prison dentistry that would involve a move to Tri-Cities, a desert region of eastern Washington.

The very next morning my heart almost stopped when I got to Deuteronomy 4:41-43 in my through-the-Bible reading. Moses set apart cities of refuge, three cities eastward toward the sunrise where criminals could flee and live in safety. I knew immediately that God was confirming His plans for our family. City of Refuge was a word God had given me for our family to be for orphans and vulnerable families. Three cities was just like the Tri-cities area we were considering moving to. Criminals were significant for Michael's job offer at the prison and ministry opportunity to those who need to overcome the consequences of bad decisions. Eastward signified a literal move east for us.

One clear word from the Lord and a move that I would otherwise dread, became exciting. Despite the sadness of moving away from family and the challenges of moving during the first outbreak of COVID, I was filled with faith, confident that I had heard the voice of God.

Our realtor warned us that selling a house in the middle of a global pandemic would be challenging if not impossible. But with God the opposite was true! We had three offers over our asking price within twenty-four hours of our house going on the market. God cleared the way for us to follow Him. It was hard to leave our friends and family, but we trusted the voice of our Shepherd.

The home we ended up purchasing was surrounded by vineyards with breathtaking views of the sunrise from the front and sunset from the back. It became an oasis in the desert. God opened our spiritual eyes and moved us to a home on Clearview Lane. We will never be the same after the two years of spiritual wilderness training the Lord had planned for us there. For a season we felt isolated, unable to form a tight-knit community, but God soon brought us friends that became like family.

Together we helped plant a church that we had the privilege of hosting in our house for a season.

After two and a half years, God spoke to us that it was time to move back by family and He again prepared the way for Michael to transfer to a different prison. The place that without God we would never have wanted to move to, became hard to leave. That's the faithfulness of our God!

There is a common misconception that wilderness seasons involve distance from God and spiritual dryness. I have found them to be the opposite! Wilderness seasons are meant to bring us closer to God through consecration and separation from everything else.

Wilderness times have become my very favorite. In Matthew 4, the Spirit led Jesus into the wilderness to be alone with the Father. During this time Satan came and tempted him. After He resisted three times, angels came to minister to Him and He left the wilderness closer to God and filled with His power. If we desire the intimacy with the Father and authority Jesus had, we need to fully embrace our wilderness seasons. Intimacy with the Lord is worth every test, every challenge and everything we leave behind to follow Him.

In seasons of wilderness, God sometimes hides us for our protection. If we are not aware of the sovereign hand of God on us, we can be deceived into thinking we are being overlooked. The desire to be seen and known was given to us by God and has to be fully fulfilled through intimacy with Him before we can experience being seen and known in a healthy community. Hiddenness can look like isolation, but it is very different. Isolation is something we do in our false identity that disconnects us from God and others. Hiddenness is something God allows in certain seasons to grow our connection to God, which in time strengthens our connection to community.

During one season of wilderness training I remember feeling like people were not sure if they could trust me, and the things I would share fell flat, lacking any weighty anointing. The exact same words would come out of someone else's mouth and be powerfully received, but out of my mouth words were questioned and disregarded. When God revealed to me that this was for my protection, I felt so much relief. He told me He was keeping me all to Himself in this season and hiding my anointing from others.

God does not leave us in the wilderness forever, but we can prolong our wanderings when we try to get out of our season prematurely. When we feel overlooked, we will be tempted to self-promote. The test is in our willingness to trust God to write our story. Christine Caine says, "God does not need to discover you, not when He has created you. You and I need to be developed, conformed and transformed into the image of Jesus Christ. That is what happens in the darkroom. God takes us into anonymity and obscurity. He takes us into the darkroom of life to forage His image on the inside of us."

In a time where it is so easy to put the spotlight on ourselves, the test is to wait for God to put his light on us. In a time where we can open our own doors, the test is to wait to walk through doors that only God can open for us and no man can shut. In a time where we can easily build our own platforms to share our message, the test is to wait for God to lay a foundation for us to stand on and implant His message on the inside of us. The result is the same if you take a caterpillar out of a cocoon or a photo out of a darkroom prematurely: destruction of the intended image.

When the time is right, the promise that seems delayed will suddenly happen, and we will cross over into our promise. Crossover seasons come with their own challenges. Seasons of transitions can be the hardest to be present in. It is easy to let our thoughts wander into the future and our desire to feel settled can tempt us to run ahead of the Lord's leading. Scripture says, "Those who wait on the Lord will renew their strength." To experience the renewed strength of the Lord promised in Isaiah 40:31, we first have to experience the weariness and fatigue of waiting on the promise.

Eventually every waiting period turns into a "suddenly" season. The word 'kairos' in the Greek that we looked at previously means, "the right season, a suddenly moment, and miraculous movement."[62] Kairos moments are characterized by things that, all of a sudden, happen quickly after being long awaited. The same seemingly contradictory language is used by the prophet Habakkuk:

> *"For the vision is yet for the appointed [future] time. It hurries toward the goal [of fulfillment]; it will not fail. Even though it delays, wait [patiently] for it, Because it will certainly come; it will not delay." (Habakkuk 2:3 AMP)*

---

62. Hamon, *Discernment: The Essential Guide to Hearing the Voice of God.*

Even though it delays, it will not delay. Confusing, right? But when applied to the different phases of transition, it perfectly describes how God moves in our lives. We experienced a kairos moment when God moved us to the Tri-Cities and another one two and a half years later when He moved us out of our wilderness season to be planted back by family.

Activating Assignments

God wants to give us more than direction for our lives. He wants to activate revelation within us. Sometimes God will answer our request for quick direction, but without revelation and wisdom our obedience to that direction is very hard. When we ask Him for revelation, the direction of the Lord comes as a package deal. When we seek to know who God is and who we are in His reflection, our true identity will lead us into our assignments.

No one likes to be at the wrong place at the wrong time, but that is how the majority of Christians live when they do not spiritually discern when God has a kingdom assignment for them.

God's assignments are always more than we are capable of accomplishing on our own. They often will seem unrealistic and even foolish. Faith is the activator of our assignments while apathy is the killer of our assignments. Apathy is the plan of the enemy to keep us inactive and shut us down as a result of overwhelm, insecurity, rejection, and fear. Apathy is surrender without faith.

Activating our assignments requires equal parts of surrender and faith. If there was no gap between what we have capacity and gifting for, and what God is asking us to do, we would not need God. Assignments that are from God always require dependency on Him. You've probably heard it said: faith is spelled R-I-S-K.

The irony of FOMO (fear of missing out) is that fear – of anything other than God – is what causes us to miss out.

When God asks us to do things that are hard, our first reach for comfort is often understanding. "Why?" is a question that quickly rolls off our lips. Yet throughout scripture we are commanded to lean not on our own understanding. Understanding can be a counterfeit comfort. We do not have to understand to obey. It is revelation that sustains our obedience. Where understanding seeks to know God's method and specific plan, revelation relies on the character of God, the principles of God and the processes of God and produces a deep trust despite lacking understanding.

Sarah Glassett, someone who experienced unimaginable childhood trauma, says when she began to heal, God told her, "Don't ask me why, ask me who I am." This is the difference between understanding and revelation.

Assignments are invitations from God that keep us on our path of purpose. God has invitations in the mail for us everyday. Not checking the mail is the same as not coming to the Lord in prayer and asking Him what He wants us to know and do each day. We come to the Lord full of expectation that He is a good Father who has good things for us (Matthew 7:11)! As a reminder of what these invitations consist of, let's use an acronym for mail.

M- Mindsets & thoughts
A- Assignments & projects
I- Innovation & strategy
L- Leading & impulses

If we do not open and accept His invitations, we will not be at the right place at the right time to experience the miracles He has already prepared for us. Likewise, if we accept an invitation that may appear good but is not from God, we will also end up at the wrong place at the wrong time. The reality is the Lord is not the only one sending us mail; Satan sends us daily invitations as well. The enemy offers us counterfeit mindsets, assignments, innovation and leadings to distract us from God appointed assignments.

The irony of FOMO (fear of missing out) is that fear – of anything other than God – is what causes us to miss out. We only miss out when we do things God did not invite us to or do not do things He has invited us to. It is sobering to consider the invitations we did not accept simply because we did not come to the Lord humbly in prayer or we let fear talk us out of action. To remain on track with our destiny, the fear of the Lord must become our one driving fear.

"Fear God and keep His commandments, For this is man's all." (Ecclesiastes 12:13)

As with all spiritual activation, activating our assignments requires us to connect to the voice of God. When I sense the change of a spiritual season I like to ask God, what would you like me to leave behind in this last season? He answers me with assignments that are out of season or offenses and attitudes that are not serving me well. One of the most powerful questions we must ask God regularly is, "What have I said yes to that you have not asked me to do?"

When we are committed to serving God, Satan's best tactic is no longer to tempt us with overtly bad things. He is much craftier than that. The enemy diverts sincere followers of Jesus with good things. Remember, we are not driven by need, we are driven by assignment. It is impossible to tell the difference between a good thing and a God thing without listening to the voice of God.

After I let go of any assignments that are out of season, I ask the Lord, "What do you have for me in this season?" He prompts me with new things to say yes to or a redirection of my priorities. Mel Robbins teaches a science backed theory called the 5-second rule. She says, "If you have an impulse to act on a goal, you must physically move within 5 seconds or the brain will kill the idea." We want to be those who are impulsed by the leadings of the Holy Spirit and respond with immediate obedience.

When God gives me a new assignment, my follow up question is always, "When, Lord?" My first action step is to find time on my calendar to act on this assignment. Our capacity grows as our tree matures. With this expanded capacity can come full lives with full calendars.

On each of our personal branches we have evergreen leaves of prayer. It is prayer that positions us for our purpose. We do not serve a transactional God, and I do not like checking boxes in my prayer life. However, the vision God has given us for our life must be brought before God daily in prayer. Each day my prayers look different, but there is a Spirit inspired rhythm to them. In prayer I often ask the Lord two questions for each of my branches.

1. What do you want me to know about this branch today?
2. What do you want me to do? Or, what leaves do you have for me on this branch today?

The encounter section of the Field Notes at the end of this chapter provides a guided prayer rhythm that can change your life. Prayerlessness is pride. To think we can do anything without utter dependence on God is foolish. Having rhythms of prayer in our lives is one of the most important assignments we have been given.

As I pray for my family branch the Lord might tell me to call a family member or friend to which I will respond, "Yes Lord, when?" as He gives me specific practical insight at that moment I must commit to obeying Him. Checking in with the Lord in prayer protects me from guilt for all the things I have not been assigned to do that day. This practice gives me insight not just on what I have grace to do each day, but what I do not have grace to do. This has brought me much freedom! My outer branches usually have less leaves on them and many days the only assignment I nourish on those branches is the evergreen leaf of prayer. When the season is right, our prayers are alway led by the Spirit into action.

> *It is impossible to tell the difference between a good thing and a God thing without listening to the voice of God.*

Very few assignments require one action step; most require recurring action. This is where we must tap into the rhythm of the Spirit. Jefferson Bethke says the main difference between chaos and shalom is rhythm. He writes about the importance of setting cadence in his book *To Hell with the Hustle*. Jonathan says that growth only happens when we are intentional to let what we believe change our daily habits and rituals.

After years of unraveling religious strongholds in my life, I have discovered that the difference between religious rituals and holy habits comes down to what our hearts value. If we say that we believe something but we do not attach an action to our belief, we do not truly value it. If I believe something to be true but I do not act on that belief, I am a hypocrite. If I act on a wrong belief, I am also participating in a religious mixture.

What we value is one part what we believe and one part how we act. In the same way that faith without works is dead (James 2:26), what we value is evidenced by our actions. I can say I believe that Christians should be compassionate and loving towards people. If I say this, but I do not act out in love and compassion towards people, I do not actually value love and compassion.

An unactivated belief benefits no one. Belief without action is religion. Action with false belief is also religion, and it often takes the form of self-righteousness. Walking in the Spirit requires action connected to truth. Our action, or lack thereof, reveals what we actually believe. If someone holds the false belief that God is a God of judgment, they may take extremely hurtful action like standing outside an abortion clinic with a sign that says, "Murderers go to hell." By their false beliefs, they justify hateful actions that are anti-gospel. The spirit of religion makes it impossible to share the compassion, forgiveness and love of Jesus with others.

If you have journeyed along this far, I assume you do not hold extreme anti-gospel beliefs like the example I just shared, but we all have false beliefs that we will have to confront for the rest of our lives. To walk in the Spirit, we must examine our beliefs and motives and take action that aligns with truth. Allow me to give you a more applicable example.

Adaline tries hard to wake up at 6am every morning to pray. One day she sleeps through her alarm and misses her prayer time. All day long she feels like a failure. She tries to pray throughout the day, but she is easily distracted. Her day goes horribly and she blames herself. She determines that tomorrow she will wake up at 5am and try harder to be better. Her *false* beliefs are: God cannot do His part if I do not do mine. God helps those who help themselves. I brought this bad day upon myself. I set myself up for a spiritual attack because I did not pray this morning. I deserve this bad day because I am not doing enough for God. Her actions from these false beliefs result in more religious striving, exhaustion and burnout.

Margaret, meanwhile, wakes up at 6am almost every day and goes straight to her prayer closet to spend time with the Lord. Each morning she is tempted to hit snooze and go back to sleep, but she wakes up because she knows she is desperate for Jesus. She starts her prayers, "Jesus, I need you today! I love you!" One morning she forgets to set her alarm. She wakes up and thanks the Lord, *"Thank you God for the extra sleep this morning. Lord, I need you today. Thank you that you are going to encounter me as I go throughout my day."* Her *true* beliefs are: God wants time with me even more than I want time with Him. He is not mad at me. His presence goes with me today and His undeserved grace and goodness chases after me. The result is that Margaret prays all day and walks in the Spirit. The next morning she wakes up even earlier than usual because she cannot wait to have time set aside alone in the presence of God and give her full attention to the one she loves.

Both Margaret and Adaline pray, but they have different motivating beliefs. Adaline's actions were self dependence, striving and performance built out of wrong beliefs while Margaret's were actions of love and surrender built on true beliefs. Adaline is motivated by a spirit of religion and pride. Margaret is impulsed by love and compelled to walk humbly.

Adaline has religious duties built into her day. Margaret has righteous rhythms. Adaline is subjecting herself to the law and coming back under a yoke of slavery. Margaret is guided and led by the Spirit.

Adaline's motivating false belief: "I *should* wake up every morning to pray." The action: she will be consistent for a short time and then give up altogether. The result: guilt, shame and condemnation.

Margaret's motivating true belief: "I *get to* wake up every morning and pray!" The action: consistent pursuit of Jesus. The result: empowered by love to produce the fruit of the Spirit.

Love does not say, "I *should*;" love says "*I get to.*" Condemnation is almost always hiding behind the term, *"I should."* When we connect to the narrative of love, we will *want* to give our time freely to the assignments God has given us rather than feeling like we *have* to. Remember, lovers always outwork doers. Our faith has to be cultivated and activated for our tree to sprout leaves of good works that God desires for us.

One New Year's Eve, I sat with the Lord going over my goals one final time before the new year when I heard Him clearly say, "I don't want you to have *to-do* goals this year; I want you to have *to-be* goals." God reminded me that since our being informs our doing, focusing on our being changes the practices and actions of our life.

Recently I have been focusing on introducing, or reinforcing, the practice of one personal and one family habit a month. Rather than starting a new year with an unrealistic amount of change, I will focus on one habit at a time. Some of the family rituals we are currently practicing are rehearsing memory verses on the way to school, afternoon tea time, and bedtime blessings. Personally, I have been practicing making sourdough bread weekly, going on daily prayer walks and lifting weights in the morning. Science has proven it takes a minimum of twenty-one days to create a habit. It has been said that people greatly overestimate what they can do in a day and underestimate what they can do in a year.

Now, rather than setting *doing* goals, I have *being* goals that I attach to a practical habit. If a habit is connected to who we are, it becomes a part of us. All our responses, good and bad, that feel automatic are connected to a habit. A goal is simply an idea unless it is attached to a repetitive practice with the potential to produce the desired growth. If I desire to grow my connection in my marriage, I must submit to the Lord's leading with habitual practice that yields connection such as morning prayer together, weekly date nights, or evening walks. These rhythms flow from our true identity and connection to the Spirit.

God has called my husband and I to be "intertwined oaks of righteousness" and says we are ten times more fruitful together than we are apart (Deuteronomy 32:20). If I believe this to be true, I will have rhythms in my life that flow from this true identity.

> "But I say, walk habitually in the [Holy] Spirit [seek Him and be responsive to His guidance], and then you will certainly not carry out the desire of the sinful nature [which responds impulsively without regard for God and His precepts]." (Galatians 5:16 AMP)

We are instructed to walk habitually in the cadence of the Spirit. God desires to give us a rhythm to our life and meaningful connective practices. We can be free of the balancing act of life when we realize life with the Spirit is a beautiful dance! He sets the pace of grace, and we remain responsive to His lead. Seasons come with different tempos, and as we lock eyes with Jesus, we step in time, side by side dancing on the timeline of our destiny.

We do not seek our assignment, we seek the Lord. Michael Kulianos says, "The great achievement of the Christian experience is finding constant communion with the Lord. The person who finds constant communion, God will absolutely work through." When we cling to Jesus, He takes us right where He wants us when He wants us there.

SPROUT FIELD NOTES
Identify when your assignments are in and out of season

Find a quiet place and start by breathing in God's love for four seconds. Hold that breath for four seconds, imagining His presence filling you up like a balloon. Now, for four seconds breathe out whatever negative emotion is weighing you down. Repeat this exercise until you feel settled and present. Ask the Holy Spirit the following questions. Then journal the free flow of thoughts that come to your mind as you fix your eyes on Jesus.

Questions:

Holy Spirit, when do I feel the most energized? What tasks and activities fuel me?

_____
_____
_____

When I was a child what was my dream? What would I do if I had no fear?

_____
_____
_____

When have I put a dream on hold? What is one assignment that has been dormant?

When was I marked with a life message? What would I share if I could only preach one message for the rest of my life?

When you created me, what problems did you destine me to solve? What problems am I currently noticing the most in my family, church and community?

When do I feel the most valued? What do I value most?

When I am in my true identity, how do I impact the world?

When have I overcome something that has given me a specific passion?

When in my day would you like me to introduce a righteous rhythm? What holy habit would you like me to practice this month?

_____

_____

_____

Use the above questions as clues and ask the Holy Spirit what your assignments are and when are they in and out of season? When is He asking you to act on kingdom assignments? List your assignments for each of your branches in two categories – In Season Leaves and Out of Season Leaves.

Activation:

Read the following poem popularized by Elisabeth Elliot. Ask the Holy Spirit when leaves are sprouting on each of your seven branches and what is the next thing He wants you to do to partner with Him. Do that thing in faith this week.

> From an old English parsonage down by the sea
> There came in the twilight a message to me;
> Its quaint Saxon legend, deeply engraven,
> Hath, it seems to me, teaching from Heaven.
> And on through the doors the quiet words ring
> Like a low inspiration: "DO THE NEXT THING."
>
> Many a questioning, many a fear,
> Many a doubt, hath its quieting here.
> Moment by moment, let down from Heaven,
> Time, opportunity, and guidance are given.
> Fear not tomorrows, child of the King,
> Trust them with Jesus, *do the next thing*
>
> Do it immediately, do it with prayer;
> Do it reliantly, casting all care;
> Do it with reverence, tracing His hand
> Who placed it before thee with earnest command.
> Stayed on Omnipotence, safe 'neath His wing,
> Leave all results, *do the next thing.*

Looking for Jesus, ever serener,
Working or suffering, be thy demeanor;
In His dear presence, the rest of His calm,
The light of His countenance be thy psalm,
Strong in His faithfulness, praise and sing.
Then, as He beckons thee, *do the next thing*.

Encounter:

Start by thanking God for the seed of the Spirit on the inside of you and praise God for who He is. "Thank you Lord that you are the King of Kings and Lord of Lords and you reign above it all! Jesus you are worthy to be praised! You are glorious! You are faithful and kind! You are Alpha and Omega! You are wonderful!" and so on. Enter His gates with thanksgiving and enter His courts with praise (Psalm 100:4).

Whenever you feel it's right, move onto praying for your identity roots as you envision them growing from the seed of the Spirit. "Jesus, how I need you! I don't want to do anything without you. Thank you God that you have made me a new creation in Christ Jesus! I am so grateful for your spirit alive inside of me, and I call my true identity and spirit to the front to lead today. Who do you say that I am? I receive the names you call me (say them back to him imagining your roots being strengthened)."

"Holy Spirit, are there any weeds growing in my soil that you would like to uproot?" Wait in His presence until He speaks. He may show you a picture, bring a verse to your mind or speak directly to your heart. Respond with repentance. This can sound like, "God forgive me for holding onto this offense. I surrender it at the foot of the cross" or "Lord, I break agreement with this lie (I confess the lie He revealed that I am believing) and choose to believe your truth (Repeat whatever true statement He speaks back to you).

Now surrender to the sap of the Spirit and invite the love of Jesus from your roots to your branches. Abide in His love and begin to pray over each branch. Ask God, "What do you want me to know and what do you want me to do in relation to this branch today?" Write down what He speaks. If He gives you an assignment, ask Him when He would like you to do it and commit to obeying Him. Speak life and bless each branch.

Lift your arms to Heaven and praise the Lord for providing all you need today according to the riches in Christ Jesus. Remain in a posture of praise as you move on with your day.

Recommended Resource:

Learn about Mountain Gateway Wilderness Intensives & Mission Training at Mountaingateway.org.

BLOSSOM X

Fig 25
developing blossoms

Fig 26
blossoming branch

Figure 25: Developing Blossoms of Giftings
Figure 26: Blossoming Branch of Activated Giftings

BLOSSOM

Chapter Ten

What gifts has God given you to blossom?
Identifying your unique giftings

Natural Blossoms

On each healthy branch are blossoms that represent our unique giftings and ways we express the love of Jesus to the world. In this chapter, we will journey together to identify our spiritual and natural giftings so we can blossom in the beauty of the Lord. When we live loved, our trees blossom with love for others. This love is given away through our giftings, talents and service.

What has God put inside your DNA to give to the world? What ways do you like to serve people? Each of us has a unique set of giftings and personality. These gifts are not meant to be buried in false humility, but discovered and stewarded.

In the parable of the talents (Matthew 25:14-30), Jesus teaches that we will give an account for how we stewarded the talents God entrusted to us. He instructs us to increase and multiply our talents. This is one of the ways we occupy the space we were created to fill by bringing the kingdom of God to the earth. The man in the story who buried his talent in the ground is dealt very harshly with. The little he had is taken away and given to someone who knew how to invest it and multiply their talents. Gifts are meant to be given away!

Our gifts, talents and strengths must be discovered. If you never look for your talents to begin with, you can guarantee they will remain buried. There are many personality tests out there that promise to help guide us on a journey of self-discovery. But who better to teach us about ourselves than our Creator? The only type of self-discovery I am interested in is the type done in partnership with the Holy Spirit. The Field Note section at the end of each chapter was designed with this purpose.

To discover our gifts and talents, we cannot be afraid to try new things that we are not any good at in the beginning. We will either improve and develop a new skill or we will learn an area we are not gifted in, which redirects us to other areas. Both are super valuable! The word for wisdom in Hebrew is often translated as "skilled." Wisdom and skill have to be intentionally developed. Like any good Father, the Lord does not just desire to help us gain practical understanding, He wants to help us develop new skills by doing things we enjoy with us. I hope to be learning and practicing new skills until the day I die.

Personality can relate to gifting, but I believe it is often over-emphasized. We must be cautious that we do not allow personality tests to lead to self-obsession, the confining of oneself, the premature labeling of others or the excusing of sin on this journey of self-discovery. To develop self-awareness, I recommend a tool called Strengthsfinder that the Holy Spirit has used to reveal unique things about myself that I did not know were unique. Often, when we are gifted in an area, we make the wrong assumption that what comes naturally to us comes naturally to everyone.

Behind our character flaws are often underdeveloped talents. In our home we call these "gifts gone awry." We love people well when we learn to identify the gift behind the struggle.

For example, a focus gift gone awry can look like a person who is uninterruptible and ignores people while they are working on something. A gift of discernment gone awry can quickly turn into judgment. A gifted communicator can struggle with listening to others when their gift goes awry. A gift of adaptability can turn into a lack of structure and discipline when gone awry.

When it comes to the talents and gifts inside of us, we want to invest well. Understanding our weaknesses is as important as knowing our strengths. Accepting our weaknesses frees us to be bad at some things.

We could spend our life getting marginally better at a skill we are not naturally skilled in, or we can invest in areas of natural gifting and reap a much greater harvest.

When I was in elementary school, my grandmother gifted me with piano lessons. It became obvious pretty quickly that I did not have a hidden musical talent. The amount of effort required for me to learn basic chords was exhausting. My older sister, on the other hand, took to the piano like a natural. It comforts me to remember that Billy Graham was not invited to preach at crusades of thousands of people around the world because of his singing voice. We do not have to have a collection of varied skills to be impactful.

My laundry room testifies to my lack of attention to detail and consistency. The wrinkles in my clothes and piles on the floor of my laundry room are evidence of my weakness. Accepting my weakness does not mean I stop doing laundry for my family, but it could mean that I lower the standards for myself and stop being hard on myself for not having perfectly folded clothes. Accepting my weakness could also look like recruiting my husband's help or hiring someone to help with the laundry so I can focus my time and attention elsewhere. Doing just that has freed up hours a week for me to write this book you are now reading. Writing, like most gifts, requires time to develop.

Another weakness of mine is focus and finishing. While my husband has a one-track mind, my mind is a multi-lane race track. If it were a computer browser it would be one with one hundred tabs open at once. We often refer to my brain as spaghetti with every thought connected and his as a waffle with separate compartments for everything. I am a natural starter, but my lacking focus can prevent me from finishing well. Even now, I am sure I have unintentionally set booby traps all over our house; jars with lids not screwed on properly and milk caps half on just waiting to spill on the next user. It has become a joke in our home that my husband has to follow me around closing doors, turning off lights, and properly putting lids on items. I struggle to finish even simple tasks because of my haste to move to the next thing.

Most often, I would rather write a completely new business plan and begin implementing it than finish a project that requires prolonged focus. Acknowledging the strengths of being a visionary with a strategic gift means that I look for opportunities to help people with planning and vision casting. I now know that spending time dreaming with the Lord and writing out ideas and visions fuels me.

Recognizing my weakness in focusing and finishing means I do my best to eliminate distractions and start my day with the tasks that require the most focus. The things that do not come naturally to us make us more dependent on God. There are times when the Lord leads me to hand off projects to someone else after the initial development stage. "Quitter," the enemy repeats to me in accusation. "Faithful," God lovingly whispers in reassurance. Serving in the first phase of projects can be a strategic use of my natural gifting when I am being led by the Spirit. Other times, I will have to trust God for the grace to complete a project from start to finish knowing that in my weakness He is strong.

Understanding our strengths can help us find the right job or volunteer position, but we must remember that none of us are above serving in small mundane tasks. If we want to flow in the anointing of the Lord, we must be willing to become a servant to the world and model our life after Jesus.

> *"Even as the Son of Man came not to be served but to serve, and to give his life as a ransom for many." (Matthew 20:28 ESV)*

Spiritual Blossoms

As well as natural giftings, the Lord gives us spiritual gifts as an expression of the Holy Spirit's working on the inside of us. In 1 Corinthians 12:1-11, Paul gives us a list of manifestation gifts that includes word of wisdom, word of knowledge, faith, healing, miracles, prophecy, distinguishing of spirits, speaking and interpreting tongues. These gifts are available to us in moments of ministry where faith is expressed. Paul says that all of these gifts are the working of the same Spirit. Anyone filled with the Holy Spirit can experience these manifestation gifts. While the passage makes it clear that these gifts are not given all at once, at different times we can experience every one of the gifts listed in this passage.

> *"There are different kinds of gifts, but the same Spirit distributes them. There are different kinds of service, but the same Lord. There are different kinds of working, but in all of them and in everyone it is the same God at work. Now to each one the manifestation of the*

Spirit is given for the common good. To one there is given through the Spirit a message of wisdom, to another a message of knowledge by means of the same Spirit, to another faith by the same Spirit, to another gifts of healing by that one Spirit, to another miraculous powers, to another prophecy, to another distinguishing between spirits, to another speaking in different kinds of tongues, and to still another the interpretation of tongues. All these are the work of one and the same Spirit, and he distributes them to each one, just as he determines." (1 Corinthians 12:1- 11 NIV)

Remember the awkward moment I shared at the beginning of this book where the Holy Spirit asked me to say the word "cabbage" to a stranger? That is an example of a word of knowledge. I could not have known except by the Spirit that the word "cabbage" would be significant to my massage therapist. After that word of knowledge was released, I was given the gift to prophecy to speak words of edification and encouragement into her life. By the Spirit, I was even able to give her words of wisdom for motherhood. All three of these gifts of the Spirit were made available to me in a spa lobby in the span of five minutes.

Until I stepped out in service of the Lord, I never experienced Him working through the gifts of the Spirit. Paul tells us that there are different kinds of working and service but the same Lord. The first time I took someone through deliverance was also the first time I was able to distinguish between spirits at work in someone's life. Now, every time I pray for someone to be delivered, God faithfully gives me the same gift of distinguishing spirits to see that person set free. This is how faith works. The manifest gifts of the Spirit are available when we are compelled by compassion to minister to someone.

If you want to experience supernatural healing, step out in faith, lay hands on people and pray for them to be healed in Jesus' name! Rest assured you can pray in authority knowing you are praying according to the will of God. While healing may not manifest immediately, we can with child-like faith believe every time that it will because healing is at the heart of the Father.

We can only be faithful to do the works of God when we surrender the outcome to Him. They are His works; we are just His hands and feet. Whether we see an immediate miracle or a miracle seed is planted that will grow, we can be confident in the power of God working through us even when we do not see it. Healing will manifest immediately or a healing process will be activated. Either way, healing is imparted when we pray a prayer of faith as James 5:15 promises, "the prayer of faith will save the sick." Laying hands on the sick and seeing them recover is one of the miraculous signs that Jesus says will *follow* those who believe. As those who carry the authority of Christ, we do not chase miracles, they follow us!

> *"And these signs will follow those who believe: In My name they will cast out demons; they will speak with new tongues; they will take up serpents; and if they drink anything deadly, it will by no means hurt them; they will lay hands on the sick, and they will recover." (Mark 16:17-18)*

The blossoming of spiritual gifts was not a part of the first twenty-five years of my Christian life. I grew up in a church born out of the Jesus Movement, a powerful outpouring of the Holy Spirit. Sadly, over time spiritual gifts became no longer welcome out of the gift box. I went my entire childhood never knowing my parents prayed in tongues, because after a couple negative experiences with manifestations of the Spirit, it was no longer encouraged by our church. We studied Bible prophecy, but I never witnessed or experienced the gift of prophecy that God gave to the Church for our encouragement and edification.

I was twenty-eight when I received my first prophetic word. I had driven an hour to go to a small gathering of women I had never met simply because I sensed Jesus leading me there. During worship a woman came up to me and asked if I was married. I said yes and recognized her courage in approaching me, a stranger, with a word for my husband. I looked down and realized I was not wearing my wedding ring. She told me that God showed her a picture of how my husband was spiritually blind, but He was going to open his eyes just as He had opened mine. When that word was released over me the Spirit of God fell on me, and I wept for what felt like hours in His sweet presence.

I was baffled that God would speak through a total stranger to confirm the exact same things He had spoken to my heart in the secret place. This is an example of a word of knowledge and prophecy, gifts that when used properly make us feel seen, known and loved by our Father.

For the next few months, my faith to believe the word God spoke to me was tested. My husband believed I was deceived and following false teaching. After I found The Collective Church, he accused me of attending a cult. If he caught me listening to spirit-filled worship music or praying in tongues, he would mock me. To say the tension was thick in our home was an understatement, but I held onto this prophetic word. God did what He promised and opened my husband's spiritual eyes! Now he operates beautifully in the gifts of the Spirit.

Like salvation, spiritual gifts cannot be earned but are freely given. God does not take back the gifts and calling He gives us. Romans 11:29 says, "The gifts and the calling of God are without repentance" (ESV). If there is a spiritual gift you are struggling to receive, I encourage you to come like a child to your loving Father. God wants to give us good gifts even more than we want to receive them. We cannot act like an orphaned child; we simply come full of faith!

There are some things like the spirit of intercession and spirit of prophecy that are caught more than they are taught. This type of cross-pollination happens by intentional proximity with others who have fruit we desire for our own lives.

Ephesians 4 is another passage that emphasizes the unity of the church and the individuality of each member. When speaking of the distribution of gifts, the same language is used in Ephesians and Corinthians. 1 Corinthians 12:7 says, "To each is given the manifestation of the Spirit for the common good" (ESV). Ephesians 4:7 says, "But grace was given to each one of us according to the measure of Christ's gift." Each gift is given by grace and often for a specific assignment, not by any qualification of the person.

> *"And He Himself gave some to be apostles, some prophets, some evangelists, and some pastors and teachers, for the equipping of the saints for the work of ministry, for the edifying of the body of Christ, till we all come to the unity of the faith and of the knowledge of the Son of God, to a perfect man, to the measure of the stature of the fullness of Christ; that we should no longer be children, tossed to and fro and carried about with every wind of doctrine, by the trickery of men, in the cunning craftiness of deceitful plotting, but, speaking the truth in love, may grow up in all things into Him who is the head—Christ—from whom the whole body, joined and*

knit together by what every joint supplies, according to the effective working by which every part does its share, causes growth of the body for the edifying of itself in love." (Ephesians 4:11 -16)

Some refer to the gifts listed here as ministry gifts because this passage outlines gifts given for the work of ministry. Many have interpreted these Scriptures as a list of leadership roles that come with qualifications like that of bishops, elders and deacons described in 1 Timothy 5. If this were the case, Paul would not have used the language "given to all" and would have spoken of specific qualifications like he did in 1 Timothy. Instead, based on the text, the logical conclusion is that the five fold ministry gifts listed in Ephesians 4 are for everyone in the Body of Christ, not just those in designated leadership positions. We are all called to be apostolic, prophetic, pastoral, evangelical, and to teach. In different seasons we may carry a stronger gifting in certain areas than in other seasons.

I learned this from Dr. Brian Davenport who also points out that Paul's lists are never exhaustive but are always exemplary. He does not list everything the Holy Spirit does, or every expression of God's character, or every gift given for ministry here in Ephesians 4. I have observed that the roles of teacher, pastor and evangelist are the most accepted in various church denominations and the roles of apostle and prophet are often not in operation.

In ministry, the gift of the prophet is given by God to energize the people of God and continually call them back to covenant relationship. The Greek word for prophet used in Ephesians 4:11 means a person gifted at expositing divine truth.[63] They often carry words of correction and conviction that protect us from becoming comfortable, stagnant Christians. In the Old Testament, prophets warned of God's judgment because they had not yet received the propitiation of sin through Jesus. They did not personally know God; they knew the law of God. Jesus says in Matthew 11:27, "no one truly knows the Father except the Son and those to whom the Son chooses to reveal him" (NLT). In the New Testament, prophets challenge all doctrine and actions that hinder love. The mes-

---

63. Strong's Greek: 4396. Προφήτης (Prophétes) -- a Prophet (an Interpreter or Forth-Teller of the Divine Will).

sage of the prophets of God are often rejected because the love of God offends those who do not yet know it.

An apostolic gift looks like being sent out to do the work of the ministry as well as sending others out to do the work of the ministry. Apostle means "sent one or messenger" that goes in the authority of another.[64] For example, if a church sends out a missionary under their authority and covering, that missionary is operating on assignment as an apostle. Those with the ministry gift of an apostle continually launch people and movements forward to advance the kingdom of God.

Gifts are meant to be unwrapped and enjoyed, not kept in a box. Unfortunately, we often quench the working of the Holy Spirit and operations of the gifts of the Spirit out of fear. Many are given the gift of the Holy Spirit and keep Him constrained in the gift box He was presented to them in. There is also the other extreme where gifts of the Spirit are emphasized over the Word of God. In 1 Corinthians 14, Paul gives clear instructions on the use of spiritual gifts in church and concludes by saying, "Let all things be done decently and in order."

While the manifestation gifts of the Spirit can be experienced by any believer, in Romans 12 Paul lists motivational gifts that are distributed among believers according to the grace given to us individually.

> **"We have different gifts, according to the grace given to each of us.** *If your gift is prophesying, then prophesy in accordance with your faith; if it is serving, then serve; if it is teaching, then teach; if it is to encourage, then give encouragement; if it is giving, then give generously; if it is to lead, do it diligently; if it is to show mercy, do it. Love must be sincere." (Romans 12: 6-9 NIV, bold mine.)*

Scripture is clear that we all should prophesy, serve, teach, encourage, give generously, lead and be merciful. Yet Paul makes a point to say each of us have different gifts in this passage because everyone of us has a primary motivational gift that affects our nature and personality.

Charles R Wade Jr teaches that each person has one of the seven

---

64. Strong's Greek: 652. Ἀπόστολος (Apostolos) -- a Messenger, One Sent on a Mission, an Apostle.

redemptive gifts listed in Romans 12. His book *Designed for Fulfillment: A Study of Redemptive Gifts* is a resource I recommend for further understanding of our unique gifts. My family and I had a good laugh when we first read his example of how someone with each of the different redemptive gifts would respond to a child spilling a glass of milk at the dinner table:

A person with the gift of prophecy would respond, *"That's what happens when you are not careful!"* The Prophet's motivation is to fix the problem by pointing out the "why."

A person with the gift of serving would respond, *"I'll clean it up!"* The Servant's motivation is to fulfill a practical need.

A person with the gift of teaching would respond, *"The reason the glass tipped over was that it was put in the wrong place!"* The Teacher's motivation is to explain what happened.

A person with the gift of exhorting would respond, *"Well, as they say, it's not worth crying over, so have I told you the one about the cow who…"* The Exhorter's motivation is to minimize the interruption and get back to the fun environment, being sensitive to the child's emotional state.

A person with the gift of giving would respond, *"No problem. It happens. Let's clean it up and keep going."* The Giver's motivation is to restore peace and move forward, to show the child how to handle it in the future.

A person with the gift of ruling (also translated leading) would respond, *"Jim, get a towel. Sue, pick up the glass. Mary, pour another glass of milk."* The Ruler's motivation is to respond to the problem to achieve the immediate goal of the group to have a nice time together.

A person with the gift of mercy would respond, *"Don't feel bad. It could happen to anyone. I spilled my milk once, too."* The Mercy's motivation is to relieve embarrassment and to empathize with the discomfort.[65]

Can you see how all of these responses have their place? Each of us have different motivations that stir us to action. Part of what makes our DNA seed unique is the redemptive or motivational gift of the Spirit each of us have been given.

Christians have many varying interpretations of scripture when it comes to the gifts of the Spirit. My goal is not that you would settle on

---

65. Wade Jr., *Designed for Fulfillment A Study of Redemptive Gifts*, 139.

the same interpretation as I have. It is my hope that you would take time to pray through these Scriptures and allow the Holy Spirit to speak to you personally.

Perhaps you have been hiding from the call of God and you have kept the gifts of the Spirit in a nicely packaged gift box. Gifts are never meant to be kept in a box. Today, the Holy Spirit is calling to you to notice the budding vines of new life that are now blooming all around you.

> *"Can you not discern this new day of destiny breaking forth around you? The early signs of my purposes and plans are bursting forth. The budding vines of new life are now blooming everywhere. The fragrance of their flowers whispers, "There is change in the air." Arise, my love, my beautiful companion, and run with me to the higher place. For now is the time to arise and come away with me."* (Song of Songs 2:13 TPT)

Influence in the kingdom of God comes as we blossom in the beauty of the Lord. It is important to remember that our effectiveness cannot be measured by societal metrics. Not all influence is from God, and influence is not an expression of God's approval. Just like in the parable of the talents, some are given more influence and some are given less. How we steward the influence we have been given can affect if we are trusted with more.

Success in the kingdom is never measured by influence; it is measured by fruit. God does not reward us for our significance; He rewards us for the fruit of our obedience. God does not need our influence; He is the one who draws all men to Himself (John 12:32). God will choose a yielded person over a gifted person any day. Christine Caine says, "If you are marked by God you do not need to be marketed by man."

Remember, we are just a seed. There will be a healthy measure of excitement and accomplishment we feel when we work with the Master Gardener and begin to flourish. We should feel honored to participate in God's magnificent creation. However, taking credit for the seed's ability to be transformed from a seed into beautiful blossoms would be ridiculous. When we flourish in the gifts and talents God has placed inside of us, the Lord is magnified. To Him alone belongs all glory!

"Now to him who is able to do immeasurably more than all we ask or imagine, according to his power that is at work within us, to him be glory in the church and in Christ Jesus throughout all generations, forever and ever! Amen." (Ephesians 3:20-21)

Before teaching on the gifts of the Spirit, the writer of Romans gives us a warning to not be self-important and arrogant about the gifts God has given us.

"Do not think of yourself more highly than you ought, but rather think of yourself with sober judgment, in accordance with the faith God has distributed to each of you. For just as each of us has one body with many members, and these members do not all have the same function, so in Christ we, though many, form one body, and each member belongs to all the others. (Romans 12:3-5)

There are far too many talented people in the Body of Christ today that use their gift to bring people to themselves, not to Jesus. This reality frightens me greatly. Our gift, our talents, our preaching, our worship leading; none of it can save people. Jesus alone saves. Crowns that are not immediately cast at the feet of Jesus will give us a big head. We can wear the weight of man's praise and our accomplishments on our head, or we can lay down our crowns and carry the weight of the anointing. This is our daily choice. Gifting will entertain crowds, but only anointing breaks through heaviness. (Isaiah 10:27).

There is a big difference between someone with a gift of communication and an anointed communicator. Someone with a gift of communication will say things that sound really good, but feel airy. The language used can be beautiful and articulate, but it does not produce change on the inside of the hearer. Someone that is an anointed communicator could use less articulate language, but there is a weightiness in the Spirit to their words.

The sign of an anointed communicator is that their words become a catalyst for change because they release the presence of the Lord. Giftings are freely given to us by God, but anointing is costly. God anoints us when we receive the Holy Spirit, but there is a continual price we must pay to walk in the anointing. Just as the Holy Spirit is freely given, but continual surrender is required to walk in the Spirit.

David was anointed to be king fifteen years before he was appointed king of Israel. For fifteen years, God trained David to walk in the anointing before he was given the authority to release that anointing as king. In the time between being anointed and appointed, David was taught how to walk in the anointing through many tests and trials. In a world full of gifted ministers, we must be able to discern the difference between the gifting, anointing and appointing of God.

Blossoming in Love

When love is not our primary motivation, we can unknowingly prostitute the anointing of God.[66] What is the difference between a lover and a prostitute? A lover invests time in the relationship, not to get something out of it but simply as a response to love. A prostitute treats intimacy like a transaction and only uses relationships to get what they want out of them. The gifts of God are to be desired but not pursued. We are only ever instructed to pursue love. When we pursue love, the desires of our heart that align with love are freely given to us (Psalm 37:4).

> *"Pursue love, and earnestly desire the spiritual gifts, especially that you may prophesy. For one who speaks in a tongue speaks not to men but to God; for no one understands him, but he utters mysteries in the Spirit. On the other hand, the one who prophesies speaks to people for their upbuilding and encouragement and consolation. The one who speaks in a tongue builds up himself, but the one who prophesies builds up the church. Now I want you all to speak in tongues, but even more to prophesy. The one who prophesies is greater than the one who speaks in tongues, unless someone interprets, so that the church may be built up." (1 Corinthians 14:1-5 ESV)*

If we have all the gifts in the world but we do not have love, we are nothing. Devastatingly, many pursue the gifts instead of the Gift-giver. The consequences of this are great. If we are to get one thing right on our spiritual growth journey, it is that God who is love must be our supreme pursuit.

---

66. Caine, "Anointing vs. Gifting."

"Though I speak with the tongues of men and of angels, but have not love, I have become sounding brass or a clanging cymbal. And though I have the gift of prophecy, and understand all mysteries and all knowledge, and though I have all faith, so that I could remove mountains, but have not love, I am nothing. And though I bestow all my goods to feed the poor, and though I give my body to be burned, but have not love, it profits me nothing." (1 Corinthians 13:1-3)

What is the standard by which we are taught to test the Gifts of the Spirit and the "good works" of other Believers? The standard is love.

"Love suffers long and is kind; love does not envy; love does not parade itself, is not puffed up; does not behave rudely, does not seek its own, is not provoked, thinks no evil; does not rejoice in iniquity, but rejoices in the truth; bears all things, believes all things, hopes all things, endures all things." (1 Corinthians 13:4-7)

Jesus served the world because He loved the world. Serving others is not the goal of the Chrisitan life; becoming love is. When the love of Christ is in us, it blossoms out of us in our service to others. The NLT translates 1 Corinthians 14:1 with the beautiful exhortation, "Let love be your highest goal!"

If you are eagerly desiring spiritual gifts, the best advice I can give you is to focus on the Gift-giver instead of the gift. If you want to prophesy, look to the greatest prophet, Jesus. If you want to pray in the Spirit, look to the Holy Spirit who reveals Himself to us through Jesus. If you want words of knowledge to unlock people you are ministering to, look to the one with all knowledge, Jesus. If you want to see the sick healed, look to the Great Physician, Jesus.

No bloom ever blossomed because it tried harder. Is there anyone more loving than a person in love?

No bloom ever blossomed because it tried harder. Is there anyone more loving than a person in love? Is there anything more beautiful than love? When we lack the desire to serve, the solution is not to try harder to love; the solution is to receive more of the love of God. Some of the definitions of the root word for "receive" in the Greek is to accept, to gain the knowledge of, and to give admittance to.[67] We receive love by getting ahold of what is already true: we are loved by God! Nothing we do will make Him love us more or less. When we accept and admit this truth, we open our hearts to living in the love of God.

One of my favorite prayers to pray is, *"God remove everything that is blocking me from receiving your love! Uproot anything that hinders love in my life. Keep me in your love today and forever."*

I do not pray that God will keep me in His love because I am at risk of losing it. No, the love of God is the most secure and powerful force in the universe! I come before God asking for His help to keep me in His love because I know how prone I am to wander away from His love. Though love remains, I distance myself from it. Falling for the enemy's deception will cause me to go looking for what I already have. My fears prove that love has not been perfected in me (1 John 4:18).

When we serve for love, rather than serve *from* love, our service becomes idolatry. Dan Moheler says, "We are called to love people, not expect of people."[68] If we need the love of others, we make their love into an idol. Our desperate need for love will either drive us into the arms of Love itself or will lead us to a counterfeit that will never satisfy. We can *want* others to love us, but when we have received the love of God, we no longer *need* others to love us.

It is because God so *loved* the world that He *gave* His son to the world to save us (John 3:16). Love must come before all of our giving and our serving. Everyone loves gifts, but our gifts are not what makes us lovable. While it is undeniable that certain talents are more captivating than others, they are equal in importance. All of our gifts come *from* God and are *for* God. The comparison of gifts can be a major temptation, and James pleads with us as the beloved of Christ to not be deceived.

> *"Do not be deceived, my beloved brethren. Every good gift and every perfect gift is from above, and comes down from the Father of lights, with whom there is no variation or shadow of turning. Of His own will He brought us forth by the word of truth, that we might be a kind of firstfruits of His creatures."* (James 1:16-18)

---

67. Topical Bible: Receive.
68. Moheler, "Becoming Love."

God has given each of us good gifts that when watered with His love, blossom with the fragrance of His love to the world. We blossom when we behold love, because what we behold, we become.

BLOSSOM FIELD NOTES

Identify what unique gifts you've been given

Find a quiet place and start by breathing in God's love for four seconds. Hold that breath for four seconds, imagining His presence filling you up like a balloon. Now, for four seconds breathe out whatever negative emotion is weighing you down. Repeat this exercise until you feel settled and present. Ask the Holy Spirit the following questions. Then journal the free flow of thoughts that come to your mind as you fix your eyes on Jesus.

Questions:

Holy Spirit, what passions and interests did you put inside my destiny seed?

_____
_____
_____

What are my talents and giftings?

_____
_____
_____

What are my strengths? (refer to StrengthFinder results)

_____
_____
_____

What way do I best express myself?

_____
_____
_____

What sparks the most joy for me?

_____
_____
_____

What comes naturally to me that may not come naturally to others?

_____
_____
_____

What is my motivational gift? (Refer to Romans 12)

_____
_____
_____

Activation:

Take the love language test with your spouse or a close friend 5lovelanguages.com/quizzes. Often the way we most like to receive love is how we give love. Practice speaking the other languages of love that do not come as naturally to you this week. Look for ways to love others the way they best receive love.

Encounter:

Imagine Jesus coming into the room where you are. His person exudes warmth and comfort. Do you feel any distance between you? If so, imagine a wall in the middle of you and Jesus. Are any words written on the wall? What is the wall called? Ask the Holy Spirit to give you a tool to take it down. Use the tool to demolish the wall. Where is Jesus? Invite him closer. If He is next to you, use your imagination to embrace him. If He is still standing at a distance, imagine there is a fence between you and him. Are there any words written on the fence? What is the fence called? Ask the Holy Spirit to give you a tool to take down the fence. Now, invite Jesus to the other side of the fence to start taking it down with you. Pay attention to how Jesus is engaging you. When the fence is gone you will be standing in front of Jesus. Look at His eyes of compassion and welcome His embrace. As He touches you, imagine your body filling from head to toe with the energizing and powerful agape love of God like warm sap running through your veins. What does the Voice of Love say to you? Ask him to keep you in His love today. When you are ready, go about your day imagining Jesus staying right beside you. Abide in His love, talk to him, listen and enjoy His presence. The moment you catch yourself disconnecting in distraction, turn your heart inwardly back towards the indwelling Christ in you and continue to walk in the Spirit.

Recommended Resources:

Take the StrengthsFinder test and learn about your unique strengths Gallup.com/cliftonstrengths.

Read Designed for Fulfillment; A Study of Redemptive Gifts by Charles R. Wade Jr.

PRUNE XI

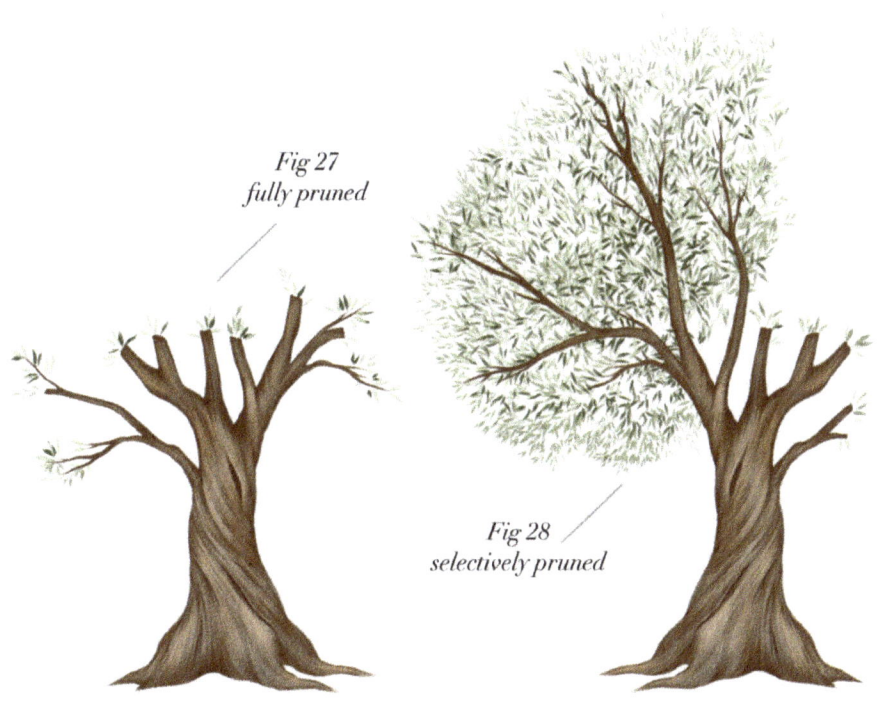

Figure 27: Fully Pruned Tree
Figure 28: Selectively Pruned Tree

PRUNE
Chapter Eleven

How do you develop and multiply?
Identifying your purpose in testing

> "I am the true vine, and my Father is the vinedresser. Every branch in me that does not bear fruit he takes away, and every branch that does bear fruit he prunes, that it may bear more fruit. Already you are clean because of the word that I have spoken to you. Abide in me, and I in you. As the branch cannot bear fruit by itself, unless it abides in the vine, neither can you, unless you abide in me. I am the vine; you are the branches. Whoever abides in me and I in him, he it is that bears much fruit, for apart from me you can do nothing." (John 15:1-5 ESV)

HERE'S THE HARD TRUTH: no eternal fruit can be produced from our tree without pruning. Pain is no one's preference, but it is a developer of character. For every promise God gives us He has planned a process of preparation for us. Prophetic words often initiate this process. Pruning is not a punishment; it is the protection of our loving Father.

We rejoice when God releases a word calling people to a worldwide ministry or an expansive kingdom business, but few feel the sobriety that comes when we actually count the cost of that call. We can grow envious of those whom God is using mightily to expand the kingdom if we do not acknowledge what they have had to endure to serve God in that way.

When we say yes to Jesus, we say yes to laying down our life and picking up our cross to follow him. Luke 12:4 says, "From everyone who has been given much, much will be demanded; and from the one who has been entrusted with much, much more will be asked" (NIV).

Ask yourself, if God fulfilled every one of the dreams in my heart immediately, would I have the quality of character to sustain me in these new positions and responsibilities? We want our dreams to be tried by fire so that we know we are pursuing God's dreams for us and not our dreams for ourselves. For this reason, I can rejoice as James instructs when I face hardship because I know that through fire gold is produced and every impure motive is burned away.

> *"Count it all joy, my brothers, when you meet trials of various kinds, for you know that the testing of your faith produces steadfastness. And let steadfastness have its full effect, that you may be perfect and complete, lacking in nothing." (James 1:2-4 ESV)*

Pruning puts pressure on unhealed places in our hearts. This can feel harsh if we do not remember that God always reveals to heal. When we feel exposed and uncovered in the pruning process, we can trust our Great Physician is performing careful surgery to heal our soul.

Surrendering to Pruning

We do not get strong without lifting weights. If we wish to build muscle, we must choose the larger weights and learn to endure as our muscles break down so they can be built back stronger. Mature, strong believers are eager to choose hard things because we know they result in our strengthening.

Choosing a hard workout, for example, does not just build physical muscle, it also builds the spiritual muscle of endurance. Choosing the longest line at the supermarket can help us resist our own hurry epidemic and strengthen our patience. Choosing to serve in the children's ministry at our church can grow our patience and endurance, a two for one bonus! In a society that loves to avoid discomfort and pain, we have to remind ourselves that God often prescribed pain for our benefit. When we surrender to the pain rather than resist it, we grow. Declare this with me, "I can do hard things!"

Are you surprised when hard things happen to you? Is there any entitlement hiding in your heart? Were you sold a false gospel that promises only prosperity, ease and comfort? These wrong theologies that hide within the Church must be confronted. God assures us we will suffer, but comforts us with the truth that He will always be with us.

> *"Beloved, do not be surprised at the fiery trial when it comes upon you to test you, as though something strange were happening to you. But rejoice insofar as you share Christ's sufferings, that you may also rejoice and be glad when his glory is revealed. If you are insulted for the name of Christ, you are blessed, because the Spirit of glory and of God rests upon you." (1 Peter 4:12-14 ESV)*

2 Corinthians 4:16 teaches that our inner man is renewed through daily adversity. One of the ways we can surrender to the pruning of the Lord is through fasting. Fasting is a supernatural tool to go on the offense against the enemy. Intentionally resisting food or other pleasures strengthens the muscle of self-control. When we actively deny our flesh, the voice of the enemy gets quieter and quieter, and the voice of God gets clearer and clearer.

Fasting was an integral part of the lifestyle of the early Church. Great breakthrough comes through fasting not because we earn it by participating in a religious act, but because God rewards us for seeking a closer relationship with Him. The Lord always responds to our hunger. When we hunger and thirst after righteousness we are promised a fresh filling (Matthew 5:6). Sometimes we have to fast to remind our body and our soul that Jesus is the bread of life, and we desire Him more than food.

When we fast we gain momentum in the Spirit, but things often feel as though they slow down in the natural realm. Fasting builds resilience which leads to resolution. Fasting helps us gain power over our flesh so we can walk in the Spirit.

Often we pray, "God empty me of my flesh and fill me with you!" This is a good desire, but emptying requires our participation beyond a prayer we utter. The physical emptying of our body from food correlates with a spiritual emptying of our flesh. God removes our sin, but He does not remove the temptations of our flesh. Instead, He commands us to rule over them. Those who live with a truly submitted heart before the Lord understand fasting as a way of life.

A fasted lifestyle is an outward expression of the heart cry, "Not my will, but yours be done!" My will never wants to fast, but when I submit my will to God He gives me His desires, that which are good for me and pleasing to Him. Fasting does not make God love us more, but it can remove the barriers in us that have kept us from fully receiving His love. Fasting tunes our ears to the frequency of heaven and often leads to divine downloads straight from the Spirit.

Fasting is humbling; it helps us acknowledge our need for God. It is meant to challenge us. When we fast our comforts, we train ourselves to rely only on God alone, our Great Comforter. Fasting requires faith. Every time we fast, the temptations of the enemy will show up in various ways. I am regularly tempted to try to work for my breakthrough rather than freely receiving it. When I fast I often hear chatter like, "You aren't praying enough during this fast," "You didn't pick a hard enough fast," or "You didn't fast long enough." These lies have to be silenced by faith. We simply ask God what to fast and trust Him with the duration and the outcome.

Revelation, breakthrough, heavenly blueprints, mental clarity, supernatural energy, and victory over the flesh are all natural benefits of fasting, but they are not why we fast. We fast because we love Jesus, and to love Him is to obey Him. Jesus said, "When you fast," not "If you fast," implying that fasting is part of following Him (Matthew 6:16). Fasting renews our connection to the Spirit whose primary role is to reveal Jesus to us. Fasting pours oil on the fire of our hearts and empowers us to burn with fiery love for Jesus. He is our great reward!

Pruning Tests

Of all the felt-board Bible stories etched in my memory from years of Sunday school, Joseph and his coat of many colors stands out to me the most because of his great perseverance in adversity. Joseph was sold into slavery by his brothers because of the favoritism his father, Jacob, showed him. From years in prison for false accusation to exaltation as the second in command in Egypt, this is an incredible trial to triumph story. Joseph saves Egypt from famine and is able to reconcile with his family who had betrayed him. He had a God-given dream, but did not fulfill his destiny until enduring thirteen years of testing. Psalm 105:19 says, "Until the time came to fulfill his dreams, the LORD tested Joseph's character" (NLT). Joseph went from humiliation and desolation to exaltation because of his faithful obedience.

The Lord guides us through various character building tests on our path to promise. God tests us not to see if we are good enough, but to see if we are going to rely on Him fully and surrender to the Spirit over our flesh. God is a good teacher. He does not test us beyond what He has prepared us for. He supplies supernatural empowerment for us to endure every test, but we have to receive it in faith. When we do not pass a test, God never fails us. Our gracious Lord gives us the opportunity to take these character tests over and over again until we pass.

It is important to distinguish between God's tests and the devil's temptations. James 1:13-15 addresses this directly saying, "And remember, when you are being tempted, do not say, "God is tempting me." To fall into temptation we have to disconnect from God and plug into a false outlet to meet our needs. God never tempts us with desires that disconnect us from Him. Temptation comes from our own desires, which entice us and drag us away. These desires give birth to sinful actions. And when sin is allowed to grow, it gives birth to death" (NLT).

Sometimes we are tempted by our own desires, and sometimes we are tempted by the devil himself just like he tempted Jesus in the wilderness (Matthew 4). God is sovereign even over the temptations of the enemy. 1 Corinthians 1:18 says, "The temptations in your life are no different from what others experience. And God is faithful. He will not allow the temptation to be more than you can stand. When you are tempted, he will show you a way out so that you can endure."

Another way we experience pruning is through persecution. The book of Acts teaches that the early Church grew exponentially under persecution. Christianity's influence also spread through their willingness to adopt. During the time of the early Church in Rome, babies were often abandoned on the temple steps, left to die in the elements. It was the Church who stepped up and took in these babies even when they did not have enough food to feed the children already in their homes. These acts of kindness and total surrender captured the attention of the Roman officials. Through much pressure and difficulty the Church remained fruitful. Because they were not afraid to die, the flame of the Spirit was unquenchable.[69]

All of us hope we would have the courage to die for Jesus if we faced

---

69. McLelland, *The Gospel on the Ground: The Grit and Glory of the Early Church in Acts.*

a moment of intense persecution. But how many of us have the courage to live for the Lord by dying daily to our own desires? One of the ways we are called to do this is by caring for the vulnerable in our own neighborhoods even when the work is costly and painful.

The early Church understood the cost of this call when James wrote one of my favorite verses in the Bible, "Pure and genuine religion in the sight of God the Father means caring for orphans and widows in their distress and refusing to let the world corrupt you" (James 1:27 NLT). One verse before, James calls out useless religion. The Greek word he uses is *thréskos* which means "careful observance of religious restrictions."[70] Verse twenty-seven contrasts useless religion by painting a picture of what pure religion looks like. The word translated "religion" in verse twenty-seven is the word *Thréskeia* in the Greek. The definition of this word changed my life. It means "worship as expressed in ritual acts."[71] Genuine religion is sacrificial worship. This pure worship is expressed through loving acts of service. Without radically loving sacrifice, religion is worthless. Pure worship requires our sacrifice but is never about us.

Throughout scripture the Church is called the pure bride of Christ (2 Corinthians 11:2). Caring for the vulnerable among us is not something we *should* do; it is *who we are*. More accurately, it is who we are becoming. I am convinced that the purification of the Church to prepare us for the return of Jesus is directly linked to our willingness to care for the vulnerable among us.

> *"Christ loved the church and gave himself up for her to make her holy, cleansing her by the washing with water through the word to present her to himself as a radiant church, without stain or wrinkle or any other blemish, but holy and blameless." (Ephesians 5:25-26 NIV)*

Like a priceless, one-of-a-kind, couture wedding gown, we are being made ready for our wedding day by the fiery love of the Father ironing out all of our wrinkles. The reality is God uses the heat of hardship to remove what is false about us. He restores us back to original intent, back to purity, to prepare us for the return of our Bridegroom.

---

70. Strong's Greek: 2357. Θρησκός (Thréskos of Unc. Or.) -- Religious.
71. Strong's Greek: 2356. Θρησκεία (Thréskeia) -- Religion.

Pruning Selfish Ambition

Jesus tells us in John 17:16 that we are not of this world. In a fast-moving culture obsessed with instant self-gratification, self-denial and endurance are greatly needed to live counter to culture.

One of the ways we can live counter to culture is by becoming the solution to injustices of our day and being *for* something rather than simply against every worldly agenda. Few things have made me more excited than when I first began to receive prophetic words about an adoption movement coming to America and that God had a role for me to play in it. The Lord connected me with other people who also carry this assignment, and I came fully alive in my calling. It felt like I was doing what I was made to do.

For one year, I had the opportunity to help build a nonprofit with the mission of equipping the Church to become the solution to the Vulnerable Child Crisis. The language for our vision and the strategies for this ministry were deposited in my spirit after long periods of seeking God for His blueprints for the Church. Our team worked hard to implement these strategies and build according to the will of God. From the outside, it looked as though I had surrendered completely to God's plan and ways. And the truth is I wanted to, but my desire to walk in full surrender was always at war with a hidden desire of my flesh to build out of my own ambition, opinions, and preferences.

> *The belief that all things are working together for good does not eliminate suffering.*

During this year, I learned a lot of things the hard way. One of those things was that God does not tolerate our ambition. He is not interested in our pride-filled opinions. He does not permit only a little bit of selflessness. Paul instructs us in Philippians 2 to abandon *every* display of selfishness. I love how The Passion Translation beautifully translates this passage.

> "Be free from pride-filled opinions, for they will only harm your cherished unity. Don't allow self-promotion to hide in your hearts, but in authentic humility put others first and view others as more important than yourselves. Abandon every display of selfishness. Possess a greater concern for what matters to others instead of your own interests. And consider the example that Jesus, the Anointed

One, has set before us. Let his mindset become your motivation." (Philipians 2:3-5 TPT)

I fell horribly short of this standard. I made God serve me as a consultant rather than serving God as my King. God graciously gave me ideas, and then I would try to implement them to the best of my ability. This method can look a lot like obedience, but true obedience flows from unrestrained surrender. Using God to manipulate the outcomes we desire is not obedience; it is actually rooted in witchcraft. Some ministry tasks were done with a pure heart, but on judgment day I believe most of these "good works" I did will burn up as my selfish motives are exposed through fire. God is altogether holy and has no desire to participate in our striving.

If the focus of "building the kingdom" is not entirely on pleasing our King, we have been deceived into building our own empire, not the kingdom of God. If we take the King out of the kingdom, we are left with "dom." Dom means rank, position or dominion. Without the pure worship of King Jesus, left to our own fallen nature, we will always seek to build on our own rank, positions and dominion. Selfish promotion often exists when we get more excited about building the kingdom of God than we do spending time in the presence of our King of kings.

> *If the focus of "building the kingdom" is not entirely on pleasing our King, we have been deceived into building our own empire, not the kingdom of God.*

The antidote is and always will be: fixing our eyes on Jesus. Revelations 1:14 says He has eyes like a flame of fire. It is in gazing at the eyes of Jesus that all the pride of life and lusts of the flesh burn away.

When we behold Jesus our desires become one with His desires, and the dreams in our heart that are not from God burn away. As we lay our head on the chest of our Father, our heart begins to beat in rhythm with His own heartbeat. We desperately need this daily alignment.

While spending time with Jesus is the remedy, it does not automatically rid us of selfish ambition and desires. During this season of my life, I spent a minimum of an hour a day reading the Word, journaling and praying. Then I would continue praying and worshiping the Lord throughout the day. Still, selfish ambition hid in my heart. So how can we know if there is impurity in our motives?

Here are some heart check questions I ask myself regularly: Am I spending more time thinking about my ministry than the majesty of Jesus? Am I focusing on what I can do *for* God more than what He is inviting me to do *with* Him? Is pleasing the Father the number one motivation of my heart? If someone else gets the credit for everything I did this week, will I still rejoice? Am I working as a means to an end or am I experiencing eternal life in this present moment? Am I trying to prove myself or am I freely giving of myself as an act of worship?

Thankfully, Jesus had a plan to set me free from the hamster wheel I was running on and rescue me from myself. Failure became my teacher. There was immeasurable value in what I learned about leadership and ministry in this year through my mistakes and the mistakes of others. It felt as though God was testing me in every area, but little did I know I still had to face my biggest test yet.

This test came after a year of pouring myself into this ministry when God asked me to step away completely and leave the ministry behind. Prior to this moment, I truly believed that this was my life assignment and walking away was almost unfathomable. But God, by His grace, did not just give me the desire to lay it down at His feet, the Holy Spirit lifted the assignment from my arms and with it all of the heaviness, control, striving, selfishness, and pride that I had become bound to.

I could blame the spiritual warfare that accompanies the goal of raising up the Church to become the solution to abortion and human trafficking. I certainly had never encountered that level of resistance and spiritual oppression before, and at times it was spiritually suffocating. The deception and confusion from the enemy had an impact on me, but I alone am responsible for the partnerships I made with these demonic forces. Ultimately, the warfare just revealed the unhealed, unsurrendered places of my heart. In many ways, I was still overcoming an orphan mindset that can have no place in the building of an adoption movement.

> *True obedience flows from unrestrained surrender.*

Walking away came with so much loss. It involved the loss of very close friends and the loss of my reputation in certain circles. I had to face personal accusations and confront my fear of being misunderstood. I had to endure the loss of a dream that I believe was from God, but He asked me to give it back to Him. Despite all of this, because we serve the Master of redemption, it turned out that the positive losses outweighed the negative ones. In short, I lost myself and I found Jesus, the All Sufficient One.

Obeying God and laying the ministry down was incredibly hard, but it was the beginning of the path of deep healing for me. My husband and I began pursuing our life-long dream of adoption and just when we thought our season of pruning was coming to an end, the deepest work began.

Pruning False Paradigms

After three months of adoption education, profile book creation, agency applications, and home study completion, we became an active waiting family with seven adoption agencies in the U.S. The excitement of pursuing my life-long dream of adoption fueled me through piles of paperwork. As we began the process of domestic infant adoption, the first thing God chose to prune was my wrong expectations. It felt like within minutes of embarking on our journey the GPS began yelling at us, "expect delays." We were immediately met with warnings everywhere declaring, "the wait is hard."

The Holy Spirit had much to teach me about different kinds of expectations. One type of expectation puts faith in the wrong things, one requires no faith, and one places faith in Jesus alone. First, I had to confront seemingly positive expectations I could have. An example would be expecting that we will match quickly and financial provision will come without effort because we are obeying God. The problem with this is that hope is placed in the circumstances and desired outcome and not in God alone.

The next type of expectation I had to confront was negative "realistic" expectations. An example of this would be the belief that the adoption process is going to be a long, grueling process and it will probably take years before we adopt a child. Negative expectations that we often label "realistic" can lead us to forfeit our faith and hope. With this mindset, negativity can easily be disguised as wisdom. The reality is, in this example, I buried my hope in a self-protective effort.

God began to teach me how to have biblical, faith-filled expectations, and I started to declare these promises to renew my mind.

I expect God will faithfully fulfill His promise to us to grow our family through adoption in His timing (Hebrews 10:23). I expect that God will write the best story for our family as the Author and Finisher of our faith (Hebrews 12:2). I expect that He who began a good work will be faithful to complete it (Philippians 1:6). I expect God will do exceedingly abundantly above what we can ask or think, and it will probably look different than we imagine it (Ephesians 3:20). I expect God will supply all our needs (Philipians 4:19) in whatever ways He sees fit. I expect that the length of our waiting (short or long) is designed by God and will be for our absolute benefit to prepare our hearts for what's to come (James 1:1-4).

These are examples of expectations in scripture that are based on God's goodness alone, not on circumstances or people. Would you take a second to surrender with me any expectations that are rooted in circumstances, people, or wrong views of God? It is a good practice to do daily. Remember, giving up all of our expectations would be forfeiting faith. We are simply asked to lay down our expectations connected to a wrong belief or bad source. The Holy Spirit is faithful to bring these to mind when we ask Him. Once we surrender our wrong expectations, we can boldly pick up expectations that are rooted in biblical assurances and the goodness of God.

When we do not actively apply our beliefs to each circumstance we face, we can end up with theoretical beliefs rather than practical ones. A theoretical belief is anything I believe to be true in my head but I have not yet applied to my circumstances and experienced good fruit from. Beliefs that are not applied to our lives in faith are not serving us at all. An expectant heart that trusts in God applies biblical beliefs to specific situations in faith.

Growing Tenacity

To continue on this path towards adoption, God knew He needed to build tenacity in Michael and me. My favorite way to think about tenacity is *courage in pain*. In the domestic infant adoption process, we received basic information about expectant mothers considering an adoption plan. If we fit their preferences, we could choose to present a letter and our custom profile book. Then the waiting began. Expectant mothers review many different hopeful adoptive families before they choose one to match with. Interceding for these expectant mothers while we waited is one of the most vulnerable things the Holy Spirit has ever tasked me with and something that required more courage than I possessed.

I could have prayed simple prayers like, "God bless her; God give her wisdom; God provide for her," and I did, but that is not the only way the Holy Spirit asked me to pray. Each time there was an expectant mom we presented our family to, God invited me to feel His heart for her. Often He would even give me a glimpse of the pain she was experiencing and the trauma of carrying a baby she could not parent.

It was not hard to pray for these mothers and families; it was an honor. But it was hard to attach to them through prayer, love them supernaturally, and then find out they chose another family. We rejoiced when each expectant mother found a family that she wanted to raise her child, but we had to grieve the fact that we would not ever get to meet the ones we had supernaturally grown to love. Thankfully, our heartache lasted only a brief time because we trusted that He had answered our prayers, just in a different way than we had hoped.

Our intercession is most powerful when we are willing to be part of the answer to our prayers. This put us in a unique position as hopeful adoptive parents to be able to pray for vulnerable families in a way others cannot. This was an assignment I did not take lightly.

"God, bring this mother a family who will respect and love her unconditionally," we prayed while being willing and wanting to be that family. "Jesus, place this baby with parents that will honor their heritage and raise them up in grace and wisdom," we prayed while willing and wanting to be those parents. "Lord, surround this family with a dependable support system and cover them with financial provision," we prayed while willing and wanting to be that support system.

Sometimes, even when we matched an expectant mother's preferences, the attorneys would decide not to present our family to her. These situations (when the attorneys made the decision for the expectant mom without even giving her the letter we had written for her), were the hardest. After one particularly hard situation when we received the familiar email, "Your family was not selected to present," I made an important confession to the Lord. "This feels like a punishment," I whispered through tears. In every moment of grief on this adoption journey, God peeled off another layer of lies I was believing to heal deeper parts of my heart. While tears ran down my cheek, the Holy Spirit responded with exactly what I needed to hear, "Waiting is not punishment, it's preparation for your protection."

Jesus used this moment of pruning to take me back to points in my life where I first believed the lie that having to wait was a form of punishment. Time outs, grounding and detention are all societal norms that teach us that having to wait is a punishment for not being good enough. Many of us subconsciously apply this to our relationship with God.

Romans 2:4 says, "Or do you presume on the riches of his kindness and forbearance and patience, not knowing that God's kindness is meant to lead you to repentance?"

Misunderstanding the Father's heart can be detrimental to our faith. God never punishes us for not being good enough, and the blessings He gives us can never be earned. He delights in giving undeserved gifts to His children. When He has us wait, it is always for our benefit.

God disciplines those He loves (Hebrews 12:6). His rod and staff are comforting to us because God does not use the rod to spank us. Maybe you have heard the famous sermon illustration of shepherds in Israel breaking the legs of their sheep and then carrying them on their shoulders to teach them not to wander off. Allow me to burst your bubble; this is not true. It is a perpetuated fallacy in the Church. Shepherds use the rod as a boundary enforcer to gently tap sheep going astray. The rod of our Great Shepherd is for our protection not our punishment.

The Lord is like a faithful coach. Paul uses physical exercise as his example for what the discipline of the Lord is like. He says, "let us run with endurance the race that is set before us, looking to Jesus," then continues with this metaphor a few verses later when he says, "For the moment all discipline seems painful rather than pleasant, but later it yields the peaceful fruit of righteousness to those who have been trained by it" (Hebrews 12:1, 11 ESV).

Once I confronted the lie that God was punishing me, I had to face the fear that people could keep me from my promise. It felt like the attorneys who decided not to present our family to the expectant mother as an option for her child were preventing us from being chosen to adopt. But that was not the truth. The decision of these attorneys could not block God's plans for our family.

One of the most common fears is the fear that people will control our future. This fear is rooted in a lie. Destiny is not an inevitability, but people cannot keep us from our promise. The only one who can keep us from fulfilling our destiny is ourselves. We do this by believing lies that Satan trips us with so that we cannot walk in God's purposes.

At a ministry event, Britt Hancok, the founder of Mountain Gateway, taught that when scripture says God has plans for us, it is always plural. Because God gave humanity free will, He has an indefinite amount of plans prepared to help us accomplish our purpose. His purpose for us never changes. Despite our mistakes or the sin of others against us, God has good plans to lead us to our purpose.

This truth brought me so much freedom! One of my most treasured moments with Jesus happened at Crestview Retreat Center after Britt preached this message. We were worshiping together when the entire room suddenly went silent. The Holy Spirit filled the chapel so powerfully that it felt as though Jesus had stepped into the room in the flesh. Every single person in the room, around 100 of us, hit our knees in unison. Surrender to God's ways is like a magnet to the power of God.

Whether we are on plan A or Z, we can rest assured that the plan currently unfolding is a perfect path to our promise. Our destiny is a journey of identity, not a destination to arrive at. I have learned that God cares a whole lot more about who we are becoming than where we are going or when we will get there.

God does not separate Himself from us in seasons of waiting; He draws us closer. The God of the universe waits with us. He carries our grief, our hopes, and the longing of our hearts. He is patient and kind and delivers His promise right on time. He is found in the waiting and His presence is the greatest reward.

Pruning Our Dreams

Sometimes our tree can have branches full of leaves that represent dreams in our heart that are not God's dreams. Submitting to the pruning process ensures that our dreams go through the process of death, burial and resurrection. The resurrection test is essential to knowing if our dreams are our own or are God's dreams. When a dream that is of God is pruned it will grow back seven times more fruitful. When a dream that is not of God is pruned, it will not grow back. Instead, in its place will grow a dream from God, much better than anything we could dream for ourselves.

It has been said that every dream has four stages: dream, distress, development, and destination. The dream of having a baby is a great example of this. Once pregnant, the distress phase hits in the form of morning sickness. If you are lucky, the distress passes after the first trimester and you move to the development phase as the baby grows. Before long, you reach the destination phase and hold your precious baby in your arms. With God, the destination is always better than the dream.

In our season of waiting for a baby, God was pruning us. Believing in the purpose of hardship does not take the pain away, but it does protect us from discouragement. I was full of faith that in the right time our branch would bear the fruit of the long-awaited promise. The branch of my tree that said "Adoption" was cut back further and further until it was just a stub. Then God asked us for the stub that remained. "Will you lay down your dream of adoption?"

At first this question confused me. Why would God ask us to give him a dream that was so clearly from him, a dream that I had carried since childhood, a dream that united Michael and I together since the very beginning of our relationship? It did not make any sense. Was this another test like Abraham sacrificing Isaac? I did not have the answers, but I knew God was asking us to be willing to step away from our pursuit of domestic infant adoption without a match.

The Lord began to change our definition of adoption from being a means to growing our family to the primary goal of growing *His* family. One day, God confronted my husband's fear of fostering and the inevitable heartbreak of goodbyes that come with it. He said, "Your biological children, Finn and Lucy, are not your own; they are mine and I want them back. You are only fostering them on this planet for a little while." God spoke to us that there would be no difference with the children who come into our care who on paper belong to the State, because in reality they belong to Him. Our fear of the temporary, unpredictable nature of foster care just illuminated our addiction to control.

We laid down our dream of adoption and picked up the dream of family preservation. Foster care occasionally involves adoption, but the first goal is always reunification. The mission of foster care is restoration of families. This mission cannot be supported when foster parents are simultaneously motivated by their desire to adopt. Through much pruning, God changed our hearts to desire to support vulnerable families no matter the cost. A desire that would have been unrecognizable in us both prior to the pruning process.

To be clear, surrendering this dream after a year of significant financial, emotional and time investment felt like a death, even greater than the pain of surrendering the ministry the year prior. But no story that involves our risen Lord ends in death. There is always a resurrection when we surrender to God's ways. In Isaiah 66:9, The Lord promises that he will not cause pain without causing something new to be birthed.

One of the things God taught us on our domestic adoption journey was how to grieve in community. When I am sad, I do not usually want to be around people. The moment I received this final email that marked the end of our adoption journey, I had just pulled up to my sister's house. God orchestrated the timing so I would not isolate myself in my grief. Instead, I got to spend the day with my mom and sister, the two women who had been my constant support on this journey. We cried together and spoke in reverence of the worthiness of God. He is near to the brokenhearted.

That same night I had my weekly women's Bible study. I wrestled with God on the way, not sure if I could trust these new friends with the tender places of my heart that I felt I was wearing on my sleeve. God had asked me to be very raw and vulnerable about our adoption journey which resulted in many misunderstanding me.

My experience taught me that, as Christians, we are so quick to try to take other's pain away or give out band-aids rather than holding space for the pain. We mean well, but sometimes declaring Romans 8:28, "All things work together for good!" can leave people feeling condemned or misunderstood rather than comforted. The belief that all things are working together for good does not eliminate suffering.

If a person is not believing the truth and is feeling hopeless as a result, then by all means we can comfort them with biblical encouragement. In my case, I was not discouraged, I was grieving and I needed people that would simply make room for my grief. When people tried to derive their own meaning from my pain it was hurtful rather than helpful.

Despite my fear of being misunderstood, I went to Bible study that night and the support I received was deeply healing. God spoke to the leader that I had something I needed to share and the group needed to listen without responding. They held space and cried with me. I felt like it was a funeral where these women warriors of the faith were standing at attention, not saying a word, just honoring what was being laid down.

John Piper says, "Occasionally weep deeply over the life you hoped would be. Grieve the losses. Then wash your face. Trust God. And embrace the life you have."

Grieving God's way is always worth it. The very next day I woke up and I felt resurrected. I was not sad, and I was not second-guessing our decision to walk away. I felt steady and excited for the new path God was leading us down. My strength had been revived for this new adventure and it felt like a dawning of a new day.

Our dream to love on vulnerable children was resurrected when we received our first foster placement and our family grew in a day. Instead of adopting a child, we adopted a vulnerable family and are supporting them on a path of restoration. We experienced further resurrection when God birthed a ministry through us to support families in the fieldwork of family discipleship. My dream to prepare the Church for an adoption movement was resurrected when I was invited to serve this mission with an established ministry that God has anointed and appointed for this very assignment; this time with open hands and having nothing to prove, just something to give.

Fruit of the Spirit

"But I say, walk by the Spirit, and you will not gratify the desires of the flesh. For the desires of the flesh are against the Spirit, and the desires of the Spirit are against the flesh, for these are opposed to each other, to keep you from doing the things you want to do. But if you are led by the Spirit, you are not under the law. Now the works of the flesh are evident: sexual immorality, impurity, sensuality, idolatry, sorcery, enmity, strife, jealousy, fits of anger, rivalries, dissensions, divisions, envy, drunkenness, orgies, and things like these. I warn you, as I warned you before, that those who do such things will not inherit the kingdom of God. But the fruit of the Spirit is love, joy, peace, patience, kindness, goodness, faithfulness, gentleness, self-control; against such things there is no law. And those who belong to Christ Jesus have crucified the flesh with its passions and desires. If we live by the Spirit, let us also keep in step

with the Spirit. Let us not become conceited, provoking one another, envying one another." (Galatians 5:16-26 ESV)

Pruning our branches that bare rotten fruit is necessary for our sanctification. Paul says in this passage in Galatians that those who produce the fruit of the flesh will not inherit the kingdom of God. In John 15, Jesus says *every* branch must be pruned to produce more fruit, the fruitful and the barren ones. A tree does not strive to produce good fruit; it simply surrenders to the care of the Master Gardener.

God is faithful even when our season is not fruitful. The Lord does not create barren wastelands. He wastes nothing! Barrenness is the plan of the enemy, but fruitfulness is our inheritance as children of God. In seasons of pruning, new life begins at the very moment our branches are cut back. The fruit of Christ's resurrection power might not yet be manifest, but we must be those who have eyes to see in the Spirit and perceive the new thing about to spring up. May we not quit right before our harvest. Fruit in us has to be realized to be released. Fruitfulness is not measured by production; fruitfulness is measured by faithfulness, gentleness, kindness, love, joy, peace and self-control.

"Behold, I am doing a new thing; now it springs forth, do you not perceive it? I will make a way in the wilderness and rivers in the desert." (Isaiah 43:19 ESV)

PRUNE FIELD NOTES
Identify your places of pruning

Find a quiet place and start by breathing in God's love for four seconds. Hold that breath for four seconds, imagining His presence filling you up like a balloon. Now, for four seconds breathe out whatever negative emotion is weighing you down. Repeat this exercise until you feel settled and present. Ask the Holy Spirit the following questions. Then journal the free flow of thoughts that come to your mind as you fix your eyes on Jesus.

Questions:

Holy Spirit, how are you calling me to do hard things in this season?

_____
_____
_____

How are you currently pruning my branches? How have I been submitting or resisting?

_____
_____
_____

How would you like me to fast? When would you like me to begin?

_____
_____
_____

Activation:

Pick an activation step that feels hard for you, but that you can commit 21 days to. (Example: Changing how you eat, an exercise that challenges you, a project you have been putting off, pursuing a relationship you would rather avoid, setting your alarm for an hour earlier, …etc.). Each time you rely on God to empower you to choose this hard activity, you build trust.

Encounter:

Ask God for a spirit of intercession to fall on you. Who is coming to your mind to pray for? Ask the Lord to give you His heart for that person. Imagine you are literally in their body. Feel what they feel. Surrender to the Holy Spirit as he prays through you in tears, groaning, words, tongues or however else he chooses. Give yourself to prayer until you feel a spiritual shift.

Recommended Resource:

Get adoption and foster care support as well as answers to FAQs at Fieldguideforfamilies.com/support.

FLOURISH XII

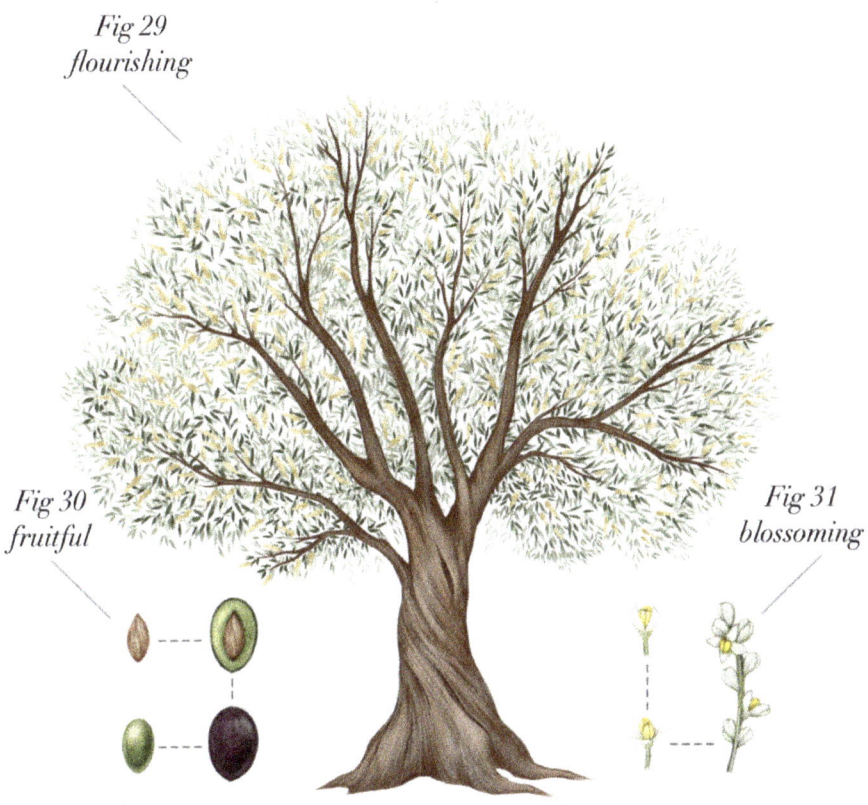

Figure 29: Flourishing Tree Growing in the Light
Figure 30: Faithfully Fruitful   Figure 31: Blossoming Eternally

FLOURISH

Chapter Twelve

Why were you created?
Identifying your mission and the motivation of your eternal destiny

Growing In The Light

To be people of the light is to be people of praise. Praise is the posture of a prayerful heart that trusts in the Lord. On this journey, we have spent time asking God intentional questions and seeking Him for the blueprint of our unique destiny seed. I pray that the Holy Spirit has encountered you on this adventure and given you more vision for your life than ever before.

Scripture goes so far as to say that people perish without vision (Proverbs 29:18). Another translation says, "Where there is no vision, the people cast off restraint" (ASV). Without clear vision we will drift, often unintentionally, off of destiny's timeline. Author and founder of Life Church, Craig Groeschel says, "We cannot do what we do not define." To live the story God has written for each of us requires us to see and grow in the light of eternity.

> *"Write the vision And make it plain on tablets, That he may run who reads it." (Habakkuk 2:2)*

As we continually seek the Lord for fresh vision, a common question is, *"What is God's will for my life?"* Did you know the Bible directly answers this question?

> *"Rejoice always, pray continually, give thanks in all circumstances;* ***for this is God's will for you*** *in Christ Jesus." (1 Thessalonians 5:16-18 NIV, Bold mine)*

The will of God for us is so simple that I am convinced 99% of Christians miss it. Rejoice always. Pray continually. Give thanks in all circumstances. God's mission for our life only becomes complex when we make it about us and not about Him.

Is Paul saying rejoicing, thanking God and praying continually is all we are to do with our life? Certainly not! These instructions come in a chapter full of numerous other things Paul instructs the church at Thessalonica to do as *"children of the light."* He tells the Thessalonians to be awake and sober, not caught off guard by darkness, to put on faith and love like a breastplate and the hope of salvation as a helmet. They are implored to live together with the Lord, encourage one another and build each other up. He goes on to instruct the church to acknowledge and honor those who work hard among them and to live in peace with each other. He does not stop there. Warn the idle, help the weak, be patient with everyone. Do not pay back wrong for wrong. Do what is good for each other. Do not quench the spirit. Do not treat prophecies with contempt, but test them. Hold onto what is good, rejecting every kind of evil (1 Thessalonians 5).

If read like a to-do list, this is quite overwhelming! Thankfully, this is not that. What Paul writes here are actions that flow from our being when we know who we are as children of light. There are only three things listed as God's *will* for us: "Rejoice always. Give thanks in all circumstances. Pray continually." This is the START HERE on our spiritual growth journey. It is also the FINISH LINE of faith. I believe that when we remember who we are as children of the light and focus on rejoicing, thanksgiving, and prayer as the primary expression of our true identity, everything else that is within the will of God for our life will come naturally. After all, Scripture assures us that it is God, not us, who sanctifies us.

> *"May God himself, the God of peace, sanctify you through and through. May your whole spirit, soul and body be kept blameless at the coming of our Lord Jesus Christ. The one who calls you is faithful, and he will do it." (1 Thessalonians 5: 23-24 NIV)*

When we forsake praise, our trees are filled with rotten fruit that weigh us down with the cares of this world. This fruit falls to the ground having no eternal impact. Our trees become heavy with anxiety when we lack eternal perspective. The opposite of anxiety is not peace, it is trust. Trust is expressed and cultivated through praise. Anxiety flees in the presence of God. Praise invites His presence, making it impossible for anxiety and gratitude to coexist. Where the Spirit of the Lord is, there is freedom (2 Corinthians 3:17). He is the lifter of our head (Psalm 3:3).

"I will bless the LORD at all times; his praise shall continually be in my mouth." (Psalm 34:1 ESV)

Gratitude lifts our spirit, shaking off everything that tries to weigh us down. When overwhelm tempts us, gratitude rescues us. Psalm 100:4 gives us the password to the presence of God. We enter His gates with thanksgiving and enter His courts with praise. We express thanksgiving by acknowledging God for what *He has done and is doing*. We express praise by acknowledging God for *who He is*.

Gratitude does not suppress our emotions or deny our reality; it settles us where we are. When we feel weighed down by hardship, gratitude lifts our heads and reframes our experience. Only with Jesus can we rejoice in suffering knowing that every hardship we face is for our benefit. When we thank Him, our souls rest in His goodness. This settling of our mind brings us back to a posture of praise as an expression of our surrender. Praise is the natural response of a heart satisfied by Him.

When we partner with complaint, fear, slander, criticism and other negative forces, the enemy's power in our life increases. The task of Philippians 2:14 to "do all things without complaining," feels impossible when we focus on what we are *not* supposed to do. Instead, we can focus on the antidote to negativity and complaining: gratitude! When we actively look for and cling to whatever is praiseworthy, we are lifted above our circumstances.

Lifting our arms in praise during trying circumstances can feel like bench pressing heavy weights. As we push through the resistance, our spiritual muscles are strengthened. When we do not feel like praising is often when we need the breakthrough of praise most.

Praise is also the remedy for the soul weighed down with earthly cares. Heaven is not an ethereal destination; it is our eternal home. Ephesians 2:6 says we are *currently* seated with Christ in heavenly places, high above the spiritual war raging below. Jesus ascended so that we could be seated next to Him with our defeated enemy under our feet. We do not fight for victory, we fight from victory. When we feel weighed down, the Spirit calls to us to ascend with Him to our heavenly seat. Just like the Bridegroom in Song of Songs 2:13, Jesus is always beckoning us to run away with Him to the higher place.

As we walk by faith, we are forced to continually confront our fears and any number of negative emotions that threaten to weigh us down. One day, when I was wrestling with the emotional rollercoaster of foster care, the Holy Spirit invited me to stop riding the ride. I had completely forgotten that I had the power to get off the roller coaster of fear. Sometimes foster care feels like a chaotic state fair, but I cannot help the spinning happening all around me if I do not first stop the spinning happening *inside* of me. The Holy Spirit gave me the key to standing unmovable, surrounded by screaming and shaking: "*Feel it all, then settle on gratitude.*"

This phrase has become a mantra for me every time I feel the pressures of foster care begin to weigh me down. Endless appointments, adrenaline and exhaustion make the first weeks with a new foster placement a blur. The joy of falling in love with another child and an unhealthy amount of coffee carry us through for a while. The joy never leaves, but as the excitement fades, we are quickly reminded of how many other emotions can coexist with joy. Even off of the rollercoaster, the ground still shakes and things continue to move around us. When we step into broken spaces, we are not called to join the chaos. To be prepared to affect positive change, we have to brace for impact.

Sometimes the unavoidable shakings of outrage come when I am presented with new information about abuse that has transpired against our foster children, but gratitude for their safety settles me. Other times, I am shaken by heartbreak during their first Christmas, first word or first steps as I live memories that are not supposed to be mine and grieve for their biological parents who are absent. In these moments, I hold onto gratitude that God redeems all things while I wait for the shakings of grief to subside.

While I have chosen to get off of the rollercoaster of fear, sometimes fear's force is so strong that it rattles the ground I stand on. More often than I would like to admit, I get knocked over by the fear that I will not be able to handle saying goodbye to my foster children if the goal of reunification is achieved.

"*I could never foster. I would get too attached,*" people are constantly telling us, unaware that getting attached is the whole point of foster care. A secure attachment to a safe and loving parental figure is the very thing children need to heal. Unfortunately, it is also the scariest thing to freely give away. We have to continually confront our fear of loss to continue to love the way Jesus has called us. As scary as this calling is, it is incomparable to the fear foster children face as they are plucked from everything they know and brought into the home of a stranger. Being a foster parent may be scary, but being a foster child is terrifying. Foster children are not given the choice of whether they want to participate in foster care or not. How then can I freely choose not to participate with fear as my excuse? Instead of abandoning this God-given assignment, I let gratitude for each moment with the children in front of me steady me.

Before I stepped into the dark world of foster care, I was met with many well-meaning warnings from foster parents, trying to prepare me for the weight of injustice I was about to feel. If there was a passcode to the hypothetical foster parent club it would be: *The system is broken.* While we worked to get our foster license, I found this phrase so entirely unhelpful that I vowed to never repeat it myself to foster parents who would come behind me. Foreboding, abounding injustice does nothing to fortify the faith of prospective foster parents, it only fortifies their fear.

Sadly, I had been a foster parent for less than a year before I caught myself chanting, "*The system is broken – the system is broken – the system is broken,*" to anyone and everyone. Focusing on the brokenness of the foster system made the weight of this assignment unbearable. My branches began to be pulled down by rotten fruit of hopelessness, anxiety, control, and bitterness until they almost snapped and I nearly broke. The more we focus on the brokenness of the world's systems, the more we lose sight of the light of truth. Jesus restores broken things; Jesus redeems brokenness.

A ray of hope glimmered in the dark one day as the truth hit me: brokenness has to precede restoration. In the light, I began to see that the brokenness of the foster care system has positioned it perfectly for revival and reformation. God revives and rebuilds from ruins. In the light of eternity, we see differently. God is rebuilding the foster care and adoption system, and we each have a part to play. We are not its Savior, that is for sure. But as His Church, we are called to be agents of restoration and redemption.

God is commissioning families to stand in the gap and rebuild their portion of the wall just like He did in Nehemiah's time. Instead of focusing on the brokenness we see around us, we are called to take ownership, pick up a brick and rebuild our part.

Praise keeps us on the pathway of eternal life. As Westerners, we often think of eternity as something that begins at the end of our life. In reality, Jesus taught us that eternal life begins at our salvation and new birth. Ecclesiastes says God put eternity in our hearts. Eternal life can be accessed here and now as we live in harmony with our Eternal King. Eternal life is not a linear concept. It exists in all dimensions, everywhere.

God does not ask us to hold on and wait until we get to Heaven. Jesus tells us to pray, "Thy kingdom come, thy will be done on Earth as it is in Heaven." He teaches that the kingdom of God is like a mustard seed. As sowers of this seed, we are to be those who bring the kingdom down to earth.

One of the most destructive doctrines that plagues the body of Christ today is escapism. There are many waiting for the rapture to rescue them from a world going to hell in a handbasket. Obsession with current events and end-times prophecy has left many with a twisted mindset, "To Heaven with me and to hell with the world."

Jesus commissions us to bring the kingdom of God to earth and to go into all the world with the life-changing gospel. It has been noted that after the Jesus People Movement in the 1970s, the Church's adoption of an escapism theology halted cultural reformation. The enemy knew that he could make us ineffective Christians if he trapped us in a holding pattern of bad theology, lulling us to sleep as we wait for Heaven. When the Church wakes up from this deception, I believe we will see cultural reformation as the natural result of revival. Revival starts in our hearts, spreads to our homes and becomes a heritage for our children. We are the ekklesia, "a gathering of citizens called out from their homes into some public place."[72] We occupy until our King returns.

When I lose my eternal perspective, it becomes incredibly hard to

---

72. G1577 - Ekklēsia - Strong's Greek Lexicon (Kjv).

stay on mission as a foster family. I desperately need the light of eternity to maintain a posture of praise in an otherwise dark environment.

In the light of eternity, I can see constantly changing visit schedules as an invitation for connection and growth for the biological family rather than the burden that they often feel like. When my hope is in Heaven, I see a phone call from a parent as a divine appointment to share the love of Jesus rather than an annoying interruption in my day. Prayer, and the heavenly perspective that comes with it, protects me from stepping into a trap of offense when a system worker misunderstands, belittles or berates me.

The remedy for my fear of not having enough time with the children I love as my own is, and always will be, prayer for eternity with them. When eternity is not in my heart, it is far too easy for me to root against the biological family rather than for them. Earnest intercession for the salvation and healing of my foster children's biological family protects me from distorted perspectives.

"It is in his light that we see light." (Psalm 36:9)

The term "permanency" in the foster care world is used in reference to the long-term care of children. The goal of the State is always for the permanent plan to be reunification with biological parents unless circumstances make that impossible. While I support this goal, there are many days when I wish the permanent plan could be changed to adoption. Keeping my heart free from selfish desire is only possible if I maintain an eternal perspective through praise and prayer.

While we support the first permanency plan being reunification, it is not our foster care mission. As we serve the foster system, our primary permanency plan for them is Heaven. Reunification with biological family is incredibly important work, but it will never be more important than our mission to see people reconciled with their Heavenly Father: Heaven for my foster children, Heaven for their biological families, Heaven for the overworked social workers, Heaven for the CASA (Court Appointed Special Advocate) and Heaven for the judge whose policies often harm the children I love. Heaven is the permanency plan we all need.

I am so glad that I did not heed the unsolicited advice to "guard your heart," that rolls off the tongue of most people when they discover we are a foster family. Do not get me wrong, "guard your heart" is excellent biblical advice when rightly applied. However, it is horrible advice in the manner it is usually presented. "Guard your heart" is not, and never will be, an excuse to withhold love.

We guard our hearts by taking captive thoughts of judgment towards birth parents, choosing instead to love and forgive. We guard our hearts by not allowing our minds to jump ahead to begin planning a future with children that are not forever ours and instead thank God for each present moment we have been given with them. We guard our hearts by confronting bitterness and practicing quick forgiveness towards a child welfare system that does not always prioritize the welfare of children. As foster parents, we must guard our hearts in many ways, but withholding our love and attachment will never be one of them.

Because of love, we have been able to develop a beautiful relationship with our foster children's biological mother. Because of love, Michael and I had one of the highest honors of our lives to baptize her into the family of God. Because of love, our relationship is not just temporal; it is eternal. And while our foster family may technically be temporary, it is also eternal because loving God's children matters for eternity.

I pray that I will get to spend eternity in Heaven with my foster children, their families and the system workers who are sometimes the hardest to love. But my prayer requests do not stop with their eternal salvation. I also pray that Heaven will invade earth where they are here and now. I pray, "Your kingdom come, your will be done, in the Clark County Foster system as it is in Heaven." Having a heavenly perspective changes everything.

What is your Matthew 6:10 prayer? We can all pray like Jesus for the kingdom to invade the whole earth, but I believe that He has given each of us specific territory for the kingdom of God. What is the cry of your heart? "Your kingdom come, your will be done, _____ as it is in heaven." We can fill in the blank with the branches of our tree. As we lift our branches in prayer and praise we grow upward in the light of eternity, bearing the fruit of our destiny.

Fruit of Destiny

The type of fruit that grows on our tree represents the different missions we each hold. Our DNA seeds all differ, therefore the type of fruit we produce will differ.

In Matthew 28:16-20, Jesus commissioned His disciples with these words, "All authority in heaven and on earth has been given to me. Therefore go and make disciples of all nations, baptizing them in the name of the Father and of the Son and of the Holy Spirit, and teaching them to obey everything I have commanded you. And surely I am with you always, to the very end of the age" (Matthew 28:16-20 NIV).

The term commission includes our unchanging mission and our seasonal assignments. It is a co-mission, meaning it can only be accomplished in connection to Jesus and community. Paul says we are co-laborers. Let's look at this passage in full context to uncover the theme.

> *"The one who plants and the one who waters have one purpose, and they will each be rewarded according to their own labor. For we are co-workers in God's service; you are God's field, God's building. By the grace God has given me, I laid a foundation as a wise builder, and someone else is building on it. But each one should build with care. For no one can lay any foundation other than the one already laid, which is Jesus Christ. If anyone builds on this foundation using gold, silver, costly stones, wood, hay or straw, their work will be shown for what it is, because the Day will bring it to light. It will be revealed with fire, and the fire will test the quality of each person's work. If what has been built survives, the builder will receive a reward. If it is burned up, the builder will suffer loss but yet will be saved—even though only as one escaping through the flames. Don't you know that you yourselves are God's temple and that God's Spirit dwells in your midst? If anyone destroys God's temple, God will destroy that person; for God's temple is sacred, and you together are that temple." (1 Corinthians 3:8-16 NIV)*

The Greek word for you in this passage is plural. It would be better translated as "you all," or "y'all," if you are from the South. We are all a part of the temple, but we are not the whole temple. One person's assignment is to plant, another's is to water, and both are needed. Peter calls us living stones. We have a destined position in the house of God, a piece of the puzzle.

> "As you come to him, the living Stone—rejected by humans but chosen by God and precious to him— you also, like living stones, are being built into a spiritual house to be a holy priesthood, offering spiritual sacrifices acceptable to God through Jesus Christ." (1 Peter 2: 4-5 NIV)

Each of us have been created in the image of God, but no one person carries the fullness of God's image. I believe the day is coming when celebrity Christianity will die and every person in the Family of God will rise up to take up their rightful, needed space. We are commissioned into community on co-mission together.

The definition of a commission according to Merriam Webster is, "a formal written warrant granting the power to perform various acts or duties; a certificate conferring military rank and authority; an authorization or command to act in a prescribed manner or to perform prescribed acts; CHARGE; authority to act for, in behalf of, or in place of another; a task or matter entrusted to one as an agent for another."[73]

God calls us His agents of reconciliation whom He has entrusted with all authority. He charges and empowers us to go and be His ambassadors to the world.

> "Therefore, if anyone is in Christ, the new creation has come: The old has gone, the new is here! All this is from God, who reconciled us to himself through Christ and gave us the ministry of reconciliation: that God was reconciling the world to himself in Christ, not counting people's sins against them. And he has committed to us the message of reconciliation. We are therefore Christ's ambassadors, as though God were making his appeal through us. We implore you on Christ's behalf: Be reconciled to God. God made him who had no sin to be sin for us, so that in him we might become the righteousness of God." (2 Corinthians 5: 17-21 NIV)

In Judges 5, we read about Deborah who was commissioned as a prophetess, leader and judge of Israel. Her assignment from God led her to public spaces where she influenced the children of Israel and was ultimately responsible for their victory over Sisera. No one else would lead

---

73. "Commission," in *Merriam-Webster Dictionary*.

the troops into battle until Deborah arose. She could have easily said, "I cannot lead an army; I am just a woman," but this false humility and disobedience would have led to the destruction of her people, not unlike the scenario Queen Esther found herself in.

Often, we are held captive by our pride and insecurity. We have to get over ourselves to step into the positions God has called us to. Women represent nearly two-thirds of the Body of Christ. The enemy knows that if he can take us out with insecurities, competition, and bad doctrine, he can have his way in the world.

"Village life ceased, it ceased in Israel, Until I, Deborah, arose, Arose a mother in Israel." (Judges 5:7)

Like Deborah, many will receive a commission from the Lord for public ministry in their lifetime. It is time for Deborahs to arise, seated in places of government, leading in all spheres of culture, mothers to the next generation in spiritual discipleship, and prophetesses who carry the word of God always on our lips. Assignments like Deborah's can function in private spaces, but it often comes with a public commission.

The victory over Sisera can be credited to Deborah's faithful obedience to go out to battle, but equal credit belongs to Jael's faithful obedience to stay home to battle. These two commissions that we receive in different seasons are both vital to the success of our mission.

Jael did not go out to battle like Deborah did. She stayed home to battle. Even though her husband was aiding the schemes of the enemy, this did not disqualify her from service. God used the deception of her husband to set her up for victory.

Many couples today wrestle with the pain of being unequally yoked. This is especially challenging when one spouse believes in God and the other denies God. Others experience a similar pain when their spouse believes in God but has not surrendered to His Lordship over their life. This tension in a marriage can be almost unbearable. God redeems all things and wastes nothing. The story of Jael assures us that no person, not even a spouse, can keep us from the purposes of God. People cannot keep us from our destiny. Everything we perceive as a setback, God can turn into a set up.

The Lord brought the enemy into Jael's home and she drove a tent peg into his head. God alone commissions us into our position, and he has the authority to change our position in each season.

In my own life, it is in the times when God is expanding my capacity and taking me into new territory that the enemy comes knocking at my door. The giants in our promised land must be confronted and defeated.

> *"Enlarge the place of your tent, and let the curtains of your habitations be stretched out; do not hold back; lengthen your cords and strengthen your stakes. For you will spread abroad to the right and to the left, and your offspring will possess the nations and will people the desolate cities." (Isaiah 54:2 ESV)*

The story of Jael gives us a prophetic picture of what to do with our tent pegs in seasons of expansion. When we stretch out our tent pegs as instructed in Isaiah 54, we must drive the peg through the enemy's skull before we can establish it on new ground. We often face the greatest resistance from the enemy right before our greatest breakthroughs. Sisera depicts a spirit of fear that can manifest in our lives in many forms when we try to step out into new territory.

I believe women and men who are able to discern and obey their assignments to either stay at their post or go out to the battlefield are the key to us taking back the territory the enemy has stolen. If we want to see the promises of God fulfilled in our own life, we must occupy whatever position God calls us to.

God promises us that in the last days, the Church will arise and shine with the glory of Christ like never before. I believe that for this to happen, we need believers who will stand confidently in their appointed positions. To be found faithfully at our posts we must first be commissioned by God.

On our spiritual growth journey, the Lord prepares marking moments to commission us into our destiny. I experienced one of these marking moments after a long season of preparation that opened my eyes to the fruit of my destiny. The Spirit of the Lord fell on me, causing me to fall flat on my back onto a concrete floor, unable to move for almost an hour. The tangible presence of God pulsed through my body like waves of electricity.

I immediately saw a vision. My spirit left my dead body, rising from a grave and went up a short stairway to Heaven. Jesus stood at the door and called me to come in. But first, He had me look back at my dead body. I saw it go even deeper under the surface of the earth. I stepped through the door into Heaven. Around me I could see groves of trees. It was like the garden of Eden. Instead of vibrant green, the trees had a gold shimmer to them. Jesus told me that all the trees were full of fruit from my life. I could not believe my eyes.

Then He had me look back through the door. I saw child graves touched by resurrection power and the children's spirits rose up. I called them, and they stepped through the door. Jesus said, "The fruit of the harvest is for the children. They are the harvesters." The children ran free and ate the fruit. I heard Jesus say, "You will rescue my children and awaken the mothers and fathers. Daughter, you are called to the nations to be a City of Refuge."

I looked down and I was carrying a boy and girl baby, one on each hip. I knew this commission was *from* family *for* family. Jesus prompted me to look back through the door. Now, I saw the spirits of mothers rising up out of their graves. Mothers came through the door into heaven and started to care for the children who were walking around the grove. Fathers soon followed. I knew I was being commissioned into ministry for families.

Then, He took me to one of the trees and showed me a purplish blue fruit that I had never seen before. He told me this was a fruit that only my life could produce. I tasted the fruit and it was sweet but with a punch to it. The flavor was potent. I held the fruit in my hands and it was like balls of power. I heard Revelation 22:1-2, "The river was flowing in the middle of the street of the city, and on either side of the river was the Tree of Life, with its twelve kinds of ripe fruit according to each month of the year. The leaves of the Tree of Life are for the healing of the nations" (TPT).

Just as God showed me in this encounter that each of us are destined to produce fruit unlike anyone else. This fruit is our mission and it is alive! From our unique DNA seed grows an individual tree that produces fruit from our essence. Prophetic intercessor and musician Christine Potter said, "God does not call us to be productive, He calls us to be fruitful." When we operate out of our true essence and remain connected to the sap of the Spirit, our trees bear fruit in every season that brings healing to the nations.

Oil to Light our Lamps

Fruit carries seeds with the potential for multiplication. Additionally, some fruit, like olives for example, serve a purpose not only in their original form but also in their pressed state. Olives are valuable, but olive oil is much more so. Throughout scripture, oil is used as a picture of the anointing of the Holy Spirit. Oil is produced after seeds grow and are cultivated into good fruit that are then harvested and pressed. Creating a supply of oil takes time.

The cost to walk in anointing is the price of full surrender. Anointing is the byproduct of abiding. As we walk in surrender, there is active releasing and receiving. We release our dead self to Him, and He puts His resurrection power in us. We release our ashes and He gives us a crown of beauty. We release our mourning and He gives us the oil of joy. We release our disappointment and He gives us a garment of praise. We release our filthy rags of self-righteousness for His white robes of righteousness. We release our shame for His glory. We release our blindness for His revelation.

> *"And provide for those who grieve in Zion—to bestow on them a crown of beauty instead of ashes, the oil of joy instead of mourning, and a garment of praise instead of a spirit of despair. They will be called oaks of righteousness, a planting of the Lord for the display of his splendor."* (Isaiah 61:3 NIV)

God wants to fill us with fresh oil. He does not want us running on oil reserves from encounters we had with Him years prior. In Matthew 25, The Parable of the Ten Virgins, Jesus gives us a parable contrasting the wise and the foolish in the Bride of Christ.

The five virgins who were carried away to marry their bridegroom were the ones who had purchased enough oil to wait for Him to come for them. The five foolish virgins went to go buy oil from the merchants only after they realized their supply was running out. The virgins who had enough oil to wait for their bridegroom would have been those who purchased oil that same day. Much like the manna God provided to the Israelites in the wilderness each day, oil also had to be purchased daily. They had to prepare, pursue and pay for the oil. Anointing comes from dedicated preparation, passionate pursuit and costly sacrifice.

In Bible times, oil was used to anoint the dead for burial and brides for marriage. Oil was also used in the temple to keep the lamps burning. Leviticus 24:2 says, "Command the children of Israel that they bring to you pure oil of pressed olives for the light, to make the lamps burn continually."

We can get around those who are burning for Jesus and temporarily catch fire, but we will not be able to maintain that fire without our own oil.[74] Each of us has to pursue and purchase oil for ourselves. Anointing comes from sacrificial worship. If we just do what we want to do all the time, there will not be oil on it.

Anointing the dead for burial is a picture of how anointing increases the more we die to our own desires. When we crucify our flesh, we receive the oil of the Spirit. And because we are now dead and our life is not our own, everything we do becomes an act of worship to the Lord.

We choose costly praise. We worship when we do not feel like it. We pray when we do not want to. There are some that experience the pressing of life, but they do not surrender to the dying process. Instead of coming out of the process with the fragrance of Christ, they reek of the rancid oil of bitterness. Crushing is a revealer of character. Rotten fruit can only yield rotten oil.

One of my favorite stories in all of scripture is the story of Mary anointing the feet of Jesus with oil that would have cost an entire year's wages. She anointed Jesus and in the process ended up smelling just like Him.

When we submit to the hard process of continual surrender, Jesus resurrects us and anoints us as his bride. Crushing produces the anointing and dying produces the fragrance of Christ on us. In scripture, kings and priests were anointed by prophets. The dead were anointed by family, but brides anointed themselves.

In Song of Songs 5, the bride made herself ready but then fell asleep, not unlike the ten virgins in Jesus' parable (Matthew 25:1-13). Ruth anointed herself before she went to Boaz (Ruth 3:3). Esther was provided cosmetics, but she was responsible for her own beauty treatments and preparations (Esther 2:12).

There is a time to receive prayer, impartation and anointing from others. Timothy tells us that gifts are imparted through the laying on of

---

74. Fomenko, "Staying Full of Oil."

hands that we are to stir up in faith (2 Timothy 1:6). And there is a time when we have to anoint ourselves. We can temporarily catch anointing from others, but to walk in anointing we must personally pursue and purchase oil to be prepared for our Bridegroom.

A pure Bride made ready for the return of the Bridegroom is one who worships in Spirit and in Truth. She is a virgin whose heart is free from idolatry and who daily buys oil in the secret place to keep the lamp of her love burning for her Beloved. She has surrendered her life not just once, but daily, even hourly.

Jesus is returning for a pure, spotless bride.

> "Husbands, love your wives, as Christ loved the church and gave himself up for her, that he might sanctify her, having cleansed her by the washing of water with the word, so that he might present the church to himself in splendor, without spot or wrinkle or any such thing, that she might be holy and without blemish. (Ephesisans 5:25-27 ESV)

The time between our anointing and appointing for the assignments of God is absolutely essential to protect us from our lamps burning out. Our anointing will flow in the areas God has given us authority. If you are a mother, rest assured you have been anointed and appointed for motherhood. You were made for motherhood and motherhood was made for you. If you feel you lack true authority in this assignment, the issue is not in your allotment of authority, but rather your belief in the authority you carry and your willingness to lay down your life. When we truly believe we carry authority, we do not have to raise our voice or use domineering tactics. Real authority is derived from self-control.

He cares infinitely more about our hearts being connected to His divine love than He does about any works of ministry that we do.

Sometimes, when we feel our words do not carry the authority of Heaven it is because we are speaking into an area that we have not been assigned to. Have you ever felt like your words go in one ear and out the other? This could be because you do not believe in the authority you have been given or it could be that you are exercising authority to speak beyond what God has appointed you for in this season.

Tragically, there are many anointed men and women of God who are not walking in purity. They may have been given a measure of authority, but they have misused the anointing of God much like King Saul. The Church has been given more authority than any empire has ever held. Unlike any earthly empire, our power does not come from our willingness to dominate, but our willingness to die.

When one of my favorite worship leaders, Steffany Gretzinger, ministers to the Lord, my Spirit can feel the purity of anointing that she flows in. She says, "When we find ourselves thinking more about what we want God to do through us than who He is to us, the lamp of first love has grown dim."

If we wish to not let the lamp of first love for our Bridegroom grow dim like the church of Ephesus did, we must buy oil, no matter how costly. The lampstand is a picture of our ministry on earth. The light in our lampstand will go out if our hearts no longer burn in love for our King. He cares infinitely more about our hearts being connected to His divine love than He does about any works of ministry that we do.

> *"I know your works, your toil and your patient endurance, and how you cannot bear with those who are evil, but have tested those who call themselves apostles and are not, and found them to be false. I know you are enduring patiently and bearing up for my name's sake, and you have not grown weary. But I have this against you, that you have abandoned the love you had at first. Remember therefore from where you have fallen; repent, and do the works you did at first. If not, I will come to you and remove your lampstand from its place, unless you repent." (Revelation 2:2-5 ESV)*

The fastest way to get oil is to remember what it was like to fall in love with Jesus. This passage says to, "do the works you did at first." What are the first works of a lover: Setting up dates, prioritizing time together, long phone calls, walks in the park, the enjoyment of each other's company, simply being in the presence of the one we love. How often do we remember what Jesus saved us from, and how He revealed Himself to us when we first fell in love?

I remember that receiving a fresh infilling of the Holy Spirit felt like seeing in color for the first time. I am an extrovert, but in this season of my life I was so hungry for the presence of God that I struggled to be around people. I craved alone time with Jesus more than food, more than entertainment, more than anything. When I feel my oil supply dwindling, I think back to this time and fan the flame of first love.

Worship connects us to our ultimate why, which is love. It is the purpose for which we were created. When we surrender to God, we lay ourselves on the altar as a living sacrifice. As we create altars of praise throughout our day – in the shower, on the treadmill, in the pick-up line at school, at the kitchen sink, while we push around fussy toddlers in a stroller, in our prayer closet – we fan the flames of first love.

The altars of love are our powersource and connection to true anointing. We read in 1 John 2:27 that there is a counterfeit anointing – this comes from the altars of the enemy. To connect to any other powersource we have to disconnect from the altar of first love. What false gods are we serving? Have we made an idol of gossip for counterfeit confidence? Shopping for counterfeit contentment? Unhealthy eating for counterfeit comfort? Excessive caffeine consumption for counterfeit energy? Scrolling social media for counterfeit purpose? Binge watching TV for counterfeit rest? Stress cleaning for counterfeit control? We stop serving these idols when we worship the one true God. His love is the most powerful source in the universe.

> "As for you, the anointing you received from him remains in you, and you do not need anyone to teach you. But as his anointing teaches you about all things and as that anointing is real, not counterfeit—just as it has taught you, remain in him." (1 John 2:27 NIV)

Ongoing anointing comes from ongoing surrender. We grow by abiding in the anointing.

When we remain connected to the Godhead, we have unlimited resources, continually flowing oil and continually burning lamps. The prophet Zechariah had a vision of seven self-filling lamps that were directly connected to two olive trees producing oil, creating a picture of perpetual supply. When Zechariah asked the Lord for the meaning of this vision, He responded, "This is the word of the Lord to Zerubbabel: 'Not by might nor by power, but by my Spirit,' says the Lord Almighty" (Zechariah 4:6 NIV).

The oil of anointing is maintained through continual, sacrificial praise, and our spiritual trees grow in the light of gratitude. Trees with fruit that remain are the ones who maintain a posture of praise in all seasons. Praise in all circumstances lifts our branches, giving us an eternal perspective that protects us from the snares of the world. With a posture of praise, we continually grow up in the light, storing fruit in Heaven to be enjoyed for all of eternity, flourishing as trees of righteousness.

The Author and Finisher of our faith has an exhilarating narrative for your life that is abundantly better than anything you could dream up for yourself! I pray that on this journey together you have aligned with the *who*, *what*, *where*, *when* and *why* of your destiny storyline. With red ink Jesus has written us into the greatest story of all time: His plan of redemption for the world. As you continue to surrender the pen to Him for His will to be written through your life, there will be many wonderful surprises and plot twists along the way. Like every good story you will experience low valleys and high peaks, but what makes the story you are living the greatest of all time is the consistent and perfect main character, Jesus IN you.

Remember that there is no arrival point. We can only thrive in our present reality when we stop trying to arrive. Heaven is our destination, but even there we will continue to grow in the depths of Jesus' love for all of eternity. We will never exhaust His all consuming, expansive love for us. As we live and flourish in His love, His kingdom comes to where we are, on Earth as it is in Heaven.

> *"For all who obey his commands find their lives joined in union with him, and he lives and flourishes in them. We know and have proof that he constantly lives and flourishes in us, by the Spirit that he has given us." (1 John 3:24 TPT)*

FLOURISH FIELD NOTES

Identify why you were created

Find a quiet place and start by breathing in God's love for four seconds. Hold that breath for four seconds, imagining His presence filling you up like a balloon. Now, for four seconds breathe out whatever negative emotion is weighing you down. Repeat this exercise until you feel settled and present. Ask the Holy Spirit the following questions. Then journal the free flow of thoughts that come to your mind as you fix eyes on Jesus.

Questions:

Holy Spirit, why does my life matter? Why was I created?

_____
_____
_____

How does having an eternal perspective change how I live today?

_____
_____
_____

How do I stay motivated to serve you with my whole life?

_____
_____
_____

How does my story connect with those you have called me to serve?

_____
_____
_____

Activation:

1. Co-creating with the Holy Spirit, write a mission statement for your life.
2. Start a vision journal for your life. Include:

   <u>Roots:</u> Your identity names and identity statements – who are you?

   <u>Branches:</u> Your biblical priorities and burdens – where are you called to serve?

   <u>Pollination:</u> Your prophetic words and testimonies – how has the Holy Spirit transformed you? What has He prophetically spoken over your life?

   <u>Leaves:</u> Your seasonal assignments — when will you act on your kingdom assignments?

   <u>Blossoms:</u> Your spiritual and natural giftings — what gifts has God given you?

   <u>Fruit:</u> Your personal mission – why were you created?

3. Write out your testimony. Commit to sharing it with someone this week.

Encounter:

Lift your hands up, fully extended towards heaven. Begin with saying, "I thank you, God that you have said _____," and rehearse his promises over your life. Then say, "I thank you, God that you have done _____," and *rehearse his faithfulness to you. Then say, "I thank you God that you are _____," and rehearse his goodness and trustworthiness.*

Once you remember the faithfulness of God, you will live in his love, trusting Him as you lay your life on the altar as a burning one.

Go on a walk or a drive and ask God to commission you in this season. Actively engage your imagination in conversation with Jesus.

Journal your experience here:

_____
_____
_____
_____
_____
_____
_____

Before you go, I would like to pray the same prayer Paul prayed over the Colossian church over your spiritual growth journey.

> "We ask God to give you complete knowledge of his will and to give you spiritual wisdom and understanding. Then the way you live will always honor and please the Lord, and your lives will produce every kind of good fruit. All the while, you will grow as you learn to know God better and better. We also pray that you will be strengthened with all his glorious power so you will have all the endurance and patience you need. May you be filled with joy, always thanking the Father. He has enabled you to share in the inheritance that belongs to his people, who live in the light." (Colossians 1:9-12 NLT)

MY FLOURISHING TREE

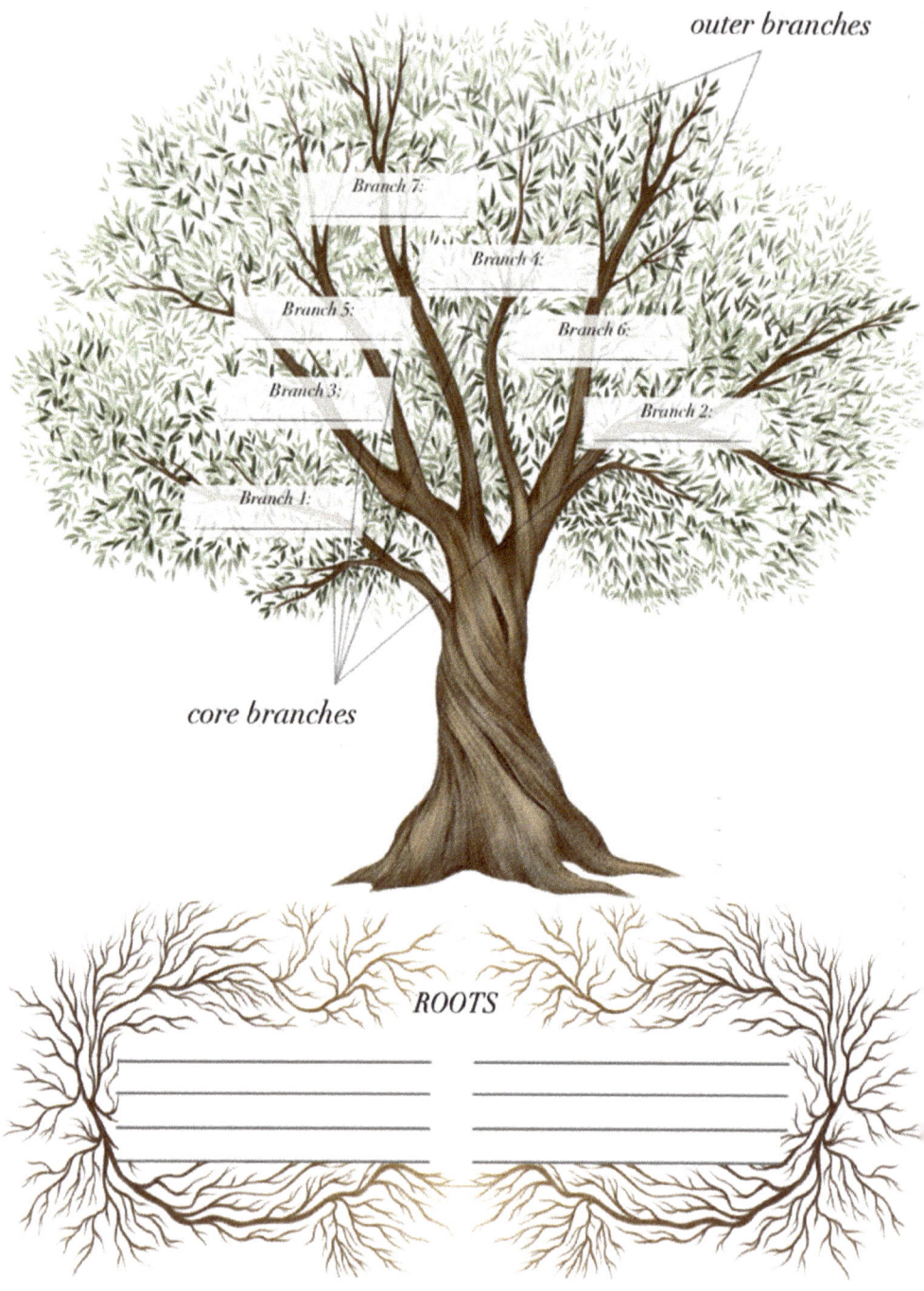

I am like an olive tree flourishing in the house of God; I trust in God's unfailing love for ever and ever. - Psalm 52:8

BRANCH 1

Leaves:

BRANCH 2

Leaves:

BRANCH 3

Leaves:

BRANCH 4

Leaves:

BRANCH 5

Leaves:

BRANCH 6

Leaves:

BRANCH 7

Leaves:

BLOSSOMS

FRUIT

Personal Mission:

Roots | Who has God created you to be?

Branches | Where are you called to serve?

Leaves | When is God asking you to act?

Blossoms | What gifts has God given you to blossom?

Fruit | Why were you created?

APPENDIX

Answering FAQs with the Holy Spirit and Scripture

Deliverance

Can a Christian be demon possessed?

{Look up the definition of possession.}

Read: 1 Corinthians 6:19-20 – What does it say?

Ask: If we are a temple of the Holy Spirit, can anyone or anything else possess or own us? If we cannot be *possessed*, can we be *oppressed* or *demonized*?

Note: Helps Word-studies says the word translated "possessed" in Matthew 8:28 *daimonízomai* (from *daímōn*) is more properly translated as *demonized* and defined as coming under the power of a demon (fallen angel).[75]

---

75. Strong's Greek: 1139. δαιμονίζομαι (daimonizomai) -- to be possessed by a demon.

Can a Christian be oppressed by demons?

Read: Matthew 15:21-28 — What does it say?

Ask: Why did Jesus say deliverance is the children's bread if deliverance is not for the children of God?

Read: Galatians 4:4-8 — What does it say?

Ask: Were we God's children before we received salvation through the Spirit of adoption?

Read: Matthew 12:43-45 — What does it say?

Ask: What does the house represent in this parable? Why would Jesus warn us about a person who has been delivered from an unclean spirit but is not filled with the Holy Spirit and is thereby at risk of being oppressed seven times more than before? Does Jesus ask us to cast evil out of someone who does not belong to God? Or is Jesus saying that deliverance is for those who belong to God and are filled with the Spirit?

Read: Acts 5:1-5 and refer to Strong's Concordance (you can access Strong's Concordance at Biblehub.com) — What does it say?

Ask: Is the original Greek word that describes Ananias, who is a Christian, "filled" by Satan to lie to the Holy Spirit, the same word used to describe the filling of the Holy Spirit in Ephesians 5:18? How can a person be filled with the Holy Spirit and an evil spirit?

Read: 1 Thessalonians 5:23 — What does it say?

Ask: Are we saved in our spirit or in our body and soul?

Read: 2 Corinthians 6:14 — What does it say?

Ask: Does it say light and darkness *cannot* coexist or *should not* coexist?

Read: Ephesians 6:12 — What does it say?

Ask: Can a child of the light be under the influence of darkness?

Read: Acts 8:13-23 — What does it say?

Ask: Why does this passage make it clear that Simon was still bound and poisoned by bitterness after he received salvation and was baptized?

How do we experience deliverance? How can we come out from under the influence of evil spirits?

Read: Mark 16:17-18 — What does it say?

Ask: These signs follow who: believers or unbelievers? — How did Jesus deliver people? Did he pray to God or did he speak to the demon in the authority he had been given?

Read: Mark 1:23-27 — What does it say?

Ask: Should we expect all demons to leave quietly if they didn't for Jesus? Whether they create a scene or not, can we expect all demons to leave when we command them to in Jesus' name like he taught us? How much authority does Jesus have– *partial* authority or *all* authority?

Read: Matthew 28:18-20 — What does it say?

Ask: In Jesus, how much authority do we have?

Recommended Reference: "Can a Christian have a demon?" Vladimir Savchuk Ministries

The Role of Women in the Bible

What was God's original design for women?

Read: Genesis 1:27-30 — What does it say?

Ask: Did God give Adam and Eve equal authority and assignment? Were they instructed to rule over humans? Was it ever God's design for men or women to dominate over other men and women?

Read: Genesis 2:18-20 and look up the original Hebrew word for helper, *ezer* — What does it say?

Ask: What does it mean? Does *ezer* ever suggest a subservient status as the one helping?

Read: Psalm 70:5 — What does it say?

Ask: Who else is called *ezer* in Scripture? Given that 16 out of 21 times *ezer* is used to describe God's character, does this word imply inferiority or honor?

Read: Genesis 3:14-19 — What does it say?

Ask: Was husbands ruling over wives the result of the curse of the fall?

Read: Galatians 3:13 — What does it say?

Ask: Since Jesus reversed this curse, is there any reason for women to remain under domination and subjugation?

Does God appoint women to speak and lead in the Old Testament? Did Jesus empower women?

Read: Judges 5 — What does it say?

Ask: Did God appoint Deborah as a judge, a leader of Israel and a prophetess?

Read: Exodus 15:20 — What does it say?

Ask: What title was Miriam given? Were there other women referred to as prophetesses in the Old Testament? What was the primary job of prophets and prophetesses? Why would God give women authority to speak the word of the Lord and lead, something quite counter to culture at the time, if he was against women speaking and leading?

Read: John 4:7-31 — What does it say?

Ask: What cultural and religious rules did Jesus defy by speaking to the woman at the well? Who was the first person Jesus told he was the Messiah? Who became the first evangelist? Why would Jesus go against cultural norms to allow women to follow him, listen to his teachings and sit at his feet when in Jewish culture women were not allowed to learn or be taught? If Jesus did not make a main point to empower women, why does Matthew, Mark and Luke all record a group of women who followed

Jesus and were present at His crucifixion and burial? What statement do you think God is making by having the testimony of women recorded and honored throughout the Bible in a time when the testimony of women was not accepted culturally? Why do you think Jesus appeared first to Mary Magdalene and other women disciples after the resurrection?

Were women appointed to leadership roles in the early church? Why does Paul instruct women to be silent and not exercise authority over a man?

Read: Romans 16:3-4 — What does it say?

Ask: Why would Paul list Priscilla's name before her husband Aquila? Refer to other five mentions of Priscilla (Acts 18:2, 18, 26, 1 Corinthians 16:19, 2 Timothy 4:19).

Read: 1 Corinthians 1:11 — What does it say?

Ask: Why would Paul refer to "Chloe's people" if she was not a leader? What about Lydia (Acts 16:13-15), Apphia (Philemon 1:2), Nympha (Colossians 4:15), the mother of John Mark (Acts 12:12)? Why do you think Junia is specifically given the title of an apostle (Romans 16:7) and Phoebe called a deaconess and overseer (Romans 16:1-2) if women were not accepted leaders of the early Church?

Read: 1 Corinthians 14:34-35 — What does it say?

Ask: What is the message and purpose of 1 Corinthians?

Read: 1 Corinthians 5:9 — What does it say?

Ask: Is 1 Corinthians Paul's first letter to the Corinthians? What main topic is Paul addressing in chapters 11-14?

Read: 1 Corinthians 11:3-4 — What does it say?

Ask: Why would Paul give instructions for women while they pray and prophesy if later he says women should remain silent?

Read: 1 Corinthians 14 — What does it say?

Ask: Why is Paul consistent with intentional language that includes both genders if his main message is that women should be silent? References: **"each other"** (1 Corinthians 12:7) **"you all"** (1 Corinthians 14:5) **"the whole church," "everyone"** (1 Corinthians 14:23) **"brothers and sisters,** when you come together **each of you** has a hymn, or a word of instruction, a revelation, a tongue or an interpretation" (1 Corinthians 14:26).

Ask: Understanding that 1 Corinthians 14:34-35 is a direct contradiction, not just to everything Paul teaches, but the entire narrative of scripture, can we assume we are missing context?

Read: 1 Corinthians 7:1 — What does it say?

Ask: When Paul directly responds to what the Corinthians wrote, "it is good for a man to not touch a woman," were these quotations in the original manuscript? What contextual clues did translators use to infer that Paul was quoting the Corinthians letter to him and refuting it? Given the understanding that quotations did not exist when the Bible was written and they had to be added in 1 Corinthians 7:1, could it be Paul is doing the very same thing in 1 Corinthians 14:34-35 and is quoting the Corinthians letter to him? If this is a quote of the Corinthians solution for order in the Church, does Paul appear to object or accept it?

Read: 1 Corinthians 14:36 — What does it say?

Ask: Does it read like a rebuttal?

Note: Throughout the book of Corinthians, Paul uses the Greek particle é to introduce rebuttal to statements proceeding it. Many translations omit the é particle (eta) but if you examine the original Greek (you can do so with Strong's Concordance on Biblehub.com) you will see Paul does in fact use an eta directly following verse 35, implying that he is rebutting a quote from the Corinthians letter to him.

Read: 1 Corinthians 14:31-37 with verses 34-35 in quotations:

"For you can all prophesy one by one, so that all may learn and all be encouraged; and the spirits of prophets are subject to prophets. For God is not a God of confusion but of peace.

"As in all the churches of the saints, the women should keep silence in the churches. For they are not permitted to speak, but should be subordinate, as even the law says. If there is anything they desire to know, let them ask their husbands at home. For it is shameful for a woman to speak in church."

(é) What! (or: nonsense!) Did the word of God originate with you, or are you the only ones it has reached? If anyone thinks that he is a prophet, or spiritual, he should acknowledge that what I am writing to you is a command of the Lord. If anyone does not recognize this, he is not recognized. So, my brethren, earnestly desire to prophesy, and do not forbid speaking in tongues; but all things should be done decently and in order."

Ask: Without the omission of the eta, does the passage make more sense contextually?

Read: 1 Timothy 2:11-12 — What does it say?

Ask: What context was this written in? What was happening in Ephesus? What was the Temple of Artemis?

Read: 1 Timothy 1:3 — What does it say?

Ask: What was Paul's purpose in writing to Timothy? Why would Paul say that he is writing to Timothy so he may "command **certain people** to not teach false doctrines" if this letter was intended to be universal doctrine and not circumstantial correction? With the understanding that when Paul says, "I do not allow" (verse 12) he uses a verb in present tense making it accurately translated, "I am not allowing," does it appear Paul is making his instruction situational or universal? Does it say **a woman** or **women everywhere**? Given the very specific corrective language of Paul directly to his spiritual son, Timothy, clearly intended as leadership instruction to pass on for a specific contextual application, how do you think Paul would feel about this being universally applied to all women in the Church today?

Recommended Reference: Vik Fomenko's Women in Ministry Series available on Youtube

Signs Wonders & Miracles

Does God still work through supernatural gifts such as tongues, prophecy and healing?

Read: Malachi 3:6 — What does it say?

Ask: Does God change? From Genesis through Revelation do we not see powerful miracles? Is God consistent with his Word?

Read: 1 Corinthians 13:8-10 — What does it say?

Ask: Does it say that spiritual gifts will cease after the Apostles? When does it say that spiritual gifts will cease? Do you think we have reached the "time of perfection?"

Read: 1 Corinthians 13:11-12 — What does it say?

Ask: Do we still see imperfectly and incompletely? If so, is Scripture not clear that the gifts of the Spirit and miraculous power of God are still in operation? Take some time to search the internet for miracle testimonies done in Jesus' name.

What are Spiritual Gifts?

Read: Romans 11:29 — What does it say?

Ask: Does God take back his gifts after He has given them?

Read: James 1:17 — What does it say?

Ask: Where do good gifts come from?

Ministry Gifts | *Read:* Ephesians 4:11-16 — *Ask:* What is the purpose of these gifts? Does this passage say these gifts are only given to some? Does it mention qualifications required to receive gifts of the Spirit? What is the difference between ministering apostolically, prophetically, pastorally, evangelistically, and through teaching? Are we all called to minister in all these ways? Do each of us have a natural bent towards one of two ministry gifts that we more naturally function in?

Manifestation Gifts | *Read:* 1 Corinthians 12:1-11 — *Ask:* Are gifts given to *each* or to *some*? Described as the workings of the Spirit, do you think these gifts manifest through any spirit-filled believer when the Spirit is working? Have you experienced any or all of these manifestation gifts?

Motivational Gifts | *Read:* Romans 12 — *Ask:* Are these gifts distributed universally or individually? Is each person given one or all of these gifts?

Recommended Reference: Designed For Fulfillment: A Study of Redemptive Gifts by Charles R. Wade

Should every Believer pray in tongues and prophecy? If so, how?

Read: 1 Corinthians 14:5 — What does it say?

Ask: Paul uses the language "every one of you" to say what?

Read: 1 Corinthians 14: 3-4 — What does it say?

Ask: Who do tongues edify? What is the purpose of prophecy? Who does this passage say prophecy is for? Is there a different word used to differentiate between Old Testament Bible prophecy and the gift of prophecy?

Read: 1 Corinthians 14:21-22 — What does it say?

Ask: Who are tongues a miraculous sign for?

Read: 2 Peter 1:19-21 — What does it say?

Ask: Where does true prophecy come from?

Read: 1 Thessalonians 5:19-22 — What does it say?

Ask: How are we to treat prophecy?

Read: 1 Corinthians 14 and Acts 2:4-6 — Compare.

Ask: Are there clear differences between the type of tongue described in 1 Corinthians: *"For anyone who speaks in a tongue does not speak to people but to God. Indeed, no one understands them; they utter mysteries by the Spirit"* (1 Corinthians 14:2) and in Acts: *"When they heard this sound, a crowd came together in bewilderment, because each one heard their own language being spoken"* (Acts 2:5)? Based off these passages are we led to believe that there is a difference between praying in tongues, also known as praying in the Spirit (Romans 8:26), giving a word in tongues to a church which requires an interpreter (1 Corinthians 14:26-28), and the supernatural gift of tongues enabling the speaking of an unknown foreign language (Acts 2:4-6)?

How do we receive spiritual gifts?

Read: Luke 11:11-13 — What does it say?

Ask: what instruction does Jesus give to us to receive gifts from the Father?

Read: James 1:6 — What does it say?

Ask: What instruction does Scripture give for how we request things from the Lord?

Read: on to James 1:7 — What does it say?

Ask: Once we request, and then realize in faith what is automatically given to us when we ask, how do we avoid instability blocking us from receiving? If we request, realize, and relax as we receive this good gift from God, is anything else required of us? Does the Holy Spirit ever force himself on us?

Read: Psalm 81:10 — What does it say?

Ask: What are we promised when we open our mouth and release a sound in surrender?

Recommended Reference: "How to Pray in Tongues: Four Keys," David Diga Hernandez Ministries

ACKNOWLEDGEMENTS

Thank you to my husband, Michael, for your dedication to me and to this project. I am forever grateful that you found me on my first day of college under that old oak tree. I marvel at how our spiritual lives have gone from resembling the smudged charcoal tree I was sketching when we met, messed by my attempts at control, to becoming flourishing trees, living a life of radical surrender with clear vision. Only God. Thank you for the ways you challenged me in the content of this book; you have contributed more than you know. You are my forever love.

Thank you to my firstborn, Finley; when you were born, it was as if the light of Heaven began shining on us. And Lucy, with your birth just thirteen months later, the light brightened and awakened your dad and me to new spiritual depths. Your lives demonstrated to me that with each child we welcome, we invite the kingdom of God to invade our home. I am so proud to have experienced this with you all the more as we became a foster family. To my beautiful children who came after we opened our home – you have taught me more about the love of Jesus than anyone. Thank you.

Thank you to my sister, Natalie, for your extraordinary commitment to supporting me in every single thing God asks me to do in prayer and practical help. I will never be able to repay you for the months you poured into editing and contributing to this book. Your storehouses of treasure in heaven are undoubtedly overflowing. I have never known anyone who gives themselves more freely for the pure benefit of others. Your love (and incredible editing skills) make me better in every way. And thank you to Andrew, my assistant editor. Having you on speed dial always willing to answer my calls with support for my last minute requests and your steady belief in this project was a huge help to me.

Thank you to my Mama for all the years of selfless service, proofreading papers and blog posts and now graciously editing my biggest project to date. I would not be all God created me to be without you. Most importantly, thank you for watering me with the Word of God from the youngest age. Thank you, Dad, for being an agent of redemption in my story through the gift of adoption. Your and mama's contributions watching my children and praying for me made this book possible. To all of my incredible family— I am so proud of you for courageously uprooting lies and growing in truth. No doubt we have experienced family revival.

Thank you to my bio Dad for teaching me that adoption, while full of loss, is chosen in love. I honor you for your selfless decision to relinquish your parental rights and your sacrifice to maintain an open adoption. My relationship with you is irreplaceable. Thank you to my bonus mom, Kim, for your encouragement. I am grateful to have shared the moment with you at my dining room table when I realized God was asking me to write this book.

Thank you to my grandparents for cultivating positive beliefs in my life and teaching me the value of family heritage.

Thank you to Pastor Ben and Heather Rose and The Collective family for being my grove; what an honor to be planted with you. I am strengthened by your deep roots and have grown so much through the pollination of The Collective Church.

Thank you to Pastors Jeho and Jana Nunez, Pastor Clyde Lewis, and our Destiny Church family for supporting me through my wilderness season. I have been forever changed by your seeds of revival and prophetic pollination.

Thank you to Pastors Bob and Jenny Donnelly and the Her Voice Team for creating a greenhouse of healing, growth and freedom for me to flourish in Jesus.

Thank you to Pastor Shawna Danberg for your dedication to loving me into wholeness in every area of my life. And to the Tuesday Night Bible Study gals, your commitment to follow the way of Jesus together is an incredible blessing to me.

Thank you to my dear friends, Gina and Shannon, for your practical support of my family, without which writing this book during the fullest season of my life would not have been possible. Before I met either of you, Michael and I joked about an imaginary support person named Grace. When the laundry piled up we would joke, "Where is Grace?" When putting the kids to bed took three hours and the dinner dishes still filled the sink at 10pm, we would look at each other and ask, "Where is that Grace?!" You two are our Grace, living expressions of God's grace toward us, and I am abundantly grateful.

MARY ALICE HALL is a mother to four children through birth and foster care. She created Field Guide for Families, a resource website, blog and podcast to equip family discipleship and activate abiding action. Mary Alice is on a mission to see the Church become the solution to the Vulnerable Child Crisis. She lives in Ridgefield, Washington with her husband, Michael. She loves adventuring with her family and is happiest with her hands full, always juggling her camera, coffee, and children in her arms.

REFERENCES

1. "Strong's Greek: 4982. Σώζω (Sózó) -- to Save," n.d., https://biblehub.com/greek/4982.htm.
2. "Number of Abortions in US & Worldwide - Number of Abortions Since 1973," n.d., https://www.numberofabortions.com/.
3. "Strong's Greek: 4161. Ποίημα (Poiéma) -- a Work," n.d., https://biblehub.com/greek/4161.htm.
4. Reasons to Believe, "Fulfilled Prophecy: Evidence for the Reliability of the Bible - Reasons to Believe," October 23, 2020, https://reasons.org/explore/publications/articles/fulfilled-prophecy-evidence-for-the-reliability-of-the-bible.
5. "Strong's Greek: 3056. Λόγος (Logos) -- a Word (as Embodying an Idea), a Statement, a Speech," n.d., https://biblehub.com/greek/3056.htm.
6. "Strong's Greek: 4487. Ῥῆμα (Rhéma) -- a Word, by Impl. A Matter," n.d., https://biblehub.com/greek/4487.htm.
7. "G1097 - Ginōskō - Strong's Greek Lexicon (Kjv)," Blue Letter Bible, n.d., https://www.blueletterbible.org/lexicon/g1097/kjv/tr/0-1/.
8. "Ginosko Meaning - Greek Lexicon | New Testament (KJV)," Bible Study Tools, n.d., https://www.biblestudytools.com/lexicons/greek/kjv/ginosko.html.
9. "Strong's Greek: 1108. Γνῶσις (Gnósis) -- a Knowing, Knowledge," n.d., https://biblehub.com/greek/1108.htm.
10. Bema Discipleship, "The BEMA Podcast," The BEMA Podcast, n.d., https://www.bemadiscipleship.com/.
11. Bema Discipleship, "The BEMA Podcast," The BEMA Podcast, n.d., https://www.bemadiscipleship.com/.
12. "Strong's Greek: 191. Ἀκούω (Akouó) -- to Hear, Listen," n.d., https://biblehub.com/greek/191.htm.

14. Ellie Lisitsa, "The Research: The Still Face Experiment," The Gottman Institute, June 25, 2024, https://www.gottman.com/blog/research-still-face-experiment/.

15. Lexi Lonas Cochran, "1 in 4 High School Students Identifies as LGBTQ," The Hill, April 27, 2023, https://thehill.com/homenews/education/3975959-one-in-four-high-school-students-identify-as-lgbtq/.

16. USAFacts, "US Suicide Rate Trends and States With the Highest Suicide Rates," USAFacts, November 29, 2023, https://usafacts.org/articles/how-is-the-suicide-rate-changing-in-the-us.

17. "Mental Health," Oxford Academic, n.d., https://academic.oup.com/aje/pages/mental-health.

18. Thomas Insel, "America's Mental Health Crisis," December 8, 2023, https://www.pewtrusts.org/en/trend/archive/fall-2023/americas-mental-health-crisis.

19. Valerie Bauman, "Is America Becoming Godless? The Number of People Who Have No Religion Rose 266% in Three Decades," *Mail Online*, April 6, 2019, https://www.dailymail.co.uk/news/article-6886705/Is-America-Godless-number-people-no-religion-rose-266-three-decades.html.

20. A.W. Tozer, *The Knowledge of the Holy* (New York: HarperCollins, 1978).

21. Anastasia Fomenko, "Destroy Fear, Panic and Anxiety with Debra Arnott," *No Longer Afraid*, March 18, 2024.

22. "O.T. Names of God - Study Resources," Blue Letter Bible, n.d., https://www.blueletterbible.org/study/misc/name_god.cfm.

23. "Cultivate," in *Merriam-Webster Dictionary*, September 14, 2024, https://www.merriam-webster.com/dictionary/cultivate.

24. "Strong's Greek: 342. Ἀνακαίνωσις (Anakaínosis) -- Renewal," n.d., https://biblehub.com/greek/342.htm.

25. Dr. Caroline Leaf, *Switch On Your Brain: The Key to Peak Happiness, Thinking and Health* (Baker Books, 2013).

26. C.S. Lewis, *The Weight of Glory and Other Addresses* (New York: Macmillan & Co, 1949).

27. Deepwater Asset Management, "Defining the Future of Human Information Consumption | Deepwater," Deepwater, September 13, 2024, https://deepwatermgmt.com/philosophy/defining-the-future-of-human-information-consumption/.

28. Jeanne Guyon, *Experiencing the Depths of Jesus Christ*, Library of Spiritual Classics Volume 2 (Seedsowers, 1981), 8.

30. Joe Griffin Media Ministries, "The Church of the Living God 09-09-27-B.FBC08-184," 2009, https://www.gdconline.org/wp-content/uploads/2018/03/FBC08-184.pdf.

31. Andrew Murray, *Humility: The Journey Toward Holiness* (Bethany House Publishers, 2001).

32. Carl Joseph, "The Whole Armor of God - Carl Joseph Ministries," *Carl Joseph Ministries - Fulfill Your God-given Potential* (blog), April 2, 2023, https://carljosephministries.com/the-whole-armor-of-god/.

33. Jamie Winship, *Living Fearless: Exchanging the Lies of the World for the Liberating Truth of God* (Revell, 2022).

34. Eric William Gilmour, *Into The Cloud: Becoming God's Spokesman* (CreateSpace Independent Publishing Platform, 2018).

35. "G3936 - Paristēmi - Strong's Greek Lexicon (Kjv)," Blue Letter Bible, n.d., https://www.blueletterbible.org/lexicon/g3936/kjv/tr/0-1/.

36. Eric Gilmour, *Enjoying the Gospel* (Sonship International, 2015).

37. David W. Augsburger, *Caring Enough to Hear and Be Heard: How to Hear and How to Be Heard in Equal Communication* (Baker Publishing Group, 1982).

38. Bob Sorge, *Secrets of the Secret Place: Keys to Igniting Your Personal Time With God* (Oasis House, 2001).

39. "Rhythm," in *Merriam-Webster Dictionary*, September 23, 2024, https://www.merriam-webster.com/dictionary/rhythm.

40. David Benner, *Surrender to Love: Discovering the Heart of Christian Spirituality* (Intervarsity Press, 2015), 61.

41. David Benner, *Surrender to Love: Discovering the Heart of Christian Spirituality* (Intervarsity Press, 2015), 63.

42. John Mark Comer, *The Ruthless Elimination of Hurry: How to Stay Emotionally Healthy and Spiritually Alive in the Chaos of the Modern World* (Waterbrook, 2019).

43. Dr. David and Amanda Erickson, *The Flourishing Family: A Jesus-Centered Guide to Parenting with Peace and Purpose* (Tyndale Refresh, 2024).

44. Jim Jackson and Lynne Jackson, *Discipline That Connects With Your Child's Heart: Building Faith, Wisdom, and Character in the Messes of Daily Life* (Bethany House Publishers, 2016).

45. "Strong's Greek: 3144. Μάρτυς (Martus) -- a Witness," n.d., https://biblehub.com/greek/3144.htm.

46. "Strong's Greek: 3330. Μεταδίδωμι (Metadidómi) -- to Give a Share Of," n.d., https://biblehub.com/greek/3330.htm.

47. GotQuestions.org, "What is impartation?," January 4, 2022, https://www.gotquestions.org/impartation.html.

48. "Why Do People Sometimes Collapse in the Presence of God?," Renner Ministries, August 10, 2024, https://renner.org/article/why-do-people-sometimes-collapse-in-the-presence-of-god/.

49. "The Neglected History of Women in the Early Church | Christian History Magazine," Christian History Institute, n.d., https://christianhistoryinstitute.org/magazine/article/women-in-the-early-church.

50. Alicia Searl, "What Is the Meaning of Proverbs 31 and Why Is It Popular?," Christianity.com, February 16, 2023, https://www.christianity.com/wiki/bible/what-is-the-meaning-of-proverbs-31-and-why-is-it-popular.html.

51. Department of State, United States of America, *Trafficking In Persons Report* (2019). https://www.state.gov/wp-content/uploads/2019/06/2019-Trafficking-in-Persons-Report.pdf

52. International Labour Office, Special Action Programme to Combat Forced Labour (SAP-FL), and Fundamental Principles and Rights at Work Branch (FPRW), *Profits and Poverty: The Economics of Forced Labour* (International Labour Organization, 2014), https://www.ilo.org/wcmsp5/groups/public/---ed_norm/---declaration/documents/publication/wcms_243391.pdf.

53. Jessica Miller, "Foster Care and Human Trafficking," Voices for Children, January 30, 2020, https://www.speakupnow.org/foster-care-and-human-trafficking/.

54. Simon G. Brauer, "How Many Congregations Are There? Updating a Survey-Based Estimate," *Journal for the Scientific Study of Religion* 56, no. 2 (June 1, 2017): 438–48, https://doi.org/10.1111/jssr.12330.

55. Empowered to Connect, *Cultivate Connection Course: Empowering Parents to Empower Children*, n.d., 70, https://empoweredtoconnect.org/training/.

56. Empowered to Connect, *Cultivate Connection Course: Empowering Parents to Empower Children*, n.d., 36, https://empoweredtoconnect.org/training/.

57. Empowered to Connect, *Cultivate Connection Course: Empowering Parents to Empower Children*, n.d., 34, https://empoweredtoconnect.org/training/.

58. John Bevere, *The Bait of Satan: Living Free from the Deadly Trap of Offense* (Charisma House, 2014).

59. "G5399 - Phobeō - Strong's Greek Lexicon (Kjv)," Blue Letter Bible, n.d., https://www.blueletterbible.org/lexicon/g5399/kjv/tr/0-1/.

60. Peter-John Courson, *A Glimpse of Heaven: A Vision of Eternity in a Moment of Hell* (CreateSpace Independent Publishing Platform, 2016).

61. Jane Hamon, *Discernment: The Essential Guide to Hearing the Voice of God* (Chosen Books, 2019).

62. Jane Hamon, *Discernment: The Essential Guide to Hearing the Voice of God* (Chosen Books, 2019).

63. "Strong's Greek: 4396. Προφήτης (Prophétés) -- a Prophet (an Interpreter or Forth-teller of the Divine Will)," n.d., https://biblehub.com/greek/4396.htm.

64. "Strong's Greek: 652. Ἀπόστολος (Apostolos) -- a Messenger, One Sent on a Mission, an Apostle," n.d., https://biblehub.com/greek/652.htm.

65. Charles R. Wade Jr., *Designed for Fulfillment A Study of Redemptive Gifts* (Free to Be Ministries, Inc., 2007), 139.

66. Christine Caine, "Anointing vs. Gifting," (Redding: Bethel Church, 2018), https://www.youtube.com/watch?v=5KahnuYJ_yA.

67. "Topical Bible: Receive," n.d., https://biblehub.com/topical/r/receive.htm.

68. Dan Moheler, "Becoming Love," (Boulder, City on the Hill Church, 2012), https://youtu.be/xfXoP9KBPGs?si=LXxXPsb829qbeWib.

69. Kristi McLelland, *The Gospel on the Ground: The Grit and Glory of the Early Church in Acts* (Lifeway Press, 2022).

70. "Strong's Greek: 2357. Θρησκός (Thréskos of Unc. Or.) -- Religious," n.d., https://biblehub.com/greek/2357.htm.

71. "Strong's Greek: 2356. Θρησκεία (Thréskeia) -- Religion," n.d., https://biblehub.com/greek/2356.htm.

72. "G1577 - Ekklēsia - Strong's Greek Lexicon (Kjv)," Blue Letter Bible, n.d., https://www.blueletterbible.org/lexicon/g1577/kjv/tr/0-1/.

73. "Commission," in *Merriam-Webster Dictionary*, September 26, 2024, https://www.merriam-webster.com/dictionary/commission.

74. Vik Fomenko, "Staying Full of Oil," (Vancouver: Kingdom Movement, 2022) https://www.youtube.com/watch?v=41OQq9JWbSA.

75. "Strong's Greek: 1139. δαιμονίζομαι (daimonizomai) -- to be possessed by a demon.," (n.d.), https://biblehub.com/greek/1139.htm.

www.ingramcontent.com/pod-product-compliance
Lightning Source LLC
Chambersburg PA
CBHW050735010526
44107CB00010B/863